Conrod and Priscilla Reining

Minneapolis , 1957

RITUALS OF KINSHIP
AMONG
THE NYAKYUSA

By the same author:

Reaction to Conquest

The Analysis of Social Change (with Godfrey Wilson)

Good Company: A Study of Nyakyusa Age-Villages

The publication of this study was made possible by funds granted by the Carnegie Corporation of New York. That Corporation is not, however, to be understood as approving any of the statements made or views expressed therein.

RITUALS OF KINSHIP
AMONG
THE NYAKYUSA

BY

MONICA WILSON

Published for the
INTERNATIONAL AFRICAN INSTITUTE
by the
OXFORD UNIVERSITY PRESS
LONDON NEW YORK TORONTO
1957

Oxford University Press, Amen House, London, E.C.4

GLASGOW NEW YORK TORONTO MELBOURNE WELLINGTON

BOMBAY CALCUTTA MADRAS KARACHI CAPE TOWN IBADAN

Printed in Great Britain by
Latimer, Trend and Co. Ltd., Plymouth

TO WHOM DO THEY PRAY?

Abanyafyale, abanyafyale bikwiputa kugu?
Abanyafyale, abanyafyale bikwiputa kugu?
Kubasyuka! Kubasyuka!

Chorus: Alikumwanya! Alikumwanya!

Abasungu, abasungu bikwiputa kugu?
Abasungu, abasungu bikwiputa kugu?
Kundalama! Kundalama!

Chorus: Alikumwanya! Alikumwanya!

Abisilamu, abisilamu, bikwiputa kugu?
Abisilamu, abisilamu, bikwiputa kugu?
Kwa Mohamedi! Kwa Mohamedi!

Chorus: Alikumwanya! Alikumwanya!

Abosigwa, abosigwa, bikwiputa kugu?
Abosigwa, abosigwa, bikwiputa kugu?
Kwa Jesu! Kwa Jesu!

Chorus: Alikumwanya! Alikumwanya!

Translation

The chiefs, the chiefs to whom do they pray?
The chiefs, the chiefs to whom do they pray?
To the shades! To the shades!

Chorus: He is above! He is above!

The Europeans, the Europeans to whom do they pray?
The Europeans, the Europeans to whom do they pray?
To money! To money!

Chorus: He is above! He is above!

The Mohammedans, the Mohammedans to whom do they pray?
The Mohammedans, the Mohammedans to whom to they pray?
To Mohammed! To Mohammed!

Chorus: He is above! He is above!

The baptised, the baptised to whom do they pray?
The baptised, the baptised to whom do they pray?
To Jesus! To Jesus!

Chorus: He is above! He is above!

(Song of Nyakyusa Christians

ACKNOWLEDGEMENT

THE material presented here was collected by Godfrey and Monica Wilson under the auspices of the Rockefeller Foundation and the International African Institute between 1934 and 1938. For leisure to complete the writing, and to revisit the Nyakyusa in 1955, I am indebted to the Carnegie Corporation of New York and the University of Cape Town.

MONICA WILSON

School of African Studies
University of Cape Town

CONTENTS

LIST OF ILLUSTRATIONS

CHAPTER I

INTRODUCTION

In the broken country to the north of Lake Nyasa live the Nyakyusa and Ngonde people who, together with those closely related to them in language and culture, number[1] nearly a quarter of a million. They stretch across the river which divides Tanganyika Territory from Nyasaland and, because they were hemmed in by mountains and swift rivers, they long remained isolated from the outside world. They are skilful herdsmen and cultivators, well fed, and practising a system of green manuring and rotation which allows of fixed cultivation, in contrast to the shifting systems of most of their neighbours.

Their villages are large. Each is occupied by a group of age mates together with their wives and young children. Father and son and grandson *must* live in separate villages and full brothers are commonly separated also. Fathers and young sons are in adjoining villages, but the villages of grown men are scattered about a chiefdom without reference to the genealogical connections of its members. The only kinship relationships common within a village are those of half-brothers and of affines, for a man often marries the daughter or sister of a village mate. But although they live dispersed, agnatic kinsmen are bound together by a strong lineage organization. Property, in the form of cattle, circulates within agnatic lineages, passing from brother to full brother in order of seniority, and thence to the son of the senior brother, who inherits, with the cattle, obligations towards his juniors and a certain authority over them. Half-brothers may also be linked by regular exchanges of cattle—'milking one another's cows', as the Nyakyusa call it. Cattle are given at a marriage by the groom to the bride's father, and distributed by him among his brothers and sons; the bulk of them usually going to one of the bride's full brothers, who retains through life a special responsibility for her and her children. Polygyny is approved. The form most favoured

[1] Throughout this book the present tense refers to the period 1934–8 when the material presented here was collected.

I

is the marriage of two sisters, or of a woman and her brother's daughter, to the same man; such 'sisters' are closely identified and their children are treated almost as full siblings.

Besides being bound together by a common interest in property —the cattle of the lineage—kinsmen join in the celebration of rituals to their common ancestors; for the very fact of their kinship is held to make them mystically dependent upon one another, and more particularly on the prayers of the most senior among them. At a funeral kinsmen will gather from many of the villages of the chiefdom, and some from other chiefdoms also. The range of kinship recognized varies somewhat with status, but the effective lineage group is normally of a span of three or four generations only, including descendants of a common grandfather or great-grandfather.

Traditionally villages were grouped in a number of small independent chiefdoms led by hereditary chiefs. Each chiefdom contained many kinsmen, but there was no fiction of common descent of all the men of a chiefdom, or of chiefs and people. There were thus three types of social group: villages occupied by age-mates, who shared common land rights, and herded and fought together; lineages bound by common interest in inherited cattle and common rituals; and chiefdoms in which the bond was occupation of a common territory and allegiance to a common chief.

Relations between the three groups are epitomized in the traditional law relating to theft, adultery, murder, and witchcraft.[1] A man was a member both of a village and of a lineage and both groups were responsible for his behaviour. An adulterer or cattle-thief was speared by the injured party and his kinsmen, if they could catch him. If they could not, they might attack any member of his age-village. This commonly led to war between the villages, but short of this, the kinsmen of the dead man claimed compensation from the thief or adulterer and his kin, not from the avengers. Both lineage and age-village were therefore corporate groups, the members of which were mutually responsible for each other, and it is significant that *both* senior kinsman and village headman of the defendant were required to accompany him when the case came to court. Murder was treated as a private delict, the kinsmen of the dead attacking or claiming compensation from the murderer and his kin, but witchcraft was treated as an offence against the

[1] cf. Monica Wilson, *Good Company* (1952), p. 150.

state, and the property of a convicted witch went to the chief. Therefore the lineage was not the unrivalled principle of social grouping among the Nyakyusa as it was among the Tallensi or Nuer, but it was a corporate body.[1]

The existence of three types of groups among the Nyakyusa made for social integration. The divergent interests of villages were checked by the fact that every man had kinsmen in many other villages upon whom he was dependent, economically and ritually; the fissiparous tendencies of lineages were checked by the loyalties of lineage members to different villages; and the villages and lineages were all held to be dependent upon their chief for the fertility of their land, control of the weather, and success in warfare.

Since an account of the Nyakyusa age-villages and an outline of their kinship system have already been published,[2] we may now turn directly to the topic of this book, their religion.

The traditional religion of the Nyakyusa people has three elements: First, there is a lively belief in the survival of the dead and in the power of senior relatives, both living and dead, over their descendants; secondly, there is a belief in medicines, that is, in a mystical power residing in certain material substances which is used by those who have the requisite knowledge; thirdly, there is a belief in witchcraft, that is, an innate power to harm others exercised by certain individuals, and in the mystical power of fellow villagers to punish wrongdoers. This last power, 'the breath of men', is akin to witchcraft. It may be objected that a belief in witchcraft is in no sense 'religious', but to exclude discussion of it in an account of Nyakyusa religion is comparable to excluding a reference to the devil in a discussion of Christianity. Evil is a reality which must be interpreted in one fashion or another in every cosmology.

The belief in the survival of the dead and the power of senior relatives, is expressed in a series of elaborate rituals, one set of which concern only kinsmen and are directed towards the im-

---

[1] There appear to be many gradations between a society with no corporate lineages, such as the Lozi, and one like the Tallensi in which the lineage is the basis of all important social groups, just as there are gradations between a stateless society in which all offences are treated as quarrels between groups of kinsmen, and a primitive state in which any serious assault is an offence against the state.

[2] Monica Wilson, op. cit. and 'Nyakyusa kinship' in *African Systems of Kinship and Marriage,* ed. Radcliffe-Brown and Daryll Forde (1951).

mediate ancestors of the participants, and another set which concern chiefdoms and groups of chiefdoms, and are directed towards
the immediate ancestors of ruling chiefs and certain distant ancestors of the chiefs' line, heroes in Nyakyusa history. The name of
one of these heroes, Kyala, has been used by the missionaries to
translate the word 'God', but all the evidence available goes to show
that Kyala was, traditionally, but one of several distant ancestors
to whom regular sacrifices were made on behalf of a large group
of chiefdoms. All the rituals of this type—those directed to family
shades, the chiefs' ancestors, and the heroes—are concerned with
that which is beneath (*pasi*), not that which is above. Men look to
the earth where corpses are buried, not to any sky god.

The theme of the present volume is the rituals celebrated by
kinsmen at death, at the puberty and marriage of a girl (the last
two events usually coinciding), at birth, especially twin birth, and
in misfortune. A further volume will deal with the communal
rituals celebrated before the annual break of the rains; whenever
public misfortune such as drought, flood, famine, or plague occurs
or threatens; before battle; and when a chief is succeeded by his
sons, and the younger generation take over power from their elders.
There is no circumcision or initiation of men other than the
'coming out' ceremony, when a whole generation takes over
responsibility for the administration and defence of the chiefdom
from their fathers. Some reference to three of the heroes—Kyala,
Lwembe, and Mbasi—is made in texts on the rituals of kinsmen,
but our discussion of them is postponed to the second book in
which the rituals directed to them are described.

A section of the Nyakyusa people is Christian and its influence
on pagan thought and practice is appreciable; however, discussion
of this is also postponed to the second book, since it is most evident
in the changing concept of Kyala. There, too, the connections
between change in ritual and other aspects of the social structure
between 1934 and 1955 are analysed.

The Nyakyusa cult of senior relatives (like any ancestor cult) is
not intelligible or significant apart from a study of kinship, and it
may be argued that this material should be presented only as part
of an analysis of Nyakyusa kinship, but we cannot discuss everything at once and some measure of abstraction is necessary. No
one ritual among the Nyakyusa is fully intelligible without reference to the whole series of rituals. The principle, propounded
forty-five years ago by Professor Radcliffe-Brown, that a symbol

recurring in a cycle of rituals is likely to have the same significance in each, holds good for the Nyakyusa: certain symbols of shaving, washing, eating, spreading banana leaves, scattering grain, and so forth were similarly interpreted by our informants in the different rituals of the cycle, and their full significance is only apparent when a comparison of their various uses is made. In this book, therefore, attention is focused on the ritual cycle. A comparison of numerous rites reveals a *symbolic pattern*, the counterpart, in the emotional aspect, of kinship organization in the practical aspect; and the comments of the more self-conscious Nyakyusa on the rites indicate the *intellectual system* linked with this pattern.

As already mentioned, the religious conceptions of the Nyakyusa include the belief in medicines, in 'the breath of men', and in witchcraft, as well as in the power of senior relatives. The importance of medicines in the rituals directed to the shades will be evident in every chapter of this book. References to witchcraft and the 'breath of men' are not so frequent, since these form what is on the whole a separate system of beliefs, and refer to a different set of relationships. The ancestor cult is concerned *solely* with the relationships of kinsmen, and of the chiefs and their peoples; witchcraft and 'the breath of men' *mainly* with the relationships of fellow villagers—i.e. age mates and their wives—though it also impinges on kinship and political relationships. Only in the relationship of spouses, and that between chief and village headmen, do the two sets of beliefs constantly overlap. An account of the Nyakyusa conception of witchcraft and 'the breath of men' has already been published, and it has been shown that accusations of witchcraft occur most frequently between fellow villagers and, nowadays, between fellow employees, that is, between non-relatives; they are also fairly frequently directed against wives and co-wives; but accusations of witchcraft against kinsmen of the same lineage are very rare.[1] Antagonism between kinsmen occurs and is expressed in accusations of practising sorcery, as well as in fear of the power of senior relatives, but most misfortunes are attributed to the lust and envy of neighbours or wives rather than to the malice of kinsmen. Evil is conceived of as having a personal cause, but as originating generally outside the circle of kin. The mystical power of senior relatives (living and dead) can never be used irresponsibly—it cannot operate unless the cause is just—and therefore misfortune emanating from the shades is always a just

[1] Monica Wilson, *Good Company*, pp. 102–4; 198–205.

retribution, not an irresponsible assault, like that made by witches.

The religion of the Nyakyusa is expressed in ritual rather than in dogma. Everyone participates, at some time or another, in a variety of rituals; a great deal of time and energy is devoted to them, and they are elaborate. By comparison, the dogma and myth are limited both in content and in influence. Many more people participate in rituals than are fully conscious of dogma and myth; many more people can describe rituals than interpret them. In this analysis, therefore, the rituals are first described and the principal dogmas are deduced from the Nyakyusa interpretation of them.

The stress is on the Nyakyusa interpretation of their own rituals, for anthropological literature is bespattered with symbolic guessing, the ethnographer's interpretation of the rituals of other people. Now it seems probable that certain symbols are universal in the sense that they express the same ideas in all societies. Many other symbols are emotionally intelligible when interpreted—the following pages are full of examples—but it is foolish to imagine that an individual schooled in one culture can understand the symbolism of another without instruction. For this reason, and at the risk of wearying the reader, many of the texts on which this interpretation is based are quoted. The interpretations of even the most self-conscious Nyakyusa, such as Kasitile the rain-maker, Mwandisi the old blind historian, Mwasalemba, Lyandileko and Kakune the doctors, do not, of course, reveal the whole truth about Nyakyusa rituals, but *any analysis not based on some translation of the symbols used* by people of that culture is open to suspicion. The texts were recorded in the Nyakyusa language by Godfrey or Monica Wilson, or one of our two Nyakyusa clerks, Mwaikambo and Mwaisumo, and the informants most often quoted were selected for their special knowledge. And very many others discussed rituals with us.[1]

Not all Nyakyusa are conscious of all the interpretations given. A few symbols, such as the association of different types of banana with male and female respectively, are known to everyone; but the meaning of many of the events in the rituals was obscure to young men and women. Most of the interpretations quoted have, however, been given by more than one informant (as is shown in the text and documents) and may be taken as *common*, i.e. current in

[1] For the methods of field-work cf. Monica Wilson, *Good Company*, pp. vii–ix.

the group. In the few cases in which our informant may have been giving his own individual interpretation, 'putting a bucket down into his subconscious and pulling it up', it was at least a Nyakyusa subconscious, and the interpretation is in terms of the culture. It is with common, not individual, symbols that we are concerned: what is offered in this book is a sociological, not a psychological, analysis.

Similarities between the symbolism of Nyakyusa rituals and the symbolism of dreams and neuroses in Western society will be obvious to readers. That preoccupation with anal and oral functions, with 'nakedness' (though the Nyakyusa habitually wore the most exiguous of coverings), with death, coition, and birth, with mastery ('overstepping') and incest, which is characteristic of the rituals we describe, is evident also in any textbook of psychoanalysis dealing with Western Europeans and Americans; and certain symbols such as a house, a doorway, a spear, seed, and so forth are common to both cultures; but here we are not concerned to trace these similarities. Our business is to lay bare the symbolic pattern of the Nyakyusa without reference to the Western tradition.

The material used for the sociological analysis of ritual consists of two types: observation or description of events, and statements about associations. The greatest difficulty in presenting it has been to choose between a chronological account of each ritual, followed by the Nyakyusa translation or interpretation of the symbolism, and then by the sociological analysis; and an integrated account combining the interpretation and analysis with the description. The advantage of the first method is that the validity of both interpretation and analysis can be more easily judged since the evidence on which it is based is fully set out; the disadvantage is that the description itself implies interpretation and analysis. The symbolism is often implicit in the description of events, and the separation of description from interpretation involves repetition; at the same time the classification of events and symbols is itself a form of analysis, and the separation of description from analysis tends to conceal this. The present study is a compromise between the two approaches. Where events and their symbolism are fairly straightforward, the interpretation accompanies the description; but where, as in the rituals of farewell to the dead, puberty and marriage, and abnormal birth, they are complicated, and the interpretation may well be questioned, accounts of the events are separated from detailed evidence on symbolism. Analysis is neces-

sarily implied all through, but since the argument can only be un-
folded step by step (for no one ritual can be fully analysed until
all are described) a discussion of it is reserved to the concluding
chapters. In interpreting the symbolism, cross reference between
the different rituals of the cycles would be too frequent to give in
the text. Readers wishing to follow up references to the symbolism
of bananas, for example, or *ikipiki* medicine, should use the index.

The link between religious beliefs and morality (in the sense of
right behaviour) is very clear among the Nyakyusa. Many misfortunes are attributed to sin, that is, wrong-doings (*inongwa*)
thought to be supernaturally punished. Indeed, to the Nyakyusa
the idea of the wicked man 'spreading himself like a green bay tree'[1]
is inconceivable, and the disciples' question: 'Who did sin, this
man or his parents, that he was born blind?'[2] cold common sense.
Here we are concerned with the form of morality[3] sanctioned by
Nyakyusa religion, with the conception of good and evil, and with
the relation between belief and behaviour.[4] A table of private misfortunes attributed to the anger of senior relatives is included in
this volume; public misfortunes will be discussed in the succeeding
one; and a table of misfortunes attributed to witchcraft, sorcery,
and the legitimate anger of neighbours ('the breath of men') has
been given in the study of Nyakyusa age-villages already published.[5] While the Nyakyusa lay great emphasis on the correct
performance, in every detail, of certain rituals, their very performance implies co-operation between kinsmen, and not only co-
operation but amity. For 'anger in the heart', if unconfessed, may
bring misfortune. Thus though the outward form is stressed, the
inward and spiritual is not totally ignored.

We proceed on the assumption that men express in ritual what
moves them most; that the form of expression is conventional and
obligatory, and that therefore in ritual the values of a group (as
opposed to those of individuals) are revealed.

---

[1] Psalm xxxvii: 35.   [2] John ix, 2.

[3] I cannot accept Professor Radcliffe-Brown's definition of morality as the control
of conduct by 'public opinion and conscience' as opposed to control by religion. Nor
do I accept Professor Macbeath's argument that primitive man has an idea of good
quite apart from religion. A. E. Taylor's view of morality comes much closer to the
facts as shown in Nyakyusa society.

cf. A. R. Radcliffe-Brown, *Structure and Function in Primitive Society*, p. 172; A. Macbeath, *Experiments in Living*, Gifford Lectures 1948–9; A. E. Taylor, *The Faith of a
Moralist*, Gifford Lectures 1926–8.

[4] The germ of the book is Godfrey Wilson's 'An African morality', *Africa*, 1936.

[5] Monica Wilson, *Good Company*, pp. 198–213.

By *ritual* we mean a primarily religious action, that is, action directed to securing the blessing of some mystical power or powers. The action may be a negative, i.e. an avoidance or taboo, as well as a positive one. Symbols and concepts are employed in rituals but are subordinated to practical ends. Ritual is distinguished from *ceremonial*, which is an elaborate conventional form for the expression of feeling, not confined to religious occasions; any emotional situation, whether religious or secular, may be clothed in ceremony, and a ceremony is not enforced by mystical sanctions, only by conventional ones. In short, a ceremony is an appropriate and elaborate form for the expression of feeling; but a ritual is action believed to be efficacious.[1] Confusion between the two arises in our own society, for what is ritual to some (e.g. a rite of baptism or marriage) is but ceremonial to others. In Nyakyusa society the distinction is fairly clear-cut: *ubunyago*, which is translated here as *a ritual*, means a series of actions directed towards the shades or heroes, and enforced by mystical sanctions, as opposed to action which is merely customary and conventional (*ulwiho*). At a burial, some actions are only *ulwiho*, others are also *ubunyago*. A negative ritual, that which is taboo, is *mwiko*.

Ubunyago is applied as a noun, and in its verbal form, *ukunyagula* (to perform a ritual), to funeral rites, especially that part of such rites in which only immediate relatives participate (*ubunyago bwa bufyele*); to the girls' puberty and marriage ritual (*ubunyago bwa busungu*), to the ritual at birth (*ubunyago bwa bufwe*), especially at twin birth (*ubunyago bwa mapasa*); to the rituals performed on behalf of the country for rain and fertility (*ubunyago bwa kisu*); to the treatment of the young chief and village headmen when authority is handed to them by the older generation (*ubunyago bwa busoka*); and, nowadays, to the sacraments of the Christian Church. *Unyago* is the specialist who knows the right medicines and observances and conducts the ritual. The word is translated as 'officiant' or 'priest'.

By a *symbol* is meant something which typifies or represents something else. Our Nyakyusa informants spoke of *ififwani*—likenesses (the word is also used for photographs)—and in expounding rituals they repeatedly said of an object or action: 'This means (*kokuti*) such and such.' Symbolism is always based on an association, a feeling of likeness between things. The intrinsic quality of an object, or relationship, or event, is expressed in terms of another

[1] cf. Godfrey Wilson, 'Nyakyusa conventions of Burial', *Bantu Studies*, 1939.

object or action which it is felt to resemble. The images men use, the things they feel to be alike, are determined in a general way by the form of the society, and Nyakyusa images are in terms of bananas, staple grains, cattle, smithing on a primitive forge, lineage organization and so on. There are cultural idioms, accepted forms of expression, which frequently recur, but the particular associations are not predictable any more than the associations made by a poet in our own society—the priest and the doctor are indeed in one aspect poets.

The essence of Nyakyusa ritual is that things which are felt to be alike are taken as causally connected. Both positive actions and avoidances or taboos are based on the assumption that like objects or actions react on one another. This was clearly recognized by an informant who remarked: 'avoidances come from resemblances.' The basis is invariably the *feeling* of likeness, but mixed up with this there is often exact observation, as in the following taboo. The husband of a pregnant woman may not hunt big game because, it is said, they will be unusually fierce and attack him particularly. The association made is between a pregnant woman who is irritable, 'fierce' (*nkali*), and the game which is fierce. The husband is identified with his wife, 'and', the Nyakyusa say, 'lion *always* attack a cow in calf'. Sometimes like things are felt to be antagonistic, as 'seed in the belly' and seed in the ground, and sometimes sympathetic. Sometimes like is thought to produce like—a pregnant woman is forbidden to sit close to someone lest she bears twins—and sometimes men mime a misfortune as a prophylactic against it.

The rituals are magical in the sense that efficacy is held to lie in the particular material form,[1] but they vary in detail with the cultural group, just as the language does.[2] The rituals of the Lakeshore plain in Tanganyika (MuNgonde) and of Selya are almost identical, but those of the Kukwe, the Lugulu, the Saku, the Ndali, the Penja, and the people of Ngonde in Nyasaland are all somewhat different. Differences in ritual are directly connected by the people themselves with differences in lineage, and the principle is maintained that every individual follows the ritual of his or her father's lineage, though a married woman will follow that of her

---

[1] For a discussion of this characteristic of magic cf. G. & M. Wilson, *The Analysis of Social Change* (1945), pp. 72–3; 88–95.

[2] An account of the various cultural groups included under Nyakyusa, and of related peoples, is given in *Good Company.* pp. 1–5.

husband when at her husband's home. Kakune, a doctor, explained: 'The ritual for a woman is that of her husband's group, always. My mother was Lugulu, but at her death we did the Kukwe ritual. If my daughter marries a Sangu and dies, they will do the Sangu ritual; she has moved.' We attended a death ritual which was actually performed in two slightly different ways by two sets of mourners. A member of a Sangu family, long established in Selya, had died; sons and daughters of the family performed what was said to be the Sangu ritual, but the children of daughters married to Selya men performed the Selya ritual. Whether the Sangu ritual is really so similar to the Selya ritual as this celebration suggests is doubtful—it seems unlikely, since the Sangu are very different from the Nyakyusa in other respects and their languages are not mutually intelligible—but some sort of adjustment had been made by this foreign family living in Selya and by others in a like position. Our informants *expected* to find parallels to the events of their own rituals in the rituals of neighbouring groups, and they expected also to find *minor* differences. Any variations are explained by the phrase 'that is the custom in their lineage', and the officiant is the final arbitrator as to what is correct. A number of informants also pointed out that the staple foods were used in the death ritual and that these varied somewhat with the area. 'We eat the principal food of the country—it differs with different people. The Kisi and Ngonde (of Nyasaland) use fish, the Ndali use goats, we Nyakyusa cannot use rice but the Swahili would. Our food is bananas.[1] The pumpkin, which we also use, is a very old vegetable and is still much eaten; it is one of the best vegetables.' The Sangu use millet porridge, the Penja maize and beans.

In this book are described the rituals of the main cultural groups of the Nyakyusa—those of the people of Selya and Masoko and the Lake-shore plain (MuNgonde)[2] which are similar, and those of the Kukwe which are different, and a few references are made to other variations. The variations are suggestive, for though the details differ, the values and attitudes expressed are identical. There are also minor differences between families of the same cultural group, and in the practice of different officiants, but their

[1] The Nyakyusa use *amatoki* as a general word for plantains and bananas, though *itoki* is properly one variety of plantain. 'Bananas' is used here to include all varieties of bananas and plantains.

[2] cf. Monica Wilson, *Good Company*, p. 2.

interpretations scarcely differ. Thus the commonly accepted idea that ritual forms are more stable than the interpretation of symbolism[1] does not hold for the Nyakyusa.

The account of the ritual cycle begins with an analysis of funeral rites, for of all the family rituals they involve the greatest emotional tension and are the most elaborate, as well as being performed far more frequently than any others. Moreover, in them are adumbrated symbolic patterns which recur again and again throughout the cycle; in them is apparent that preoccupation with fertility characteristic of the cycle—they are a rite of creation as well as a farewell to the dead—and in them lies the key to an understanding of the conception of the *abasyuka*, 'those who have risen from the dead', that is, the shades.

The principal participants in the rituals are immediate kin—parents and children, siblings, grandparents and grandchildren—but the circle included varies with the particular ritual concerned and more distant relatives and neighbours are involved in varying degrees. In order to bring out these differences and avoid repetition, the detailed discussion of who takes part is deferred until after all the rituals have been described.

Should any Nyakyusa, reading this, feel that matters have been revealed which should remain secret, I would remind them that the interpretation of traditional ritual reveals a profound similarity in the phantasies of the Nyakyusa and those of other races; and such understanding of the dark places of men's minds as the *abanyago* possess may swell that body of knowledge which is the heritage of men of all races and cultures.

[1] A. R. Radcliffe-Brown, *Structure and Function in Primitive Society* (1952), pp. 155-7; A. N. Whitehead, *Symbolism: Its Meaning and Effects* (1928), p. 75.

CHAPTER II

BURIAL RITES[1]

(a) The form of burial

WHENEVER a death takes place, whether of man, woman, or child, a series of funeral rites lasting a month or more begins. The first of the series is the burial (*ifwa*) which, in the case of most adults, lasts three or four days, though for a rich man it may continue for a week, and for a child it is over in a day. For the sake of convenience the account of burial is given mainly in reference to the burials of men; those of women are very similar and occasional references are made to them; but the constant qualifications of statement that would be necessary to give a complete description of both would be wearisome and are unnecessary for our purpose.

As soon as death occurs the women who are present begin wailing and messages are sent to the chief, the village headman, and the dead man's kinsmen and affines, to announce the fact and bid them to the burial. The first message is sent to the father, or to a senior brother, if one is still alive, or failing them to the heir of the dead man, and he it is who sends out the other messages. If the father or a senior brother is alive the burial may take place at his homestead, the body being carried there at once; otherwise the dead man is buried at his own home: the choice rests with his father. A married woman is buried at her husband's home if she has borne children, otherwise at her father's; an elderly widow is buried by her son.

Messages must be sent to all the fathers-in-law and all the sons-in-law both of the dead man and of the senior kinsman who buries him, to all the dead man's full and half-brothers, to the husbands of his sisters, to any classificatory brothers with whom he exchanged cows, to his mother's father or brother, to the full and half-brothers of his father, and to his sons. If any one of these

---

[1] This description is an amended version of that published by Godfrey Wilson in 'Nyakyusa Conventions of Burial', *Bantu Studies*, 1939. The theoretical analysis differs somewhat from that offered in the paper, for the ritual element appears to me to be dominant at the burial as well as in the later 'farewell to the dead'. Between us we attended thirty funerals, in whole or in part.

13

is forgotten he will be angry: 'It happens sometimes that a kinsman comes in later, after the man is buried, and is very angry
because no message was sent to him; he comes in a passion, and
perhaps he beats his brother [the one who should have sent him a
message]. Then the others catch hold of him and say: "Why do
you not come soberly and greet us decently with the appropriate
words? Come now, why?" And if he does not stop they beat him.'

These kinsmen and affines, with their wives and children, are
under obligation to come to the burial, unless they are sick. Young
children under the age of 10 or 11 are not obliged to come, though
they often do, but older children must do so. One reason for the
continuance of the burial ceremonies for three or four days is that
this gives time for relatives from a distance to receive the messages
and come. Deliberately to refuse to send a message or, on the
other side, to refuse to come to a burial for no good reason, is a
symbolic breaking of the bond of kinship and no one ever does
either, unless there is a serious quarrel and all economic and social
relations are being broken off between the two families concerned.

The village neighbours also are obliged to come to every burial
in the village. They normally wish to do so, but, even if they do
not, they still come for shame or for fear of being accused of witchcraft if they stay away. Where there is friendship the neighbours
come in grief and sympathy and quarrels are softened by the
fact of death, but, if the memory of enmity still persists, then the
last sanctions are shame and fear: 'Some people mourn more
than others.' 'The men who knew him say: "Let us go and
mourn him." ' 'Those who did not know him intimately mourn
because each thinks: "He has died, my neighbour, and so will it
be with me one day." ' 'If I have quarrelled with my neighbour
and he dies, I go to his burial for I say to myself: "It is true that
while he lived we quarrelled, but now he is dead and we shall never
meet again. I too will go to his burial and mourn him." ' 'If a
village neighbour does not come to a burial we say he is unkindly
and unsociable.' 'And if a man does not go to his neighbour's
burial then at once people say: "It was you who bewitched him.
Why else do you not come to bury him?" ' Several of the accusations of witchcraft recorded had been occasioned by a man's absence from a village neighbour's funeral. For it is believed that
witches are chary of going to the burials of their victims lest the
dead should rise and denounce them.

A chief normally goes to all burials in his own country, except those of very young children. 'He goes because it is his subject who has died: he is like the senior kinsman of the whole country, he rules all.' 'If a chief omits to go to a burial people say nothing, they know that he is always going to burials and they think that perhaps he has some urgent business. But if he constantly misses burials then people say that he has no affection for his people, that he does not come to bury them as is fit; and if a chief hears them saying this then he is ashamed.' Sometimes a chief who is busy will send a son to represent him. And he sends the drums to beat the lament. 'The drum *is* the chief . . . they cannot beat the drum before the chief has spoken.'

Besides the chief, the villagers, the relatives, and the drummers, there come also personal friends of the dead man from other villages and chiefdoms. And beyond all these there often come others who are attracted not so much by grief and sympathy, nor even by the obligation to express these feelings, but rather by the dancing, the crowds and the possibility of getting some meat to eat. Not all those who come stay the whole three or four days, while the relatives who live at a distance often do not arrive until the second or third day.

The Nyakyusa believe that in order to protect the living and avenge the dead it is most important to discover the cause of death. To do this they summon a doctor to perform an autopsy,[1] an operation fearful and repugnant, but felt to be necessary. The symptoms are interpreted in terms of witchcraft or sorcery, or other supposed causes of disease.

On the first, or early on the second, day after death, the burial takes place. The grave is dug in the swept and beaten earth that immediately surrounds the huts. The first spit of earth is always turned by the eldest son of the one who has died. At one burial we saw the young eldest son of a dead man being helped to do this. He was too small to manage a hoe by himself so he caught the handle near the blade while an older relative held it behind to steady it for him. The digging after the first spit is done by a skilled grave-digger, who may be a kinsman or not, with the help of others. The grave is ten or more feet deep with a cave at the bottom to one side. Some graves are oblong, some round or oval,

---

[1] This is certainly traditional, cf. D. Kerr-Cross, 'Crater Lakes North of Lake Nyasa', *The Geographical Journal*, V (1895), p. 119. The custom is also reported for the Nyamwanga. For a description of the autopsy, cf. Monica Wilson, *Good Company*, pp. 247–50.

according to lineage custom. In the round and oval graves the body is placed in the cave in a sitting position; in the oblong graves lying at full length on one arm; but in both the dead man is set to face the direction from which he and his people have traditionally come. The bulk of the Nyakyusa say that they came from the east, eight or ten generations ago, down the Livingstone Mountains into their present country; and it is to the east that they face in death. Those in the north of the district, whose local name is Kukwe, face in death towards their most recent centre of dispersion near Rungwe Mountain, although they have traditions going farther back to a migration from the Livingstone Mountains through the present Sangu country.

Digging a grave is traditionally a dangerous activity, but nowadays it is no longer so much feared as it used to be. Formerly only mature men helped to dig a grave and they were given a whole leg of the burial meat to eat by themselves. Nowadays young men —often Christians—do it.

Before the burial the body is carried in procession round the homestead. The chief mourners surround it wailing, and the dead man's cattle are driven in front. 'We do this to honour the dead man.' Then one of the cattle of the lineage is taken 'to look into the grave'. Two or three people get down into the grave to receive and bury the body. In the case of a man, his chief wife, his sister, and a male kinsman or village neighbour usually bury him. These three line the cave with mats and cloths which are passed down to them; then the body, previously washed and shaved[1] and now wrapped in cloths, is handed down, and they put it in position in the cave together with a few personal possessions such as a pipe, an eating-pot, a little calabash of ointment, and one of beer; nowadays also a looking-glass and perhaps a pencil and a cup. 'He goes with them to the place of the shades.' A woman is given barkcloth belts and rouge, and a winnowing basket in place of the pipe and pot. They take off the strings of such utensils as are normally hung up. 'If the strings are left on the utensils will still be hanging up and he will be looking for them.' More cloths and mats are then put in with the body, and the cave is closed either with a stiff mat or with the door of the dead man's house, in accordance with local custom. Often there are hot disputes be-

---

[1] The Kukwe wash the body just before death, the Nyakyusa and Penja after. The Kukwe fear lest their children should die of 'water in the stomach' if they wash a corpse.

tween the kinsmen about the amount of property to be destroyed. Once we saw the sons of a dead man tugging at two fine mats which his sister was folding into the cave. She wished to put them in but the sons opposed her, saying: 'Why should we spend all the mats? We have buried him, he is dead.'

It is held to be most important that earth should not touch the corpse's face, but once the cave has been closed the chief mourners each push a few handfuls of earth into the grave, the rest of the earth is filled in, and the dancers stamp it hard. Soon no sign of the grave remains.

(b) The terror of death

Death to the Nyakyusa is a fearful thing. They believe that the spirit (*unsyuka*) of a dead man survives underground (*pasi*) in the place of the shades (*ubusyuka*) and that it can and does visit surviving relatives in dreams and materially affect their destinies. The shades of the dead are one of the final causes with which their religion deals. But contact with them is feared and the function of the ritual at the funeral is 'to drive the shade away'. This ritual begins during the burial (*ifwa*) and continues in a series of rites which last for a month or longer. At the burial itself people's attention is mainly concerned with the death as an emotional event, with the fact that a father, a mother, a kinsman or a neighbour has died; but into the emotional quality of death their religious beliefs enter. With the shades they desire no close contact, for the most usual dreams of the dead are those in which they reproach a man for some sin, or foretell his death; their commonest activity is believed to be the sending of madness and misfortune upon sinful men. Nor is it desirable to join the shades oneself. The place of the shades is a vague and shadowy land where no certain happiness is traditionally believed to be. 'No one', said an old man, 'has ever been there and come back to tell us about it. When the dead come to us in dreams they do not show us where they live nor tell us about their life. We do not know what we shall find there. But we do not think that we shall have happiness, or friendly intercourse.' 'He has died and we shall never meet again,' said another man of his dead neighbour. Some old men, however, have definite theories about the place of the spirits, and all agree that wealth is important there; but these theories have no certainty: 'We are just guessing.' It is certain that the dead continue to live somehow, for they are believed to affect the lives and enter the dreams of their kinsmen; but the nature of their survival is uncertain.

A man, when he dies, is believed to join his ancestors. Until the end of the funeral rites, they say, he is on the way and if the ritual is not properly performed he does not reach them, but troubles the dreams and lives of the survivors until he is properly driven away. 'If you do not perform the ritual for your father or mother you may go mad or else have a slow and lingering death.'

Many of the younger pagans, however, are affected by Christian belief. Young men spoke confidently of going after death 'to a fine country with dancing and feasting and a chief to rule us'. But many old men scoff at such beliefs. 'They have learnt them from the missionaries—how do they know, have they been there to see?' Among some of the younger men also the ritual of death is less important than it used to be. As one Christian said: 'The pagans no longer fear to die away from home—they used to fear very much to die in a strange country (and many still do), they thought: "If I die far from home I shall never reach my ancestors, for people will not bury me properly." Nor do all the young men now fear if they fail to attend a father's funeral ritual.' 'We no longer believe in the old rituals,' said a sophisticated young pagan, 'because we see that the Christians do not do these things and nothing happens to them.'

An additional reason for fearing death is the Nyakyusa belief in the contagious character of many diseases. Death is thought to be caused sometimes by witchcraft, and sometimes by one of a variety of diseases. Of these diseases some are held to be hereditary and to run in families, and they are usually non-contagious; others, and they are usually contagious, are believed to be due to the sorcery of enemies. And the contagion is thought to be spread by an autopsy. It is especially dangerous to relatives; other people do not fear these diseases unless they actually hold the corpse in their arms, or dig the grave, or help to bury it, but all relatives are afraid.

Besides the contagion of specific diseases, the corpse itself is held always to have a vaguely defined, but none the less fearful, contagion of its own. And, because of this, all who have had any close contact with the body go to bathe immediately after the burial. Those of the chief mourners who hold the body in their arms, the grave-diggers and those who get down into the grave to bury it, all go to bathe. 'Even when death is no due to a contagious disease it seems as if there was another disease in the corpse itself, it is a stinking mass of disease.' Traditionally they use two medicinal plants to wash with, but in some chiefdoms near mission stations they now wash without them. The chief of one such country explained: 'In the old days they feared very much to eat before bathing—but now sometimes they just wash their hands and eat. Of old they feared death, they feared lest the disease should spread, they wished to rid themselves of the contamination of the corpse. They used to wash with two plants—as medicine. Now they just bathe in the stream or sometimes only just wash their hands.' But, particularly in chiefdoms at a distance from the centres of European influence, the fear of the contagion of death is still very strong.

Death then is, for the majority of pagan Nyakyusa, a fearful as well as a grievous event; less fearful than it used to be to their fathers, but more fearful by far to them than it is to their Christian neighbours.

(c) The sacrifice

At all except the very poorest burials one or more head of cattle are killed. Cows are provided whenever possible, but, if no cows are available, bulls may be used instead. If the man who has died left cattle of his own, one at least of his herd is killed; if he has left none, his family make every effort to buy or borrow one, or else they provide one themselves from their own herds. If the dead man was rich, several of his cows will be killed. If his senior son has cattle of his own, he should kill one for his father (*ikumbamba*) and if there are a number of grown-up sons the senior of each group of full brothers will offer a cow.

Not only the immediate family of a dead man but also the fathers (or brothers) of his wives and the husbands of his full sisters and daughters are expected to provide cows for killing at his burial, and if he is buried at his 'father's' place then his 'father's' affinal relatives also are expected to bring cattle or cloths. When a married woman dies, her husband and her own 'father' are expected each to provide a cow or a bull. Occasionally other affines of her husband bring calves, but less usually. More cattle are killed for men than for women. For a young child nothing is killed.

The cattle are killed either by the dead man's 'father' or by his heir; if a woman has died, then by her husband. At a man's burial the killing has a legal implication, for the death of a man involves the transfer of his wives and property to another. If the inheritance is quite clear and disputes are unlikely, then a 'father' of the dead man tells the heir to kill the burial cattle. All the people present see him do this and know that he is the heir. And if the inheritance is, after all, denied him later, then the fact that he killed the cattle at his brother's (or father's) funeral gives him a strong *prima facie* claim to its recovery in the courts. If the inheritance is doubtful then a 'father' of the dead man kills the cattle. It is known that he himself cannot inherit and his killing of the cattle is an assertion of his authority to decide who shall do so.

When a man of the chief's lineage dies, a live cow is buried with him and the more general custom of taking a cow or bull to look into the grave is interpreted as being 'like burying the cow'. The cattle used in this way must be of the lineage stock and are reserved for sacrifice.

All the cattle killed are thought to go with the shade to the land of the dead (*abuke nasyo kubusyuka*) and it is believed that if he goes without any cattle he may be rejected by his kinsmen there. Tales are told of meeting dead men in the bush with their cattle which were killed for them. A cloth is a substitute for a cow and cloths which are buried likewise go with the dead. 'We will meet in the land of the shades and he will be wearing these cloths.' At one burial we saw, the dead man had left no cows of his own but his brothers killed two cows for him, three beasts were brought by affines, and sixteen cloths were brought by kinsmen, affines, and friends. 'Why', we asked, 'do you spend so much wealth at death?' 'Because, we say, as the owner has died let him take his wealth with him to the place of the shades. If he dies in lonely poverty he goes with nothing.' At another burial two beasts were brought by kinsmen, six by affines and one by a friend. There were thirty-two cloths, fifteen brought by kinsmen, twelve by affines, and five by friends. 'The bringing of cloths is to express sympathy (*kukuti ndaga*); we bury many of them with the corpse, and some we leave over, which we bind on as mourning belts (*amakiba*). Of old, people brought the cloth the Safwa weave, and brass body-rings. It means: "May our fellow go with them; may he swagger with them—with the cloth and body-rings (*ko kuti umwinetu abukege nafyo, a mogege nafyo*)." And we pour out food that he may take it with him.'

During the course of the war-dance (described below) the young

1. *Sacrifice and drums round the open grave*

2. *Leaping on the newly filled grave*

men cut down some of the bananas which surround the huts and the open place in front of them. 'The owner has died, it is a sign to men that someone has died there.' 'We do it so that it should not seem as if he was still alive; if the bananas were not cut but all stood they would cause us to remember that he was recently alive.' 'We wish the dead man to take them with him to the land of the shades.' And for exactly the same reasons some of the calabashes and pots of a dead woman are broken at her burial, and saplings of the *ficus* used for making bark-cloth are cut down. We have seen older men get up and check the dancers from destroying too many bananas. They told us that 'in the old days we used to cut down all the bananas of a dead man and any crops that were growing near the house also; but now we think that if we destroy all the food his children will die of hunger! So we just cut down a few bananas.' This destruction of food is connected with the belief that a man, when he dies, takes the fertility of the land with him, and this loss of fertility can only be avoided by the proper performance of the funeral ritual. The present moderation of the ritual destruction of food is, we think, an index of the decline of the power of the old belief; for the fear of future hunger, which now restrains them, used to encourage them to a greater sacrifice.

(*d*) *The wailing and dancing*

From the time of the death until the end of the three or four days of the burial rites, wailing continues intermittently. 'We weep because we grieve and tremble with fear.' The old women are the most persistent, next come the men and boys. 'The women weep all the time; even at night they only sleep a little, weeping and sleeping and then weeping again! But we men weep just once, when we first arrive, we do not go on and on.' The chief mourners (*abenemfwa*: lit. owners of the death) among the women, that is the mother, stepmothers, wives, sisters, daughters, and brothers' wives, spend most of the time inside one of the huts, which is the centre of the wailing. The other women spend some time inside the hut, wailing with the chief mourners, but then they move to make way for others and sit just outside. On the plain and in Selya they sit packed close together and sway rhythmically as they wail in chorus, following a leader who stands in their midst. Tears roll down her face as she chants short phrases ending in the high-pitched wail: 'Alas father! Alas! Aaaaaaaaaaaa! Farewell! Go So-and-so, farewell . . . we long for you, Father, farewell!' In the

c

hills the women who are outside do not bunch together, and the wailing is both less rhythmical and less abandoned. The people of the plains laugh at them for not wailing properly. 'In the hills their funerals do not go well; each one wails separately. Here we listen to one another.' 'In Selya they lament a death properly; here [in the hills] they do not; they wail higgledy-piggledy, each one on her own. But we of Selya, and the people of MuNgonde and Masoko, we lead the wailing properly. There is always one person as leader and others follow her. If a woman does not follow, the leader will drive her away from the funeral saying "Wail alone". And if a widow wails out of time, they reprove her also saying: "Friend, we have come to lament at your funeral, but if you want to wail alone we will go and leave you with your husband." Then she agrees. . . . The leader speaks of the childhood and adult life of the deceased and concludes: "And then you died, farewell!" '

The chief mourners among the men—father, brothers, sons—go into the hut at first and wail with the women, but then they come out and sit with the men. Other male relatives, neighbours, and friends, as they arrive, go to the door of the hut, or just inside, and greet the women sympathetically; then they go and greet the chief mourners among the men and sit down with them. We asked the reason for the sympathetic greeting and were told: 'It is the custom at a burial; and when I die they will come to greet me also.' No exact line of division can be drawn between the wailing of the chief mourners and others, for some of the more distant male relatives go right inside and spend some time wailing and shedding tears. And both among the chief mourners and others the extent to which grief is thus expressed varies considerably.

In the groups of men and boys there is no wailing. The group of women outside wail intermittently at first, but later their attention is diverted to watching the burial dance. Those within the hut wail continuously before and for several hours after the burial, and on succeeding days they begin again each time new arrivals come into the hut to sympathize, and at nightfall as the crowds move off home.

Before the actual burial the body is kept in the hut and the chief women mourners hold it in their arms. One man expressed the opinion that, if a death occurred late in the evening or at night, the body should not be buried before noon the next day, so as to give people time 'to weep and assuage their grief, for they always wail more before the body is buried, when they can see the dead man'. Sometimes, immediately after the burial, the chief mourners, both men and women, wail outside near the newly-filled grave.

Very many of the women relatives, a few of the men relatives, and some of the neighbours smear their heads and faces with mud or pot-black as a sign of grief (*kyo kesa*). Such an expression of grief is thought extravagant by the Christians who have themselves abandoned the custom. One Christian explained: 'The pagans smear themselves with mud because they tremble with fear at a death—but we do not tremble; the pagans are very sorrowful because they say: "Our friend has vanished from our eyes and we shall never meet him happily again." '

It is also the custom for the women relatives to bind one another's bellies with strips of bark-cloth, and for their woman friends to bind them also. These bark-cloth belts are called *amakiba* and symbolize the fearful grief and mutual sympathy of the mourners, and the sympathy of their friends. One women, who was taking two belts to tie up the bellies of two mourning friends whose husband had died, explained: 'I give them these to tie round their bellies because they are all a-tremble, they are full of fear.' And when she was asked why men did not thus support one another, she replied: 'They are not afraid like women, they do not tremble much.' But there is evidence that, before the coming of the Europeans, men also wore *amakiba* 'and even now if a chief dies his men often wear *amakiba* for one day'. The Christian women have kept the custom, but they emphasize more the aspect of sympathy and less that of fear. 'If a woman wears many belts at a burial that means she has many friends; her passionate grief is comforted by their friendship.'

Sometimes on the first day, and usually on the last two or three days of a burial, there is dancing as well as wailing. Dancing begins late in the morning to the accompaniment of three or four drums, in the swept courtyard of the dead man's homestead; gradually it attracts more and more dancers, more and more of the attention of the onlookers, until the wailing is confined to the chief women mourners inside the hut, and the dance is the most conspicuous part of the proceedings. It is led by young men dressed in a special costume of ankle-bells and cloth skirts and, traditionally, bedaubed with red and white clay. All hold spears and leap wildly about, stamping down the soft earth of the grave as they dance. There is little common movement, each dances alone as if fighting a single combat. Among the men some of the women move about, singly or in twos and threes, calling the war-cry and swinging their hips in a kind of rhythmical walk. Under a tropical sun in a damp heat, with the thermometer often over 90° F. in the shade, they dance for hours. In the dust and noise and excitement there are no very apparent signs of grief; and yet if you ask the onlookers what it is all about they reply: 'They are mourning the dead.'

This burial dance is traditionally a dance of war; now, as also in former times, it provides those men who are most affected by grief and fear with a violent and passionate means of expression, in which their feelings are assuaged by the touch of life; for the others it was, in the old days, an assertion of their own and their dead neighbour's warlike quality, and this significance is still vividly present to their minds; but, after a generation and more of peace, its content is changing and the sexual element, always present in it, is rapidly dominating the old memories.

'This war-dance (*ukukina*)', said an old man, 'is mourning, we are mourning the dead man. We dance because there is war in our hearts. A passion of grief and fear exasperates us (*ilyojo liku-tusila*).' Since this statement is the clue to both the present and the traditional meaning of the war-dance for the chief mourners, we must examine the language carefully. *Ilyojo* means a passion of grief, anger or fear; *ukusila* means to annoy or exasperate beyond endurance. In explaining *ukusila* one man put it like this: 'If a man continually insults me then he exasperates me (*ikusila*) so that I want to fight him.' Death is a fearful and grievous event that exasperates those men nearly concerned and makes them want to fight. The chief mourners and personal friends among the women assuage their feelings in the wailing, among the men in the war-dance. 'A kinsman, when he dances, assuages his passionate grief (*ilyojo*); he goes into the house to weep and then he comes out and dances the war-dance; his passionate grief is made tolerable in the dance (lit. he is able to endure it there, in the dance), it bound his heart and the dance assuages it.'

This exasperated and fearful grief was linked in traditional expression with a general salute to the warlike quality of man. Those of old said: 'The dead man was a lively dancer in battle, and now he is dead we dance for him, he too was a fighting dancer!' 'He was a warrior (lit. a man of the spear), we dance now, as he danced himself, the dance of war.' And this salute at the same time gave to the dancers a heightened sense of their own warlike quality: 'We used not actually to fight at burials so much as to dance and become conscious of our strength for future wars against other chiefdoms, when, on another day, we would go to raid their cows.'

But although an actual fight was not a necessary part of the funeral it very frequently occurred; and burials are still one of the most usual occasions of spearing. 'In the old days, before the country was at peace, we men often fought at burials; we ran in front spearing one another, while our wives ran behind calling the war-cry and watching the prowess of their husbands.' So far from rituals having the sole function of promoting social integration, as some would have us believe, the burial rites of the Nyakyusa were occasions on which existing antipathies continually found overt expression in fighting and new antipathies arose; but the quarrels were not within the mourning lineage.

The fights normally followed the lines of division between chief-dom and chiefdom, village and village. Kinship and affinity have always for some men extended beyond the single chiefdom; and to the burials of these people, if they are in any way eminent, the young men of other chiefdoms often come to dance. And while to-day, with a well-established tradition of peace, there are fewer smouldering enmities between chiefdoms, forty or fifty years ago it was scarcely possible for the young men of two chiefs to meet peaceably; cattle-raids, abductions of women, defeats and victories in battle were too hot in the memory. Sometimes an accidental jostling, sometimes a deliberate insult was the occasion for a running fight.

At burials there was often war. If the men of two chiefdoms were there together at a burial they would quarrel and fight. Sometimes the fight began when one hurled his spear into the ground and then pulled it up so as to pitch earth on to another man. Perhaps there would be only a few men dancing at first and many sitting down; but when a neighbouring chief was heard coming with his men, and the sound of the trumpet and flute[1] came to us, then we said: 'If we sit still they will say there were no men but only women at that burial, let us dance too!' So we would get up and dance, and then if the others did any-thing there would be war.

And fights sometimes occurred between two villages of the same chief.

---

[1] The trumpet of horn and the bamboo flute which used to accompany the war-dance. They are now seldom heard; drums have superseded them.

Besides fighting, the dancers indulge in an orgy of destruction, slashing at the bananas and *ficus* saplings (which surround the swept courtyard) with their spears.

The dance was thus, traditionally, a common form for the expression by the dancers of a considerable range of emotions, varying from an intolerable burden of grief and fear to a recognition of and salute to the warlike quality of the dead man and a vivid consciousness of their own. And this last feeling passed easily into actual fighting.

To-day it is not so much into the excitements of warfare that the feelings turn, but rather into those of love. Burial dances are the occasions of much sexual display, of the beginning of some love affairs and the consummation of others, and this is nothing new. 'At a death people did not want war (though it came sometimes), they wanted love-making: they displayed the pride of their strength!' 'We speared one another . . . our wives called the war-cry when they saw the strength of their husbands.'

Dances of sexual display, on occasions other than burials, are traditional among the Nyakyusa; but all our informants are unanimous in declaring that both these other dances and the dances of burial are far more frequently followed by lovers' meetings than they used to be. For the enforcement of peace among the Nyakyusa has been accompanied by the prohibition of violence of any kind; and this has freed sexual passion from its rigid traditional bonds. Girls are married young and engaged younger; and while formerly any man who seduced or even flirted with another man's betrothed or wife was speared or tortured by the husband and his friends if they caught him, such punishments are now illegal and the present fine of cattle is a far less effective deterrent. 'In the old days love-making only went on in secret; if a man stood and talked to a woman he expected to be speared. But now the Europeans have introduced the custom of making love openly!' (i.e. by forbidding the previous penalties.)

For all the younger men and women, save the chief mourners and close friends, the quality of the burial dance is now predominantly and openly sexual. But the older people are, on the one hand, more conscious of its warlike associations and, on the other hand, inclined to regard the whole occasion more soberly than their juniors. 'There are two reasons for coming to a burial: the old men come to mourn their friend, they say: "Let us go and mourn him"; but the young men say: "Let us follow the

tradition of the leaping dance and show ourselves to the girls!"
And so it is with the women, some of the young women do not
come to mourn but to call the war-cry to the boys! Those who
come to mourn go into the hut and weep and weep. The young
men say that they dance by reason of the women. The old men
say that in the past it was different, it was war; the women ran
behind the fighters watching the battle and calling the war-cry.
And we all say that the present custom of dancing is the softer
custom of a peaceful land.'

As the old significance of the dance to the majority of the participants was a lively salute to the dead man's fighting quality and
a heightened sense of their own, so now it is his sexual quality
which they honour and their own which they enjoy. 'Why', we
asked a young man, 'do you dance nowadays at burials? There is
little or no warfare and the dead man was never a fighter!' His
answer came almost in the traditional form of words: 'We think
that he too danced before the women, he was a brave dancer
(*mogi*), and so we too dance (*ukukina*) at his death.'

'He too was a brave dancer (*mogi*).' The word *mogi* is from the
verb *ukumoga* which refers to the ordinary dances of sexual display
in contrast to the war-dance (*ukukina*). It is the war-dance which
is still normally danced at death. Not only, however, is its significance being assimilated to that of the ordinary dances of recreation, as this quotation clearly shows, but these other dances are
now often performed at burials. Near Rungwe Mission the pagans
dance the war-dance on the first day of a burial and sometimes on
the second day as well, but always on the third day the dance is
changed. The men abandon cloth skirts, spears, and ankle-bells
and put on their best clothes, an ample white toga being particularly fashionable; the women adorn themselves with great care and
some put roses in their hair. The dance is no longer a wild mêlée,
but is slow and graceful; and its sexual significance is now apparent, not only in the faces of the dancers and the comments of the
bystanders, but also in the forms of movement.

This custom is new. None of the chief mourners takes part in the
dance, though they watch it. In the war-dance, however, the chief
mourners among the men are expected to participate, and some
of them always do so. 'The (men) relatives dance if they have
strength, they weep first and then dance. For if they all sit still and
no one of them dances we others say that they have not mourned
him properly.' But they do not all dance. One old man whose

brother had just been buried said: 'Those who are really sad sit quite still and silent.' But he was an old man with little strength for dancing; on the first day of his brother's burial he sat still, but on the second day he danced a little.

As for the women who participate in the war-dance, running about among the men and calling the war-cry, their behaviour is clearly distinguished in accordance with their relationship to the dead man. 'The distant (women) relatives dance in their dirt, they cannot adorn themselves much, but non-relatives adorn themselves. The wives and sisters of a dead man and the nearer women relatives are the chief mourners and they cannot dance at the burial. They are truly grieved. If a wife danced we'd say she did not love her husband—well, perhaps she might wander round distraught to the sound of the drums, but with grief on her face and without looking at the young men! If she looked at the young men we'd say she did not love her husband. If a brother's wife danced we should laugh at her and say she was no kinswoman of the dead man! But for a man it is different, he dances with his grief to enable his heart to bear it. In the old days, if there was a fight, the chief women mourners did not follow and call the war-cry, but the others; all the men went to fight but not all the women to watch.'

Our observation shows that there is just as much dancing at the burials of women as at those of men. Here too the dance, as now performed, combines the two functions: assuaging the fearful grief of some people and providing a sexual display in honour of the dead: 'We dance at her burial, for she too was a brave dancer (*mogi*).' But in the old days also there was dancing at women's burials: 'For a woman', one old man explained, 'bears us men, so that she too is a warrior.' 'In the past,' said another old man, 'we did dance at women's burials, only a little, not so much as at men's; we said that she was only a woman, but that none the less she also was concerned in war.'

The change in the quality of the burial dance is one of emphasis only; in the past also the sexual element was present: 'We danced so that the women should see our strength'—but it was not dominant. And the warlike quality which was then dominant has by no means disappeared; we heard of many spear-fights at burial dances. At one of them the chief, in order to prevent its continuance, made the dancers abandon the war-dance and finish the funeral with the ordinary dances of sexual display.

The emotional quality of mourning (*ukulila*) is different in

Nyakyusa pagan society from its quality in England. The word *ukulila* in other contexts means to cry, weep, or complain aloud; at burial it is used to refer specifically to the wailing, and by extension to the whole of the ritual. The quality of Nyakyusa mourning is both more openly terrified and grief-stricken and also more lively than in England. And these two qualities of fearful grief and vivacity are very closely connected.

That some at least of those who attend a Nyakyusa burial are moved by grief it is easy to establish. We have heard people talking regretfully in ordinary conversation of a man's death; we have seen a man whose sister had just died walk over alone towards her grave and weep quietly by himself without any parade of grief; and we have heard of a man killing himself because of his grief for a dead son. But, even among the chief mourners, they are not all grieved: 'There are some men', said an old woman, 'who have no sorrow when their wives die. J., when his wife died, was quite unmoved; and some women are not much upset when they lose their husbands. L. was not when her husband died; perhaps she was thinking of marrying again, for she was quite young. But old women are always grieved for they cannot marry again.'

Whatever their private feelings may be, however, the chief mourners and other relatives are obliged for very shame to show signs of grief. The chief women mourners, as we have seen, may not dance; the more distant women relatives may not adorn themselves; and all the chief mourners, both men and women, are expected to weep and shed tears. We have seen an old man weeping at his half-brother's burial, although the two had, notoriously, been on very bad terms and had hardly spoken to each other for years. And all relatives, however distant, who come to a burial are expected to greet the chief mourners sympathetically. Very many non-relatives do so too, but they may omit the greeting without offence, if there is a great crowd present.

We have plenty of evidence that the grief at death is largely mixed with fear. It is, indeed, probable that the fear of death (fear of their own future death, fear of the shades, fear of the contagion of the corpse) touches some people at a burial more deeply than grief. Be this as it may, it is clear that the mourning is, for some, an expression of real fears. And it is the relatives, above all, who are afraid. Neither contagious diseases nor subsequent affliction by the shades, nor the vague contagion of the corpse concern any non-relatives, except those who dig the grave and bury the dead man; but all kinsmen and affines fear contagion, and the family fear spiritual afflictions as well.

These fears are dealt with in two ways: fear is an immediate state of feeling which the Nyakyusa, on this occasion, express and make tolerable in the wailing, the dancing, and so on; but their terror is also rationalized[1] as a fear of certain specific events proceeding from religious causes, and thus is pacified by various ritual actions which are believed effectively to prevent those happenings. The killing of cows, the washing with magical plants, the subsequent ritual of protection—all these are designed to check the occurrence of fearful events.

But still the fear, as an actual state of feeling at the time of a death, has to be expressed in some tolerable form. Its expression in the wailing associated with grief is already clear; and it is also proved that the war-dance is, for the men most affected, both an expression and an alleviation of their terrified grief: 'There is war in our hearts—a passion of fear and grief exasperates us—it is made tolerable in the dance.'

It is the attitude of the chief mourners that is the clue to the whole ritual; and the contrast between terrified wailing and lively dancing, which seems very strange at first to a European observer, is explained by it. The fear and sorrow of death are only emotionally tolerable if their expression is followed by, or combined with, an assertion of life. This is certainly true of the Nyakyusa, and possibly it is universally true. Having no confident expectation of happiness in a future life, these pagan Africans turn at burial to a realization of present life in its most intense quality, to the war-dance, to sexual display, to lively talk, and to the eating of great quantities of meat.

And to this emotional reaction of the chief mourners the sympathetic vivacity of other people is essential. The Nyakyusa were astonished to hear of the sobriety of an English funeral: 'We talk and dance to comfort the relatives. If we others sat sad and glum, then the grief of the relatives would far exceed ours. If we just sorrowed what depths of grief would they not reach? And so we sit and talk and laugh and dance until the relatives laugh too.' And they were even more surprised at the suggestion that anyone might wish for privacy. 'We are quite different: we keep people company, when a relative has died, to cheer them. I am com-

---

[1] The word 'rationalize' properly implies neither truth nor falsehood of thought, but simply the fact of its existence.

forted, I think people follow the custom, many have come to see me.'

There is no criticism of men or women who come to a burial to dance rather than to weep: 'They are not relatives—it is our custom of mourning.' They are saluting the dead and 'seeing him on his way', they are helping 'to comfort the relatives'. The presence of non-relatives at a burial is variously determined by feelings of affection and grief, of respect and sympathy for the family, by a sense of shame, by fear of being accused of witchcraft, and finally by the attraction of the crowds, the lively conversation, the dancing, and the meat.

At the burial of a Nyakyusa Christian there is little unrestrained wailing and no dancing; instead the young men of the congregation gather round the grieving relatives and sing cheerful hymns, full of the certainty of Heaven, 'to accompany him on his way to God' and 'to comfort the mourners'.

(e) Prestige at funerals

As has already been indicated, the length of the mourning depends upon the status of the deceased. It is short for a child—there is no sacrifice and no crowd; for a rich man it is longer than for a poor man; for the kinsman of a chief longer than for a commoner. Mwaikambo explained:

Many conceal their position (*ubufumuke*), it only appears at death. People may never know that a man is rich—only those who build close to him will know—but when he dies many know; many people come to the funeral. For a commoner, an ordinary person, the drums usually play a lament for two days only, sometimes for three, but for a village headman they play the lament for four days, or perhaps a week, and also for a man who has married a chief's daughter it continues for four days or a week. Then people ask why the drums are playing for so long and the reply comes: 'He married into the chief's family. The chief honours him in kinship.' Drums follow the importance of a man.

Those who stay longest at a funeral are kinsmen. If a man has many kinsmen then the funeral will last long because his kinsmen do not return home quickly. A chief has many kinsmen, more than anyone else, because the people of his chiefdom are all like kinsmen. With a village headman also the people who build with him are somewhat like kinsmen, and his funeral lasts a long time.

The size of the crowd at a funeral depends very largely upon the amount of meat provided, and this in turn depends upon the wealth of the family in cattle and the number of its affines. There is a direct relationship between the number of cattle killed and the number of people who come to a burial. On one occasion we were told: 'There are not many people here because there is little meat; they only killed one bull!' And this connection can be observed at any burial; hundreds of people come to mourn the rich, only a few to mourn the poor. And if no meat is killed there is usually no dancing at all. But once a crowd has gathered it is in itself an inducement to others to come. When men were dancing the funeral dance in the rain a neighbour commented: 'They will say there is no rain for many women are present.' We have seen a crowd of 2,000 or more at a funeral, with 100 men dancing at once.

The meat is divided among the chief, the relatives, the neighbours, and the non-relatives from a distance. To the chief of the country is given the breast and ribs of one beast: 'This is to honour him.' To each affine who brings a beast a whole leg is returned to be eaten. To the various groups of non-relatives from other chiefdoms is given sometimes a side, sometimes a leg, and the rest of the meat is divided between the relatives and neighbours who have come from the same or adjoining villages. At large funerals, where many cows are killed and where people gather from all the villages of the chiefdom, a portion of the meat is presented to each of the various village headmen to eat with his men; at smaller funerals the division is made less formally.

'A man's very own cow, that of his lineage, is eaten by the people of the country, not the relatives, because the people [non-relatives] always looked at it thinking: "It's ours." ' A picture of ghoulish expectation? That indeed is an element of Nyakyusa thought. While we were in the country a number of chiefs forbade the offering of funeral meat to non-relatives, for, it was believed, gluttonous neighbours sometimes killed a man by witchcraft[1] in order to feast at his funeral.

The kinsmen of the dead man gain prestige from a lavish funeral. They are compelled to sacrifice by fear lest the anger of the shades, or the 'breath' of their neighbours, should bring misfortune upon them, and they are rewarded by the admiration of men when they do so.

Social pressure is not always exerted upon the members of the dead man's family to provide cattle themselves. If he left sufficient cattle to sustain the family dignity they only kill from his own

---

[1] cf. Monica Wilson, *Good Company*, p. 93.

herd. But if he has not left sufficient, then they are ashamed not to make good the deficiency. 'If no cows are killed at a burial we others [non-relatives] say that it was a mean burial, that the dead man was a pauper without kin, for if he had had kinsmen they would have killed cows for him. So then the relatives grieve their poor griefs alone, we others don't go to that burial.' To a poor burial the members of the same village do in fact come, as they are obliged to do; but few other people come, and there is seldom any dancing.

There is one other situation in which a member of the family is under obligation to kill. If the dead man is buried by his 'father' at his 'father's' place, then one of his 'father's' cows must be killed. But if his 'father' does not choose to exercise his privilege of carrying the body to his place for burial (and he need not do so unless he wishes), then there is no such obligation.

Upon affines, however, the obligation is absolute, unless they actually have not got a cow or bull available. 'If a father-in-law brings no beast to his son-in-law's burial, then his daughter is estranged from him, she asks angrily why he does not bring one, seeing that her husband has died.' 'If a son-in-law does not bring a cow to his father-in-law's burial, though he has one that he might have brought, he is ashamed before men. They say to him: "Your wife's father has died, why did you not bring a cow? Perhaps you think you have a father-in-law still alive (i.e. the dead man's heir, to whom all previous obligations are due, and with whom the relationship of affinity continues very much as before), but he himself, your own father-in-law, has died."' And thus, if insufficient cows are killed to maintain the family dignity, both the family and the affines are made to feel ashamed.

Occasionally a friend of the dead man, who is no relative, brings a bull to kill, as a sign of friendship and affection, but he has no obligation to do so.

Social position, both in its practical aspect of authority and in its emotion aspect of prestige, depends primarily, among the Nyakyusa, on the generous use of wealth, or, to put it more simply, on feeding people. The Nyakyusa insisted on this again and again in explaining the relative status of different people: one man is great and distinguished (*nsisya*) because he feeds people, another who feeds people less is less distinguished. At a lavish funeral, where many people gather and eat meat, they go home in the evening saying with admiration that it was a most impressive (*nsisya*) burial; months or years afterwards it is still remembered and described with pride by the family, with admiration by the neighbours. What is chiefly remembered is the number of cattle killed and the number of people present; sometimes the vigour of the women's wailing and of the men's dancing is also described.

(f) A particular burial (recorded by G. W.)

It is the second day; the man, who was quite young, died yesterday afternoon and was buried early this morning. I arrive at 7.30 a.m. to find that the wailing is the dominant activity. The dead man's house is full of weeping men and women, shedding tears and wailing in the conventional high-pitched voice. His sister, his young wife, a step-mother, a classificatory brother and two half-brothers, with many other women, are inside the house. The noise is considerable. The rest of the women, fifty or more, are seated just outside, in and around an un-finished bamboo house which he died leaving half-built; they too are weeping and wailing. A few men are seated in a group on the opposite side of the swept place facing the women; they are either silent or talking soberly.

The emotional pitch is very high. The classificatory brother leaves the house and walks about round the new grave with his hands to his head, shedding tears and calling: 'Alas! Alas! What kin are left? Alas! What kin are left?' He is a mature man about forty years old. Then he takes by the hand a half-sister of the dead man, a woman of thirty or more, smothered in mud and pot-black, her belly supported by many bark-cloths, and with a baby on her back; together they walk over the grave weeping and wailing, addressing each other in words that I fail to distinguish, and stumbling about as though blind with grief. The baby sleeps quietly all the time. Then comes an old woman, stepmother of the dead man, leading a daughter in each hand (his half-sisters), all wailing, shedding tears and calling out indistinguishable words. They sit down on the newly-filled grave with their arms on one another's shoulders rocking to and fro and weeping. More people keep arriving and in the background now is the insistent wailing of seventy or a hundred women in and outside the house.

For the first hour after my arrival the drums are only occasionally beaten, and a few young men rush across the grave brandishing spears, but only spasmodically.

The two half-brothers, after wailing in the house, come outside and walk up and down together still weeping. Then they each take a spear and run back and forth several times wailing the dead man's name.

One of the half-sisters, meanwhile, rolls over and over in the fresh earth of the grave in passionate contortions, with the tears running down her cheeks. Gradually a group of women relatives collects on the grave, eight or nine of them; they sit huddled up together with their arms on one another's shoulders wailing. One woman, before she sits down, makes a series of trembling gestures towards the grave, crying out 'Avaunt!' in fearful grief.

Then, at last, the drums begin in earnest and the young men start to dance. The insistent vital rhythm of the drums contrasts sharply with the grief and despair of the wailing. The situation begins to change. Still in the house the wailing is loud and continuous, but the women on the grave give place to the dancers and return to the house, while the group of women outside gradually ceases wailing and turns all its attention to the dance. The conversation among the men changes also, none are silent now and the talk is more eager than before. Soon the dancers begin to cut the bananas; one stem falls full on a young man's head, causing loud laughter among the onlookers. But at first the dance, though always lively, is by no means wholly gay. The male kinsmen dance with grief in their looks, calling out 'Alas!' as each shakes his spear.

No women are yet dancing at all; two or three kinswomen wander about distraught, and one of the half-sisters in particular seems quite blind to the dancers, who have to get out of her way. The situation is, however, a lively one, and it becomes livelier still as the young men from another village come to join in, bringing three more drums with them. Six drums are now being beaten and about thirty young men are dancing. Two hours have passed since I first arrived.

At 4.30 p.m. I am back again to find the scene changed once more. There is no sound of wailing, not even inside the house. About a hundred men are either dancing or standing round looking on, with a number of girls walking rhythmically about among the dancers. These girls are non-relatives and adorned with great finish.

The young men leap and dance, some with more agility than others; they stamp, roll on the ground, leap in the air, turn somersaults, hurl their spears into the earth and fight invisible enemies. All the spectators, save the chief women mourners and one or two of the men, seem lively and excited. I see the young wife of the dead man looking tired and sad, and she and the other women chief mourners spend most of the time in the house; but one of the half-brothers, on the other hand, who appeared to be so greatly affected seven or eight hours before, is laughing gaily as he dances.

Two cows have been killed and are now being cut up. As the sun sinks and the dancers go away home, taking their meat with them, the relatives and near neighbours gather round fires and begin to roast and eat the meat. Some is given separately to the groups of friends from other chiefdoms; and by the next morning the whole of the two cows is finished. Wailing and dancing continue for two days more. 'It was a grand burial' people say afterwards, 'we have seen him on his way (to the land of shades) properly.'

CHAPTER III

FAREWELL TO THE DEAD

AFTER spending three or four days weeping, and feasting, and dancing, the main body of mourners scatter to their homes, but the close kinsmen remain for a week or two sleeping at the home of the deceased, awaiting the ritual of farewell. The Nyakyusa themselves distinguish three main events in it: the 'picking up of pumpkin-seeds' (*ukusala inyungu*) when the chief mourners first begin to wash; the 'shaving of the sprouting hair' (*ukutemela ilite-melo*) when the beer of inheritance is brewed and the estate divided; and the 'ritual of the gasping cough' (*ingotolo*) when the widows, having lain with the heir, go to visit their parents. The details differ appreciably between Selya and MuNgonde on the one hand, and Kukwe country on the other, and we describe them separately.

I. IN SELYA AND MUNGONDE

(a) The events

i. '*Picking up pumpkin-seeds.*' The picking up of pumpkin-seeds begins with the formal recognition of the heir, if the deceased was a married man. The heir and widows are suddenly seized and hustled, resisting, into the mourning hut. If they go willingly 'it seems as if they wished their relative to die'. The officiant smears their chests with ash and puts a strand of the *ilingolongofwa* creeper on each one's right shoulder. These are both signs of mourning, and the creeper is also 'a sign that we have given him the inheritance'. After a few minutes the heir and widows are formally summoned to come out of the hut, and they go off to wash away the ash and creeper in the stream. But first, the flowering head of a banana is buried in the courtyard near the door of the mourning hut and the grave of the deceased. If he was not a married man and there are no widows to be inherited, the ritual begins with this. The banana flower is explicitly identified with the corpse: it must face in the direction from which the ancestors came, as the corpse does; if the deceased is a male the flowering head is from a plantain (*itoki*); if a female from a sweet banana (*injali* or *indefu* or

D

37

iselya); and it is wrapped in a leaf (of the same species as the flower) which represents a blanket. The symbolism is interpreted in terms of the habit of growth. A trunk of plantain or sweet banana flowers and fruits only once, then dies and is pruned away, being replaced by a sucker from the same root, hence the association between the flower and the corpse. *Ilitoki* is a large variety of plantain, eaten when it is green and hard; *injali* is a smallish banana eaten when it is ripe and sweet, and it takes nine months to develop. 'When an *injali* stem forms and a woman conceives a child at the same time, the bananas will be ripe and the woman bear her child together.' No one hesitated about this identification of plantain with male, sweet banana with female; it is as obvious in Nyakyusa as the associations of 'breeches' and 'petticoats' in English.

The officiant sprinkles a powdered medicine on to the earth of the grave and all the participants (that is, the heirs, widows, children, and certain siblings of the deceased) rub themselves in it. They rub forehead, right elbow, right knee, and right toe in the pile of earth. Only chiefs and their close relatives and twins refrain, for they have been drinking medicines, and such close contact with a corpse would 'spoil their medicine': 'The medicine would go rotten if they touched the grave which contains medicine,' so the chief's forehead, etc., must not touch the grave. He merely touches the earth with a finger-tip.

Having touched the earth, all the participants go to wash in a stream, and when they return they wash again ritually in the doorway of the mourning hut, the doctor pouring out medicated water from a small calabash and each participant catching the water in his hands and rubbing them and his mouth and knees with it. Then they oil themselves. Until this ritual they must remain dirty and dishevelled with the mud and ash of mourning on them, and any who steal away to wash are fined by the other relatives.

Next the officiant takes roasted bananas and sticks into each one or more pumpkin-pips (*inyungu*) and one or more lentils (*inandala*).[1] She half-buries these in the earth at the doorway of the hut, or sits in the doorway holding a banana near the ground, and each participant approaches in turn and stoops and bites off the banana, and eats it.

The *ulufumbo* (the litter of dry banana leaves on which the

---

[1] Some also add cowpeas (*imbange*), others oil-seeds (*inyemba*).

mourners sat) is sprinkled with powdered medicine and carried out by the officiant and burnt, or thrown away under the bananas. If the deceased has been buried elsewhere still a bunch of banana leaves representing the *ulufumbo* is taken out. 'Until then the rubbish (*imindu*) is kept in the house and not swept out because they are grieving—a person cannot be clean, it would seem as if he did not grieve.'

Next the officiant takes an old pot and, holding it, circles round the hearth while her assistant drops pumpkin-seeds, beans, lentils and cowpeas into it and the participants sing: 'The croaking bird, the croaking bird (*ilinwanwa*).' The food is transferred to another pot and put on the fire and the officiant touches the hearth with different parts of her body (or makes gestures as if to do so), she and the participants saying as she does so: 'The knee is also put on (the fire), the heel is also put on, the backs of the knees are also put on, the loins are also put on, the belly is also put on, the back of the head is also put on.' Then she stamps noisily on the hearth, and the participants sing: 'It startles him. . . .'

Relatives and village neighbours are expected to bring small gifts of millet at this ritual and these are formally received by the officiant, who sits outside the mourning hut with two large baskets beside her and acknowledges each gift as it is brought and emptied into one or other of them. The one is for the millet of kinsmen, the other for that of neighbours. She addresses each giver in terms of his or her relationship to the deceased, announcing: 'Your grandchild has brought a measure, your daughter has brought a measure, your fellow (i.e. neighbour) has brought a measure, etc. . . .' This is spoken of as 'measuring the measures' (*ukugela imigelo*); it is 'to greet the shade', and if millet is not available at the time the ritual is performed it is done symbolically.

A fresh piece of bark is stripped from the species of *ficus* used for making bark-cloth, hammered a little and placed on a fresh banana leaf and sprinkled with powdered medicine. A grindstone is lifted on to it and the officiant grinds some of the millet just presented and allows it to fall on the bark. During the grinding the officiant says: 'The knee is also ground, the heels are also ground,' and so on, mentioning the belly and loins. From the time of the death until this ritual, hammering of bark-cloth in the home of the deceased is taboo (*mwiko*), for hammering bark-cloth is a symbol of sexual intercourse and 'the hammer belonged to him who died'. The first millet ground is made into a paste and later smeared on the heads of the participants as a preparation for shaving 'the hair of the corpse' (*inwili sya mfimba*), the rest is made into porridge.

The participants stand in a line in the mourning hut while the officiant sweeps the dust (*imindu*) on to their legs, and they begin to wail and sing the farewell dirge: 'Good-bye, So-and-so, good-bye. . . .' The other mourners join in the dirge and the women weep. The participants are then told to stand with their legs apart and the officiant pushes a winnowing basket of millet, mixed with a few pumpkin-seeds and lentils,[1] between their legs. She crawls along the ground to do this and then puts the basket on to the head of each participant in turn, and a pinch of the millet flour on each one's shoulder. She takes banana leaves and, after touching her own body in various places with them, she girds them round the waists of the participants. She puts down a stem of bananas[2] and a hen (or a bunch of feathers representing a hen) and each participant in turn sits on them. She holds a banana sapling across the doorway and as each participant passes out of the hut, stooping, he bumps his head against it. Another line is formed in the courtyard and again the basket of millet is put on the head of each participant. Some grains of millet are thrown over them and some sprinkled on the ground. They sing a song, the leader starting: 'The rubbish (*ilindu*) . . .' and the others replying in chorus: 'The rubbish, we were startled at the rubbish (*tunyomwike ilindu*)' and they dance the stamping dance for a few minutes.

Then they go off to bathe, taking with them the stem of bananas and the hen and the bark on which the millet was ground. The leaves they wear and the bananas are thrown away in the stream; the bark and hen are dipped in the stream and taken home by the officiant as her perquisite. They separate to bathe, the men from the women, the older from the younger.

Returning home, they all run into the mourning hut and out again, one by one, as the officiant pours water, mixed with powdered medicine, on the thatch above the doorway, and the water drops on their bodies. Then each sits down in the doorway and is washed again with water and medicine by the officiant.

A mash of beans and banana is made, and a few pumpkin-seeds and lentils are mixed in. Some of it is salted, some left unsalted. A little of the unsalted mash is handed to each participant to eat,

---

[1] Some also add beans.   [2] i.e. the whole fruiting head.

but the salted is mixed in a ball with the millet porridge previously prepared, and plastered against the wall of the hut and on the hearthstones, whence the participants must bite it off. They compete for it, jostling one another. Sometimes the officiant also puts some watery porridge in a leaf of the bark-cloth tree and squeezes it into a basket. Again the participants fight to take a little each.

Some of the millet paste, previously prepared, is smeared on the head of each participant in the form of a cross, drawn from the forehead and the nape of the neck to the crown, and from each ear to the crown. The officiant then shaves each of them, beginning with the lines along which she smeared them. As she does so she says: 'Alas, he (or she, if the deceased was a woman) stole. . . . They cut his head.'

If the family is wealthy at least one cow is killed by the heir—Kasitile insisted that a sacrifice is essential at the pumpkin-seed ritual—and the authority of the heir is acknowledged at the same time. Lubalelo, discussing the funeral of his kinsman Mwafyuma, remarked that, at the ritual of the pumpkin-seeds, when they had called together all the dead man's children, his son would kill cows. 'Then when he has killed the cows the children will be told "He is your father", and all of them will fall down before him clapping their hands to say: "Thanks be! Father has risen from the dead (*Ndaga! Ndaga! Asyukile tata*)." '

ii. '*Shaving the sprouting hair.*' The remaining millet brought by relatives and neighbours is usually put to soak immediately and, when it has sprouted, the wives of relatives and village neighbours are called to come and help grind it for beer. The women of the village bring firewood to boil water for the beer and, when the brewing is ripe, 'those whose wives came to grind' come to drink. The participants are given some of the beer mixed with *ikipiki* and a powdered medicine in a small calabash at the grave. Then the officiant smears their faces with soot and draws lines on the head of each with a piece of banana stalk dipped in the lees of the beer to which the *ikipiki* and powdered medicine have been added. Again the lines are drawn from forehead and nape of neck to the crown and from each ear to the crown. She shaves the sprouting hair on the forehead and at the nape of the neck of each of them, and also makes some small cuts in these places and rubs in the lees of the beer. Or she may do this for the senior participant only, who then does it for his juniors. This is 'the shaving of the sprouting hair' (*ukutemela ilitemelo*) and implies the lifting of a ban. If the deceased was a man and wealthy, the heir kills a bull or cow for a feast.

According to one account, 'the heir kills a cow saying: "This is your cow, Father." Then he takes the praying calabash and fills it with beer and goes to the banana grove. The others sit in the courtyard watching from afar. He blows beer and then pours out a little, several times, mentioning the dead man's name and those of three or four prominent dead relatives, and prays for children, health, and food. He takes his own senior son (or the son of his dead brother) with him to see what he does, for he (the son) will do it after his death. Then they come back and the meat is eaten and beer drunk.' But we never saw this happen nor was the prayer in the banana grove mentioned by other informants.

If the millet put to soak fails to sprout, however, there must be prayer. It is thought that there has been disagreement among the mourners and the shades are angry and have spoilt the millet. The kinsmen gather to confess their quarrels and pray before preparing another batch.

At the shaving of the sprouting hair (or some other time during the death ritual) the sisters of the dead man formally admonish his widows on their behaviour as wives. One admonition recorded lasted two hours, and the main theme was the stinginess of the widows in entertaining their sisters-in-law when the latter had come to visit.

On the morning after 'the shaving of the sprouting hair' the participants shave their whole heads and are anointed with ointment by the officiant. In the evening comes the formal handing over of the inheritance, if the deceased was a married man. The heir sits in the doorway of the mourning hut and the senior wife of the deceased hands him a bill-hook, such as is used for pruning bananas. He is adjured by his relatives, his village headman, and his neighbours to care for the children of the deceased as if they were his own, and the widows are told: 'This is your husband who will hoe for you always.' If there is any division of property it is formally made on this occasion, the dead man's sisters and the village headman being primarily responsible for a just allocation. And though, traditionally, women were given no choice about inheritance, this was in fact the occasion on which their protests and preferences were expressed. Then the heir is thrown into the hut with the women he has inherited 'on to the ashes' (umfwandelo), and must have intercourse with all of them that night. One of them knocks on the wall when he has succeeded, and the officiant raises the *akalulu*, the trill of applause and triumph[1] which is also the war-cry, and shakes a basket of seeds by the door shouting: 'Ours, ours, we marvel at the thing!' Until this ritual connection the heir and the widows remain continent, and great importance is attached to the success of the heir in having intercourse with all the widows. Should a widow refuse the heir after touching the ash it is said that she will either die herself or cause any man she lies with to die of 'the ash'; but if she escapes before being smeared with ash then she is safe. The heir is also in danger if a widow should refuse him after he has touched the ash.

The morning after the ritual union the heir is formally summoned out of the hut by a man knocking on the door and crying: 'Come out, war has come (*Soka! ubwite bwisile*),' i.e. sexual intercourse has begun. He sits on a stool in the doorway of the hut and is greeted by the children of the deceased: 'Good morning, Father.'

iii. '*The gasping cough.*' Each of the inherited women goes off to her own father's homestead with the filth (*indafu*) of intercourse on her. She does not even wash her hands, and she takes with her cooked bananas which she has smeared with her husband's semen and her own emission. This she buries in the banana grove in her father's homestead in which he prays to his ancestors. She takes meat to her father if an animal has been killed at the 'shaving of the sprouting hair'. The heir similarly goes to his father's homestead (or that of his father's heir) with cooked bananas to be buried in his father's sacred grove. Each wife drinks beer mixed with medicine with her father and other close relatives. From the time when the heir sleeps with the widows until this ritual is performed, they cannot visit their parents nor can their children do so (though usually children come and go freely in the home of their mother's people) and, more particularly, a widow must not drink from her mother's cup, or eat with her, or sit over her fire, or touch her hand. It is believed that, if the ritual is neglected, those for whom it should have been performed will be seized with a racking cough (*ingotolo*) and diarrhœa. Even Christians, who eschew the other parts of the death ritual, often participate in the *ingotolo*.

When a woman has died she should be replaced by a sister or brother's daughter, just as the dead man is by a brother or son,

[1] The closest equivalent in our society is cheering, but the *akalulu* is raised by women.

and the widower should refrain from sexual intercourse with his other wives until the ritual union with the 'wife who replaces the dead' (unsasi) at the 'shaving of the sprouting hair'. Nowadays, however, widowers do not keep this taboo strictly, and many lie with their other wives after the 'picking up of pumpkin-seeds'.

Before the 'shaving of the sprouting hair' for a dead woman her brother (or, if he is dead, his heir) goes to cut down the bananas at her former husband's home, as a sign that kinship between them is at an end, but he is persuaded to desist. Mwakwelebeja, an elderly man who had just performed it after the death of his sister Seba, the wife of the chief Mwaipopo, in company with his neighbour Mwaiselage and his wives, thus described the ritual:

We arrived and our wives and the wives of Mwaipopo went into the house to wail, and we men went in too and cried: 'Alas father! Alas father!' Then we seized my umwipwa, the girl Ijonga, the daughter of Seba, and went off with her. The women, the chief's wives, fought with us and cried: 'Bring a cloth, bring a cloth!' They gave us a cloth and we left the girl. Then I seized a bill-hook and began to cut down the banana grove. I cut indeed! They cried: 'Not the banana grove!' and gave me another cloth.

QUESTION: What does this mean?

MWAKWELEBEJA: When we seize the girl it is as if we said: 'My child has died, the kinship is finished, it is finished here, I'll be off with my sister's children (abipwa), they are my children.' And when they give me a cloth they pay saying: 'Father, we pray you, don't! There is still kinship, Father, you are not a stranger! Do not terminate the kinship, it is still there.' And when I cut the banana grove it means the same; it means my child has died here, it is finished here, the kinship has ended. And when they give me a cloth, they beseech me saying: 'Not the banana grove, Father, the kinship is not yet finished, it still exists!' Formerly, if they were rich they gave a bull. . . . We were unfortunate, Mwaipopo paid us nothing.

After I had cut the grove I gave bananas and meat (from a cow I had brought to kill) to all my sisters' children, on the roadway (outside the homestead). I stood with my back to them and handed the bananas and meat over my shoulder. They came up behind me one by one, and took the food in their mouths. [This was demonstrated, dramatically.] Yes, it is a ritual. If we do not give them bananas and meat, their legs swell up, they fall ill and become mad.

Some of our informants maintained that this ritual of cutting the bananas was performed only when the deceased's family had no girl to send in her place. Mwakwelebeja and Mwaiselage, however, insisted that it was performed whether there was a girl to send or not, but if several sisters were married to the same man it was carried out only for the eldest of them.

We do this whether we are substituting another woman or not, but we do it only for the senior sister. There were three Sebas married to Mwaipopo, and when the two junior ones died we did not go to cut the bananas, but now the senior Seba has died, we do cut the bananas.

Mwaiselage explained that his brother-in-law would come to cut bananas when his senior wife, Lyandileko, died, whether she died before or after her junior sister who is her co-wife, but the brother would not cut bananas at the death of the junior sister.

MWAKWELEBEJA: We cut the banana grove again when all the children of those women, the kinswomen married to one man, are dead. That is, their mother's brother's son (*untani*) does it, for their mother's brother will be dead by then. It means the same thing: 'The kinship is finished.' They pay to say: 'No, Father, it still continues.'

A woman to replace the dead is asked for even though her husband has predeceased her. X, describing the ritual added:

And when my mother dies (if my father has died first) still her relatives, my *abipwa*, come to cut the banana grove. I throw them a cloth crying: 'Not the bananas.' Also they bring me another woman. If they do not, I go to them and say: 'Give me another mother to look after me.' They give me a girl whom I give to a half-brother (as his wife). If there is no girl they give me a cow, saying: 'That's your mother.'

Ibaso and Mwaijamba explained:

If, when a woman has died, her people are poor, having no child to replace her, they say: 'We are sorry, but there is nothing at all here, this cow is for drawing water with.' And formerly they returned all the cattle later on; but now, since we have stopped claiming calves, we divide the cows. . . . But when there is a daughter and they give her to me, the husband, we give marriage cattle again. Kinship does not come to an end.

To recapitulate, the main events of the ritual of death are the formal recognition of the heir (if the deceased was a married man); the burial of a flowering head of bananas and the rubbing in earth from the grave; washing; a ritual eating of bananas with certain seeds; sweeping out the mourning hut; circling the hearth and putting an old pot on the fire with various foods; the presentation of millet by relatives and friends, and a ritual grinding; a second washing and the throwing away of a stem of bananas and leaves in a stream, and bringing back a hen and bark-cloth; eating a mash on the hearth; the brewing of beer with the millet presented; a ritual drinking and further shaving when this is ripe; an admonition of the heir on his duties and acknowledgement of him as 'father' by the children of the deceased; sexual intercourse between the heir and the widows he inherits; the burial by each inherited woman of some of the fluids from that intercourse in her father's banana grove, and a ritual drinking of beer with her father and other close relatives.

If the deceased is a woman her brother comes to cut her husband's banana grove and seize her children, as a sign that kinship between the lineages has ceased, but he is dissuaded with gifts, and treats his sister's children with medicines. A sister is sent to replace the dead woman, the widower has intercourse with her at 'the shaving of the sprouting hair', and she returns home to bury some of the fluids in her father's grove, and drink beer with him ritually.

An account of one of the rituals which we attended in Selya which is quoted in the documents (p. 234) may give some reality to this stark outline.

(b) The overt purpose and symbolism

When asked why the ritual of death is performed the first reply of Nyakyusa informants was that they were driving away (*ukukaga*) the dead and that if it were neglected those for whom it should have been performed would go mad (*ukubopa ikigili*). Angombwike explained: 'In the death ritual they drive away the shade (*unsyuka*) saying: "Why are you always at me, nagging at me, in dreams?" It is to swear at him (the shade) and drive him away.'

Another informant explained: 'The touching of the earth is the expression of the wish that he will not come into our dreams and thoughts any more, and he does not!' Another confirmed this saying: 'The powdered medicine and touching the earth are alike; they wish to stop him (the deceased) coming into our dreams.' And an Ndali informant said: 'Shaving is to get rid of the shade which was on their bodies.'

There is also the implication of speeding the deceased on his way to the land of the shades, for it is believed that if the ritual is not performed he will not be welcomed by his dead kinsmen and will continue to haunt the living. Of an unfinished death ritual people say: '*Tukali ukunkesya unsyuka* (We have not yet bidden farewell to the shade),' *ukukesya* being the word used for bidding a courteous farewell to departing guests. Mwaisumo elaborated the point. He said: 'The death ritual is a saying good-bye, it is to see off the dead man accompanying him on his way (*ukunsindikela*); to demonstrate that we have buried him indeed, and to pray that forgetfulness may now come on us.' Another informant explained: 'Touching the earth is to say "Good-bye, friend." '

The danger of madness was given as the reason both for the whole ritual and for many separate actions in it. 'You go mad if you do not shave after a death,' said the wife of the chief Mwaihojo. 'You go mad if you keep the hair of the corpse (*inwili sya mfimba*),' said Mwandisi, the old blind historian, and he went on: 'Yes, much madness comes from the shades if you have neglected the death ritual for a wife or for parents, and the ritual at puberty also. Madness comes from the shades and from Kyala. And if a woman refuses to perform the ritual for her husband who has died, and refuses to lie down with the heir, she also goes mad.' If someone does go mad the cause is usually said to be neglect of the death ritual or some mistake in its performance.

Other types of illness are also attributed to neglect of the death ritual. Kasitile was ailing and thought that his illness was due partly to the fact that he had not completed the death ritual for a relative. Mwilabe said of the sweeping in the ritual: 'They sweep round their legs lest their bodies become swollen and sick. It is said that their bodies will swell if they attend the ritual of someone else and this is done and they themselves have not been swept over.' Several informants mentioned 'a lingering and painful death' (a terror often spoken of by the Nyakyusa) as the penalty for neglecting a ritual, and the last part of the ritual is expressly interpreted as a prophylactic against the 'gasping cough'.

Finally, it is said that the crops will not flourish if the ritual is neglected. Kakuju, a village headman of Selya, was explicit on the point: 'If you do not bury your father properly the food will disappear. They (the diviners) will tell you to find something and when beer has been left overnight outside in the banana grove you pray to the shade.' The fear that the crops will not flourish is not mentioned so frequently as the danger of madness, but it is a general notion.

The danger of madness or other illness coming on one is thought to be greatest if a man tastes the ritual food or beer, or is sprinkled by the dust, at some other funeral without having completed the ritual for his own parents, and the danger of the 'gasping cough' exists only when a widow, having lain with the heir, eats or drinks with her own relatives.

Everyone knows the connection between madness and the performance of the whole ritual and between coughing and the final act, but not everyone is conscious of the symbolism of the various events. For example, Mwakisisile, a middle-aged pagan man whom we knew well, could not interpret the details of the symbolism and he explained: 'Some ask about these things in the ritual, some do not ask. I have not asked. We only know, many of us, that in the ritual we drive the shade, who is here, away from the body, and that if we do not drive him away we run mad. But we do not understand the details of the ritual such as straining water through a leaf, or passing the baskets between the legs, so as to be able to say: "This detail means this." ' Those most conscious of the symbolism are the *abanyago*, the officiants at the family rituals and the priests of the communal rituals. Kasitile, the hereditary rain-maker of Selya, who was a close friend of Godfrey Wilson's, and formally presented him to his dead ancestors urging them 'not to be startled at a white face', was our foremost authority on the symbolism of the Selya ritual. He was more conscious of the symbolism than most people, but his interpretation was confirmed at almost every point by others. Kasitile was not paid for information—none of our informants was—but he and Godfrey Wilson exchanged gifts from time to time in the manner customary among the Nyakyusa, and he often had a meal with us. Mwandisi, a very old blind chief living on the Lake-shore plain (MuNgonde) who was regarded by the Nyakyusa themselves as an authority on history and custom, was also a friend prepared to expound the rituals. His interpretation contradicted Kasitile's on one point only—he denied that one purpose of the ritual was to bring back the shade into the house. Other informants, though less coherent, corroborated Kasitile's interpretation, which may therefore be taken as a general, not a personal one.

There are nine main themes in the ritual: first, the driving away of the dead from the dreams of his close kinsmen, and measures to prevent him 'brooding over them' (*ukobatela*)—the word is that used of a hen brooding over her chickens. Widows, in particular, must be separated from the shade of their husband before the heir (or any other man) dare have intercourse with them. Secondly, the identification of the mourners with the corpse and the separation of the shade from both of them. 'What they do to the participants they do to the deceased. . . . If they are not cleansed he is still muddy. . . . We throw away the corpse, the contamination of death, into the river . . . we drive the shade away off our bodies to join his fellows . . . we separate the corpse and the shade.' Thirdly, bringing back the shade as a beneficent spirit into the home. 'In the ritual we tell the shade to go away and join his fellows, and then to come back with them and warm himself by the fire in our house. . . . At first the shade is in our bodies, we cast him out . . . at first it is as if we were still holding the corpse in our arms, but we throw the corpse away into the river . . . the shade we bring back into our house.'

Fourthly, a miming of the actions of a madman in eating excrement as a prophylactic against behaviour of that sort. The dead, if not separated from the living, bring madness upon them, and simulating madness is a protection against it.

Fifthly, the corpse and faeces are identified: 'The corpse is filth, it is excrement. And so when a madman for whom they have not performed the ritual eats filth that is the corpse, he is still holding it, they have not done the ritual for him.'

Sixthly, the shades are identified with semen and seeds and their control over potency and fertility is recognized. The Nyakyusa think that they are always present in sexual intercourse, and symbols of sexual intercourse are interpreted as a means of driving out the shade from the participants' bodies.

Seventhly, 'the food which he hoed' is symbolically 'given to the shade' of the man who has just died and he is urged to be satisfied: 'You, shade, do not think there was little food at your ritual. . . . The food which we have eaten you have eaten . . . do not create hunger.'

Eighthly, the shade is acknowledged as a kinsman by eating with him food and beer mixed with *ikipiki*—the symbol of agnatic kinship—before he is driven away.

Lastly, a dead man is formally replaced by his heir, a woman by her sister or her brother's daughter.

These conceptions are expressed in the following texts which are given as they were recorded by Godfrey Wilson. No attempt has been made to systematize Kasitile's or Mwandisi's arguments, but the statements made during numerous sessions have been placed in sequence, and are separated only by dots.

i. *Kasitile's interpretation*. (Recorded by G. W. in Nyakyusa and translated by him shortly afterwards.)[1]

KASITILE: We go to bathe wearing leaves, we throw them away, we bathe, then we come back and shave our hair. This means we are driving away the shade (*unsyuka*), for at first he is in our bodies. Our fathers told us: 'When I die I shall not reach the place of the shades unless you do the ritual for me; those who preceded me will drive me back saying: "You are not one of us, you cannot come, they have not yet done your ritual." For the shades linger on the way at first, they do not reach their place.' We do the ritual so as to tell the shade: 'We have given you everything, now go away and may your fellow shades receive you, do not come here.'

When we return from bathing we put a banana in the ground with a pumpkin-seed and a lentil in it. We stoop and bite a piece off, and then we shave the hair. There is much idiocy (*ubulema*) if you do not perform the ritual, and madness (*ikigili*), or perhaps you will have a lingering death. The shade is in the body, he causes madness (*ikigili*), he says: 'Why have you not done the ritual?' The shades pound and stamp the body.

Mwambuputa (a village headman) joining in the conversation said:

All this round us [with a sweeping gesture] is the place of the shades. What we have buried is only the body, to prevent it stinking, but the heart (*indumbula*) stays here.

KASITILE: The banana which we bite in the ground is like the sausages of porridge of the Kukwe, it is excrement, it is filth; because I think that if I do not perform the ritual I may run mad and eat filth. Also before this they beat up a mash of cowpeas, they take it with a spoon and put it against the wall, and one by one we come and eat. This also is eating filth so that we may escape and be clean.

Madness (*ikigili*)[2] is of two kinds, one comes from Kyala (but we used to say from Mbasi, we did not say Kyala) and one from ritual. Mwaipopo (the chief) had the madness (*ikigili*); it is in his family on his mother's side. This is the madness of Mbasi, they do their rituals all right. Mbasi is he who lived with my father here. He called 'Kanjuki! Kanjuki!' from the hillside; then my mother would cook him some food and my father would put something out for him.[3] When we perform the rituals the shades are very pleased to see it; of old you might hear them clapping their hands in the evening here, after we had finished a ritual. But they have gone away now. . . . Yes, the shades are filthy

---

[1] I have made minor changes in the translation.

[2] Distinguished from a trance or epileptic fit, *ukukoma amalago*.

[3] See *Communal Rituals among the Nyakyusa* (in preparation).

(*banyali*), they are in the body at first, they shake it and you fall ill; they say: 'You are still muddy, you have not done the ritual.' . . . When a man dies his heart (*indumbula*) and his body (*umfimba*) separate, they are divorced, the heart with the blood (*ililopa*) and the shadow (*ilisyungulu*) are separated from the corpse which rots in the ground. The corpse is filth, it is excrement. And so when a madman, for whom they have not performed the ritual, eats filth, that is the corpse, he is still holding it, they have not done the ritual for him. If they have not done the ritual for the shade his fellows drive him back and say: 'You cannot come yet, you are still muddy, they have not bathe you in the river.' . . .

Yes, that which they do to my body, to me the heir (or the relative) they do to the shade himself. He, the corpse, is earthy, muddy. That is why we smear ourselves with mud, we mourners; it is this earth that we drive away in the ritual, it is mud, it is the corpse. . . .

The hair of the mourners which we shave in the ritual is one with the hair of the corpse, it is his. We wash and shave and anoint him and he goes to his own place. . . .

First we bite the banana with the seeds stuck into it in the ground, and then we eat bananas and seeds in the usual way. It is the food which he, the shade, ate. . . .

They seize the heir and widows at the pumpkin-seed ritual. The officiant is there, she smears ashes on their chests and puts a strand of *ilingolongofwa* creeper on their necks, then if the woman refuses the man later there is a case and she must pay the fine for adultery. If she refuses before this there is no case, and she does not pay. The ashes and creeper are signs of death, of mourning, of the corpse—they cast them away into the river.

QUESTION: The rubbing in earth—what does it represent?

KASITILE: The banana flower is the corpse. We are saying to him: 'You corpse, we have finished with you, do not come here again, it is finished for ever, do not look towards us, go away.' This earth is the same as the mud with which we smear ourselves at the burial. We bathe, we cast it away.

QUESTION: The washing at the door with medicine?

KASITILE: We wash with powdered medicine at the door because we are just going to take filth (*indafu*) in our hands—to take the bananas and pumpkin-seeds. We bathe, we wash, and then they give us the bananas. It is taboo (*mwiko*) to eat before washing. The calabash used for this washing is hung up in the porch and used for the beer later, the beer which they drink on the path after anointing themselves.

QUESTION: The bananas and lentils and pumpkin-seeds?

KASITILE: At the eating of bananas and pumpkin-seeds we do not separate them, everything is then pressed together in one place; but the banana flower we bury is separate, that is the corpse. And at the water when we bathe we make a separation—they take a stem of bananas, and a bark-cloth, and a hen to the water. The bananas they throw away—that is the corpse; the hen and the bark-cloth they bring back to the homestead and the officiant takes them home with her—that is the shade, is not the shade in the house with us? Do we not pray to him?

QUESTION: Putting food into the pot?

KASITILE: This food is the filth of the body. We say: 'We cast you from us, let our hearts be purified; the mud we smeared on our faces we cast it away, all our body casts you away. We are not corpses; we are putting you to rights and shaving your hair, go away to your fellows.' We begin to get rid of the earth we had on our faces so that we may anoint ourselves again. In our lineage we eat only bean mash, not bananas and millet porridge, we differ in our rituals.

QUESTION: The sweeping of rubbish on to legs and the weeping?

KASITILE: This means: 'We begin to cast you off wholly, let all the ritual that is left come to us, we throw it away.' The measures of millet are to tell the shade that So-and-so has brought millet and is doing his ritual. 'Do not think he is angry with you,' we tell him, 'he has brought this millet.' The throwing of millet from the winnowing basket on to the participants' heads as they stand in a line outside means that we cast him away, we are taking him to the river—at the river we throw away the corpse. They throw away the leaves and the stem of bananas.

QUESTION: Hitting the heads with a banana sapling in the doorway?

KASITILE: They hit the participants on the head, that is the *ndweka* disease of the dead man,[1] we are setting them to rights.

QUESTION: The stem of bananas, hen, and bark-cloth?

KASITILE: The stem of bananas is the corpse, they leave it in the water with the leaves; the bark-cloth and hen are the shade which they bring into the house.

QUESTION: The circling with the pot and putting in of food?

KASITILE: This is the shade whom they bring into the house (*bikumbeka*) when they have brought him from the water. The banana flower they bury is the same as the leaf they wear, it is the corpse which they throw away in the water.

Yes, we separate the corpse and the shade with all our might, the earth we rub our bodies in is the corpse, we throw it into the water and the shade we bring back to the house. The eating of the bean mash on the wall (the old custom) and on the hearth (both old and contemporary) that is the shade in the house. He warms himself by the fire in the house, we pray to him. Putting food into the pot means: 'Leave our

---

[1] Not clear to me.—M. W.

bodies altogether, go away to your friends, sit here by the hearth and warm yourself.'

QUESTION: The grinding of millet flour on to bark and the subsequent anointing of the participants with this flour in a paste, before shaving?

KASITILE: This means: 'This is your food that you ate, we give it to you.' And the smearing on the hair means: 'We have finished your ritual for you, we have left nothing out, bear us no grudge.'

QUESTION: The sweeping of rubbish (*imindu*) on to the participants' legs?

KASITILE: The rubbish is the rubbish of death, it is dirt. 'Let it come now,' we say. 'Let it not come later, may we never run mad.' The wailing (during sweeping) means: 'Go away, farewell!' We have finished the burial now, it will never be done again save once more at the beer.

QUESTION: The basket of millet between legs and over heads?

KASITILE: That is to drive him away, to tell him: 'Do not return to these your relatives here, you were in their bodies, now you are separate, we have driven you away, you are no relative of ours!' All that we do in the house there means that he is in our bodies and we are going to cast him out. The flour on the shoulder is like the flour paste in the hair, this is the corpse, we throw it away.

QUESTION: The song 'We are startled by the shade' (*Tunyomwike ilindu*)?

KASITILE: The *ilindu* is the shade, we are startled.

QUESTION: How startled?

KASITILE: Ha! Are you not startled when you run mad?[1] The heart is terribly startled, it curls upwards; when they say this phrase: 'We are startled by the *ilindu*' they quiet the heart and make it lie down again. Let him go away and be startled with his fellows!

QUESTION: The word *ilinwanwa* (the croaking bird)?

KASITILE: That is the shade that broods on the body. 'Friend,' we say to him, 'we have put you to rights, do not come to us, oh croaking bird.'

QUESTION: The ritual as a whole?

KASITILE: It means: 'We have given you everything, we have eaten filth on the hearth'—for if one runs mad one eats filth, faeces. . . .

QUESTION: What is the symbolism of pouring water on the thatch and running through the drops?

KASITILE: The ritual has many parts. We teach a person that he should do it properly and not leave out anything. Do we not fear (*ukutila*) the water for washing, the water of the corpse? When heavy rain falls do we not flee from the downpour and enter the house? That is how it is then. We mimic what he did when he was alive. . . .

---

[1] *Ukunyomoka ilindu* is used also for an epileptic fit.

E

It is forbidden for the heir to lie with the dead man's wives before the ritual is over. But at the time of the beer, when the drinking is finished, we put him into the house and he lies with them. If he has lain with them previously the semen refuses to come. . . . But if all goes well the officiants raise the cry of triumph (*akalulu*) and shake a winnowing basket of seeds by the door and cry: 'Ours, ours, we marvel at the thing, we marvel at the thing (*ifyitu, ifyitu, tunyomwike ilindu*).' If he fails they go to divine and the diviner says: '*Mindu* (sickness from the shades), he has forestalled the ritual (*akindile ubunyago*).' Then they pray in the bananas. He must have intercourse with all the women he is inheriting; yes, however old they may be, he must lie with them that night or else they will lose their strength of body or mind, or else their legs will swell. With the old ones he will never lie again! He drinks fresh milk to give him strength beforehand! Fresh milk gives strength, it produces semen.

The next morning each of the wives goes off to her father with *ilibalaga* and with meat; the first is buried in the bananas, it goes to the place of the shades, the meat is eaten. And the man too goes with his *ilibalaga* to his own father. Each wife makes her *ilibalaga* by wiping her own and her husband's genitals with her hands and then taking cooked bananas in them. He himself does likewise at the end.

The *ilibalaga* goes to the place of the shades, it is to drive away the shade of the dead man; before this he had not reached the place of shades but was on the way. In this manner we tell the shade that we have put another in his place, we tell him to go and join the other shades now and to come back with them to warm themselves by the fire in his old house.

QUESTION: How can a chief who inherits many wives lie with them all in one night?

KASITILE: I do not know how. Kyala gives him strength! . . . He has intercourse with them all. Yes, really this does happen. . . . But if the man is old and fails to lie with them all, perhaps the wives will conceal the fact. He lies on one side of a partition wall with his wives and the people (for many come to sleep in his house that night) on the other. Then if he fails altogether . . . no one beats the partition with a stick, they all stay quiet till morning; but if he succeeds at first, and fails at the last few, they may perhaps conceal it. One of the wives is told by the officiant to beat the partition with a stick when he has lain with all his wives. When she does this the officiants who are in the doorway shake up lentils and millet and pumpkin-seeds in a winnowing basket and call out: 'Ours, ours! We marvel at the thing!' If he fails altogether they stay quiet and next day go to divine; the diviner says: '*Mindu.*' Then they pray and pray, and praise all the shades of old, and that night he tries again and the semen comes.

The seeds of lentil, millet and pumpkin are symbols of the shades, the lentil is the shade, the millet is the shade, the pumpkin-seed is the shade. The doctor takes them away home and eats them, that means that the shades have gone away. The words they say: 'Ours, ours! We marvel at the thing!' mean: 'The semen is ours, the shades have supported him, they have given us the semen, they have not bound it.' For if the shades are angry they bind him and the semen does not come. . . . If the heir and his dead father (or brother) were on bad terms then, although the ritual is correctly done, yet still the shades will bind his semen at the end of the ritual. Fertility (*imbapo*) does not belong to the shades but to Kyala, but if the shade is angry he binds it.

There are three symbols: the banana is the corpse and the seed is the shade. It is the filth which madmen catch hold of, it is the faeces which they eat. And the banana is the body of the man and the seed is his semen. Eating is sexual intercourse. It is this he has done during his lifetime. It is to send him away and say that we are about to put another in his homestead. It is the body and semen of him who has died. Also when a woman has died the husband eats . . . it [the banana and seed] is what we did. . . .

The seed is the shade, and it is the blood for creating a person [i.e. the semen] because the shade and the semen are brothers.[1]

Yes, they are intermingled, all are together in the ritual: the corpse, and the shade, and the body of the man [i.e. his penis] and the blood [semen] and the filth of madness; all are intermingled. You understand, Mwaipaja (G. W.), you are a priest now, you are a real priest. . . .

When they shake up the millet and lentils and pumpkin-seeds at the beer when he has finished coitus with the women it also has a double symbolism (*fyope fyo fifwani fibili*); the seed is the blood [semen]—Ours, ours—and it is the shade who has gone. Also at puberty it is like this. . . .

Those who say the *ikipiki* is one and the same for birth, puberty and the death ritual are right. It is one only. . . . The *ikipiki* is our blood, it is kept in the house of the senior wife. It pertains both to men and to the shades, for when we marry we do a ritual with it, so the shade says: 'I have eaten it during my life, I was born with it (for it went into his stomach), I married a woman with it (we wash and shave our hair with it at marriage), now that I am dead they perform the ritual with it.' It is one and the same. The *ikipiki* is our intestine.[2] It is one and the same in all lineages.

One day at a funeral roasted bananas were brought. A man started scraping the ash off his with a spear. Kasitile asked him: 'Do you scrape bananas?' He answered: 'Yes, but if there were the litter in the house we would avoid doing so.'

---

[1] cf. *Ulukungu*: semen; *inyungu*: pumpkin-seed.
[2] *Ubula bwa kikolo*: 'the intestine of the lineage'; the large intestine.

Then they explained to me that formerly it was forbidden to scrape bananas at a death, you eat them with the ash on, for if you scrape you will scrape your body also, that is, you will scratch and scratch. But now that custom is finished. Three men were scraping away.

Mwaikambo said: 'In all rituals it is forbidden to scrape bananas —in the puberty and twin rituals also.'

KASITILE: It is forbidden to scrape bananas only at a death ritual, not at other rituals. If you scrape bananas you scrape your own body. It is the corpse. We have died, we are the corpse. . . .

The mother's brother (*umwipwa*) hands bananas and meat over his shoulder to the children who are treated, then he goes off home and they go home without looking back at one another. If they do look back at one another the child will grow feeble and go mad. If the mother's brother does not come to cut the banana grove and do this, if the child sees others eating that banana it becomes feeble and goes mad. The banana and the meat are the filth which madmen take hold of, they are filth. Yes, it is like the banana which they eat at the pumpkin-seeds ritual.

QUESTION: Why the mother's brother?

KASITILE: Who should give it to them? Their kinsman (*unkamu*) should give it to them, he who looks after everything for them.

ii. *Mwandisi's interpretation.*[1]

QUESTION: What do you do in the death ritual, what does it mean?

MWANDISI: When a child has died I do not approach the women, my wives, until we have finished the ritual. On the night of the day we drink the beer then we come together. It is a ritual! Yes, the coming together of man and woman is a ritual (*bo bunyago*). If we come together before the beer then we overstep our child, Lubabelo, he will be impotent and not beget children. No, his children are not relatives (*bo bandu*) they are my comrades (*bobinangu*) but if Lubabelo forestalls (*ukukinda*) the ritual with his wife then he oversteps (*ukukinda*) his children. And when we have finished the ritual Lubabelo begins[2] and goes first to his wife. We follow him at our home. If we begin we would overstep him, it is taboo (*mwiko*). At the ritual of pumpkin-seeds, we drive away the shade, we say: 'Do not rise from the dead and come to us, go to the land of the shades, that we may bear and beget another child, you prevent us doing so!'

[1] His son Lubabelo, who was with us during the earlier part of the conversation, left so that we could speak freely. There was no difficulty about Mwandisi's wife being present.

[2] Mwandisi was referring to a ritual performed on the death of his son Lubalelo's child.

QUESTION: The banana and the pumpkin-seeds?

MWANDISI: These are the ritual which we—I the man, and she the woman—perform at the end, they are the sexual intercourse. The pumpkin-seed and the lentil and the millet are the blood of the man, the banana is his procreative power (*mbapo jake*). The pumpkin-seed ritual is important—when we have finished it then I go to my wife and do not fear her, but Lubabelo begins. Before the pumpkin-seed ritual it is completely taboo.

QUESTION: And the beer?

MWANDISI: That is not important, but the pumpkin-seed ritual is. But when a man has died then his wife must not approach the heir until the beer ritual.

QUESTION: Then the lust for copulation always comes from the shades?

MWANDISI: Yes, desire comes from the shades. If they are angry you are impotent and cannot beget a child; and sometimes also you are impotent because the umbilical cord (*ululela*) has fallen on your mother.

MWANDISI'S WIFE: When my husband says in his heart: 'I shall go to my wife', that comes from the shades.

QUESTION: The umbilical cord?

MWANDISI'S WIFE: It is completely taboo for it to fall on the loins, then the child will not develop, it will be sterile and not bear (or beget) a child. And the mother herself will not bear again, she will not conceive again. . . . A woman cries a great deal with the pain in her belly until the cord comes away: when it has come away then she is filled with wonder and does not cry.[1]

MWANDISI: Pumpkin-seeds are used by us and the people of Selya; the Kukwe perform the ritual with beans, and the people of Ngonde with fish and beer. . . .

QUESTION: Why do the heir and wife appear to refuse when caught in the ritual?

MWANDISI: Because someone has died. Should they rejoice therefore? If they rejoice it seems as if they wished their relative to die.

QUESTION: Do they fear the dead will harm them if they appear to rejoice?

MWANDISI: No, they fear those above [i.e. the living] lest they laugh at them. They are ashamed. But sometimes a woman really refuses. She fights and fights, and struggles and struggles, and says: 'No.' Her friends (the women) hit her and put her in the house, then when she has come out of the house she runs off, she flees.

QUESTION: The ashes and the *ilingolongofwa* creeper?

MWANDISI: They are signs of mourning, they give them to the

---

[1] The umbilical cord, *ululela*, is literally the 'cord of weeping'.

heir. It is the ritual we are performing, they are signs of widowhood (*fya bufwele*), of lamentation (*kyo kesa*). The ashes are a sign of lamentation and the *ilingolongofwa* creeper is a sign of lamentation. Yes, all these things are part of the ritual, we cannot leave them out, it is taboo. (If we did) those below [i.e. the shades] would be angry and say: 'They have startled me and caused me pain in the heart; they have injured the ritual by foreshadowing evil.'

At the end the heir sleeps with the women in the house—before the beer. He performs the ritual with them, the officiants wait for them and ask them: 'How was it?' If he says 'No,' they say: 'Kyala does not stand in the house.' They go and divine at a doctor's who says:' So-and-so is angry.'

QUESTION: Kyala does not stand in the house (*Kyala akema nnyumba*)?

MWANDISI: It is the shades, they say Kyala does not give support. Then again he performs the ritual (*ikunyagula*, i.e. he attempts to have coitus) and they ask him: 'How was it?' They say: 'Yes, they (the shades) have stood with us, Kyala has stood with us.' [He gave both forms as alternatives: *batwemile* and *Kyala emile*.] Then they clap their hands and raise the shout of triumph (*akalulu*).

QUESTION: Is that the cry: 'Ours, ours!'?

MWANDISI: No, that's the cry of the hill people. With us it's taboo. Then in the morning someone shouts: 'War has come.' They come out immediately and run away to the pasture-lands.

QUESTION: Is this 'coming out' (*ukusoka*) the same as that in the coming out of chiefs (*ubusoka*) and in the twin ceremony?

MWANDISI: Yes, they run because their legs were heavy (*nsito*) in the house, now they have grown lighter and are strong; because in the twin ceremony the seclusion in the house lasts four months, at the coming out of chiefs two months, and that is hard, but at death it is only one, so it is light. But at death and the birth of twins it is the war (*ubwite*) of the mats. Is it not war with women? [*ubwite* is used here for sexual intercourse.] Then when they have come out they give one another beer to drink in the doorway. The heir takes beer in his mouth and spits it out and hands the vessel on to his wives and children. Each does the same. They do not swallow it. To do so causes diarrhœa. The man and his wives are burning. They have come from the bed. This giving one another to drink, when each spits and does not swallow, happens after the eating of sausages of porridge on the road.[1] It is the same in the twin ritual except that whereas it is only the principals who give one another to drink at the death ritual, in the twin ritual not only they, but all relatives, and even non-relatives do it as well!

QUESTION: How about the eating of millet porridge with powdered medicine on the road?

---

[1] No other informant mentioned this in the MuNgonde death ritual.

MWANDISI: The sausages of porridge stuck in the ground and sprinkled with powdered medicine which each stoops and bites mean that you should be heavy in your belly (*musito munda*) and not have diarrhœa, it is to make faeces hard (not watery). Some we leave and bury [the end of each sausage of porridge is left in the ground]; that means that people should step over it and take away the disease, may they have diarrhœa at their homes! They will get it really!

QUESTION: Why do the dead man's sisters admonish their sisters-in-law, his widows?

MWANDISI: Because we have all met together. They say: 'Do not grudge him food, go on cooking for him. He dies of hunger! Begin again! And why do you not cook for us when we come? You grudge us food!' We scold them very much and they weep tears.

QUESTION: They say in Selya that you both drive away a shade and bring him back to the house.

MWANDISI: No, we drive him away, we do not bring him back to the house.

QUESTION: But you go to the stream with a stem of bananas, a hen and a fresh strip of bark, the bananas you throw away, but you come back with the hen and the bark. Is that the shade?

MWANDISI: These do not come back home. The officiant has them and takes them to her house. . . .

The stem of bananas we throw in the stream, it is sickness, it is the corpse, it goes to Kyala there. The hen and the bark we give to the doctor, the officiant, because it is she who caught hold of the sickness. She is always an unrelated person, not a relative; we pay her. If we have not performed the ritual we run mad, the shades have not come out, they are still there within.

QUESTION: You performed the ritual for Lubabelo's child yourselves?

MWANDISI: Yes, she was our grandchild. We grandparents don't matter, we carry out the ritual but it's not important; if, however, it is our own child [who has died] then it is taboo. It is taboo up to the point that connections are not relatives. [A grandchild in this context—though not in other contexts—is treated as not a relative]. The ritual *must* be performed for all *relatives* (*abakamu*). . . .

First the stem of bananas and then the millet and pumpkin-seeds are passed between the straddled legs of the principals. The winnowing basket (containing millet and seeds) is pushed along with the officiant's elbow. In performing this ritual we finish the mating of man and woman, for that which comes out of the man in front [i.e. the semen] is the shades, when the participants have spat out we drive the shades away. If we have not performed the ritual we go mad. The shades have not come out but are still within. When, however, we have finished, then they have come out of the body. But they come again, we always have them. (*Apa tukunyagula tukumalesya mboleli nunyambala nunkikulu, po ifi fikusoka kukyeni nunyambala bo basyuka, bo baputile abasyuka tukubakaga: lenga tukanyagwila tukubopa ikigili! Abasyuka bo bakasokaga bikujamo; papo lenga tumalile po basokile munda. Loli bikwandesya kangi tukuja nabo bwila!*)

What we do comes from the shades and from Kyala himself. The blood is theirs and his together. Those who create (*ukubumba*) a child say: 'I am just eating at a woman,' but Kyala creates a child! If Kyala and the shades do not 'cook' [i.e. do not cause desire] you will do nothing, the penis is flaccid, but if Kyala has 'cooked' then you really do something, your heart (*indumbula*) is full of desire. Always the shades are there and we drive them away, they are there and we drive them away. . . .

A shade is resurrected in the body of his child (*Unsyuka ikusyuka itolo mumbeli gwa mwanake*). . . .

Passing the basket of pumpkin-seeds, millet, and lentils between the legs and on to the head and throwing to one side means: 'Here between the legs there is work, may they go out in intercourse, and from the head where we dream, may they go out also.' Because in the ritual we say: 'Let them come into the body' at first, then we drive them away. Rubbing ourselves in the earth and passing millet between the legs means: 'May they come';[1] throwing millet and so on to one side it is to drive them away, that they may go out.

QUESTION: Which shade do you drive away?

MWANDISI: He who has just died, we drive him away.

QUESTION: What about the first ancestor?

MWANDISI: He is there at their place [the place of the shades], we drove him away long ago, he just receives him [the newly deceased].

QUESTION: Why the pumpkin-seeds in the bananas?

MWANDISI: It is the semen (*ulukungu*) for begetting children. . . .

QUESTION: Do the shades always come when a man dies?

MWANDISI: Yes, they always come, they receive their fellow. Yes, even though he has died from sorcery they come and receive him, and even though he has died from witchcraft they come, the shades receive him, and if it is from illness he has died they also come. There is no death without the shades, they always come to receive their fellow.

When the witches have 'eaten' someone the shades come to receive him. No, the witches eat him alone, but the shades receive him. Someone may get up in the morning and say: 'I dreamed they ate me and I was with the shades!' Then he is about to die. Sometimes someone dreams and says: 'In the night I was in the land of the shades with so-and-so, I left him there, I escaped myself and came home.' Then his friend is about to die.

If you do not perform the ritual you go mad (*kukyembela ikigili*) or perhaps you get very thin, and are unable to die, you are ailing and do

---

[1] i.e. the participants identify themselves with the deceased.

not die. That comes from the shades when they are angry and say: 'We shall see!' It is to be finished off.

QUESTION: So the shades always come at death?

MWANDISI: Yes. See, Mwafyuma who died [the old Mwafyuma, a classificatory brother of Mwandisi, died the day before yesterday]. I dreamed at night of Mwakalukwa [a classificatory son of Mwandisi who died about 1932] and in the morning I told X here [his son-in-law who lives near was sitting with us and at once assented, 'Yes, he told me'] that I had dreamed of Mwakalukwa, and there were many deaths in the country—the people of Kisale were mourning and the peopleof Ndemba and that Mwakalukwa had said to me: 'Where are we dead to care for those who come?' And I said to X: 'If someone comes from Mwaya you will see that someone has died.' That very day my son here [Pugana his son was sitting near] came and said: 'Mwafyuma has died.'

This dream of Mwandisi's was cited as a proof that the shades come to receive a man at death. They came to Mwandisi in a dream—the shade of Mwakalukwa came, which he took to mean that the death was to be in Mwakalukwa's country, not Mwakalinga's.

QUESTION: You said the shades come to receive a man killed by witches. Have they no power to drive away witches?

MWANDISI: No, the shades have not the power to drive away the witches but Kyala drives them away.

QUESTION: Kyala? You mean the headman of the village!

MWANDISI: Yes, the headman drives them off, Kyala gave him the power (or duty).

iii. *Evidence of other informants*

KISSOULE: We begin by burying the flowering head of an *ilitoki* banana—that is a person—then we rub forehead, elbow, and knee in the earth there and go to bathe. We push away the earth, that means our business above here (in the world of the living) is finished, we have really buried you, do not come here above, go to your place (below), in the world of the shades.

MWAILAPE (a Christian): They throw the stem of bananas into the water and the bark and feathers, but if it is a fowl and the bark is good, they take them back and they belong to the officiant. Throwing away the stem of bananas means: 'We are driving you (the shade) away. Be off!' The millet which is tossed in the faces of the participants is also thrown away in the water. Tossing it in their faces means: 'This is your food which you cultivated, go away with it.'

MWAKISISILE AND OTHERS: The touching of the ground is the expression of the wish that he will not come into our dreams and thoughts any more, and he does not.

QUESTION: Why the medicine?

MWAKISISILE: It is a ritual, a custom. The medicine and the touching of the ground are the same thing, they wish to stop him coming into our dreams.

QUESTION: Why do you eat bananas?

MWAKISISILE: We eat the main food of the country.

QUESTION: Why the fighting for the porridge?

MWAKISISILE: This is still to wish him good-bye, it is the end of the ritual. We must finish or he, the dead man, will not go away, half of him will still be there.

QUESTION: Why the beer?

MWAKISISILE: Beer is the drink of the country just as bananas are the food. The drinking is to finish saying good-bye. When we have eaten and drunk then we have done with him altogether. Before this he comes time after time into our dreams. If you do not perform the ritual some people say that when you get sick you will never die, but always be sick. If you are sick they will remember and say: 'Let us make beer for ritual.' That is why all must bring some millet to the ritual to ensure a quiet and easy death. Eating and drinking like this is the custom. Something bad will happen to the lineage if it is not done. To refuse to participate is to separate from your lineage.

MPOGO: At the ritual there should be many foods. The bean is there and we eat it; the lentil is there and we eat it; millet is there and the banana and pumpkin-seed. That means: 'You shade, do not think that there was little food at your ritual; the food which we have eaten with you, you have eaten.' Yes, the shade himself eats. We sprinkle on the earth (*pasi*)[1] whither you (the shade) have gone, meaning: 'Do not create hunger, bless the children that they may eat food and not just wander about.' If we do not perform the ritual properly the children will get thin, the shade says: 'You have not unloosed me, I am just on the road.' There should be many foods which means that we have given you (the shade) all the food which we men eat. The banana in which we put seeds is the corpse. The shades eat food, we dream that we eat with them, and if they are angry the beer in the house goes bad, and the milk goes bad.

Angombwike (the Christian son of a famous doctor) agreed, in answer to questions, that 'the eating of filth by madmen is like the filth of death, those faeces are the corpse'.

MWANDISI'S FRIEND (a man of 35 or 40): We perform the ritual that Kyala may receive him, that the shades may receive him, because the

---

[1] *Pasi*: *below* and implies both *on* the ground and *underground*.

ritual is powerful. If you do not perform the ritual for your father or perhaps that of your wife then you won't be a person, your body comes to an end and you die, but you are present, you are still alive, you do not die when the body comes to an end, you take faeces as in the ritual. But when they bring millet and say: 'This is so-and-so's, and this so-and-so's' (naming him whose ritual you have omitted) and brew beer and drink it, then you die.

QUESTION: How do the dead appear to us?

ANSWER: They appear before our eyes at night. You dream and in the morning say: 'I was with the so-and-so's in the night, with the so-and-so's!

QUESTION: Where do you go (at death)?

ANSWER: When we die we go above.

QUESTION: That's a new thing?

ANSWER: Yes, indeed, formerly we said we went below; our fathers and grandfathers said that. But we now say we go below to rot and stink only but since we look toward home when they bury us perhaps the heart (*indumbula*) goes above (*kumwanya*) and that is home. We have seen this in European times in books. No, I am not a Christian and I cannot read, I've just learnt this. . . .

KALUNDA (a doctor) AND MWAIJUMBA: The *ikipiki* medicine put into the beer and lees at 'the shaving of the sprouting hair' is the same medicine as that which we eat at the pumpkin-seed ritual. The *ikipiki* of the death ritual and the puberty ritual and the birth ritual is one and the same, but the medicine for twins is different. . . . There is one *ikipiki* used in all the three rituals—puberty, birth, and death—but to it is added another medicine which is different for each of the three. *Ikipiki* is our kinship, it is our blood (*ikipiki bo bukamu bwetu, lyo ilopa lyetu*); when my wife has borne a child and no one wipes its mouth with the *ikipiki* it means it is not my child, it is just a bastard from the veld, it is no relative of mine but a stranger. In the puberty ritual it is the same, we treat the girl with the *ikipiki* of her husband. She moves from our lineage, from that of her father, she is now a stranger, not their relative (*ikusama nkikolo kyetu, kubagwise, mundu leleno, aka nkamu gwabo*). When someone has died it is the same. We eat food together with the deceased, the shade, and his blood. It is like the Swahili custom of eating each other's blood to create kinship. It means: 'You were our kinsman from afore-time, but now it is finished, you are a stranger.' But the medicine for the twin ritual is separate, it is quite different.

2. IN KUKWE COUNTRY

The Kukwe ritual of death differs in detail from that of Selya and MuNgonde, but it is performed with the same overt purpose: to drive away the dead from the bodies and dreams of the

mourners, to prevent him 'brooding' over them, lest they run mad
or become feeble in mind and body; to speed him on his road to
the land of the shades and bring him back as a beneficent spirit
in the house. The power of the shades over potency and fertility
is acknowledged and the widow goes to her father's house with the
'filth' of intercourse with the heir on her and there drinks beer
ritually, lest her relatives die of a gasping cough. In short, the
themes which characterize the Selya ritual occur also in the Kukwe
ritual.

Many of the symbols employed in the Selya ritual are employed
by the Kukwe also: the elaborate washing with medicine and
shaving and anointing to separate the mourners from the corpse,
the casting away of leaves they wear in the stream, the sweeping
out of the litter in the mourning hut, the miming of the action of a
madman in eating faeces as a prophylactic against becoming mad,
the use of the *ikipiki*—the medicine representing kinship—all these
are common to both rituals. But each has distinctive symbols also.

(a) *The events*

The ritual begins in the evening, four or five days after the
death. The participants wash with *nyasati* medicine in the doorway
of the mourning hut, and lick lumps of porridge off the mid-rib of
a banana leaf. The porridge is prepared by the officiant who
grinds the millet at the doorway and then puts the mixture on two
banana leaves, one of plantain (*itoki*), the other of sweet banana
(*indifu* or *iselya*), which are used throughout as male and female
symbols respectively. After sunset, a pot with medicine in it is put
on the fire, and each participant in turn throws in a few beans
mixed with medicine, and then some water, saying as he or she
does so: 'This is the ritual of my mother' (or father, etc., as the
case may be). A stem of plantains is 'stolen' from a friend's banana
plantation (he having agreed beforehand that it should be taken),
then the participants gather round the hearth and bid farewell to
the deceased. They circle round the hearth to the music of a harp
and sing. As they circle, the participants crumble pods of oil-seed
(*inyemba*). Sometimes they also sing: 'It's the twisting up,' and twist
up cloths as they do so. Then they dance the stamping dance,
(*ukukanya nganya*,) and raise the cry of triumph (*akalulu*). When day-
light comes they eat the beans which have stood overnight in the
hut and sweep out the rubbish (*imindu*) with a medicine (*imitwati*)
and throw it in the banana grove. This is 'clearing out the litter'

(*ukusosya ulufumbo*). Rich people kill a cow 'to clear cut the litter' which, like those killed at the burial, is said to go with the deceased to the land of the shades.

Some time later (the date varies from one ritual to another) they build a little hut at the intersection of two paths—cross-roads—or, if there is no cross-roads near, on the path to the stream, and in this hut they make a hearth with fire-bricks (*amafiga*); a fire is lighted and each participant in turn puts oil-seeds from the *unsyunguti* tree into a potsherd on the fire, saying as he does so: 'This is the death of my mother (etc.).' The seeds are mixed with medicine and, when they are roasted, are ground for ointment. Then beans are put on with water in the same fashion, each participant pouring a little water and saying: 'This is the ritual of my mother (etc.).' Next, the participants are made to sit down on a bark-cloth. The officiant draws lines on the head of each with a bunch of *ikisajelo* grass dipped in the lees of beer, and as she shaves him she mocks him saying: 'Poor fool, it found its mother was dead, went stealing, and they have speared it on the head.' Then the participants go to wash, each wearing two banana leaves round his loins and two round his neck. One of each pair is a plantain, and it is put on first, the other is a sweet banana and it comes on top. And each participant sticks a plantain into his (or her) waistband in front, and a sweet banana behind. When they come to the stream each participant sits down in it and the officiant puts pebbles between his fingers and toes, in the crooks of his elbows and knees, in his mouth and ears, and on his head. These, and the leaves and bananas he wore, are allowed to flow away in the water. They return to the temporary hut carrying flowers, *kalengelenge* and *kakesefu*, which they throw on to the roof, and the officiant pours water she has brought in a little calabash on to the thatch above the doorway, while each participant in turn runs through the drops, out at a back door, in again and out through the drops. As they come home millet is scattered on the ground before them, then they eat roasted bananas with lentils (and sometimes pumpkin-seeds) stuck in them as in the Selya ritual, boiled bananas and beans, a bean mash, and roasted chicken or, sometimes, meat. The bananas are from the plantain stem they stole and from a sweet banana stem provided by the family, and some of the food is salted, some unsalted. As they eat they look in the direction from which their lineage came, then the officiant anoints them with ointment (made from the oil-seeds prepared earlier) and ties a strip of medicated banana bark round the neck of each, and with these necklaces on they must sleep. In one lineage they take little horns and blow into them and walk round calling out: 'We are driving you away, you are a stranger to us, do not come in dreams repeatedly.'

Next morning sausages of millet porridge mixed with medicine are half-buried in the earth at the cross-roads—or somewhere on the pathway—and each participant in turn bends down and bites off a piece, leaving some in the ground. They take off their bark necklaces and throw them into the little hut, which is then destroyed. After they have bathed again the officiant strokes each one on the forehead with a razor.

When a married man has died the heir is formally recognized, and the widows are asked whether they accept him as their husband, at some point during the ritual; when Mwaikambo's father died the recognition of the heir preceded the whole ritual; more often it follows it and there is a formal drinking of 'the beer of inheritance'. In any case the first intercourse between the heir and the widows is always delayed for some months and, until it has taken place, the widows may meet their relatives; after it each widow returns to the homestead of her father (or his heir) for the 'ritual of the gasping cough' (*ingotolo*). Old Fibombe, a Christian elder, described it vividly:

The parents of the girl brew beer and call her to the beer of *ingotolo*. They also call their relatives. She brings a hoe or a goat (or now a cloth or 1s.). First of all she lifts up the pot of beer into which an officiant has put powdered medicine (*imbondanya*) and takes a mouthful, stirring the rest, then she hands it to another participant and when he has taken a mouthful she spits out, then she stirs and hands it on, and when the next has taken a mouthful she spits, and so it continues until all present have done this. Nowadays people do not take the beer in their mouths, they simply stir and pass it on. Pride prevents them. They say people will laugh at them if they do the things of old. Time is passing and things are like *Mambo Leo* [the Swahili newspaper] now. All pagans, however, still do this ritual in a modified form, only the Christians leave it undone.

This informant omitted two significant points in the ritual which we saw for ourselves: the widow brings a spear belonging to her new husband and thrusts it into the earth outside her father's house. It stands beside the vessel of beer while her kinsmen drink until her brother plucks it out and takes it into the house. Then she goes in and steals a piece of firewood from the loft[1] and runs off with it, laughing. The officiant pursues her and makes her drop it and gives her medicine, while the company cry: 'A thief, a thief!' She takes the firewood back to her husband's home. 'It is a sign that she has entered her father's house, just as the spear is a sign that she has entered the house of another husband.' In rich families the new husband sends a bull which is killed and eaten at the ritual.

Our informants were agreed that 'there is no fear of the gasping cough if a woman runs away from her husband and goes to a lover', and in practice no ritual is performed when she visits her father after divorce and re-marriage, but it is perhaps significant that such a situation could scarcely have arisen in the past, since divorce by agreement rarely, if ever, occurred. An adulterer fled, if he could, with his lover to another chiefdom, breaking off all relations with her kin.

(b) The overt purpose and symbolism

Now we turn to the Kukwe interpretation of events. Our two principal informants here were Mwasalemba, an elderly pagan man, brother to the chief Porokoto, whose wife, Syungu, acted as officiant at rituals in the chief's family, and Kakune, a young doctor who had learnt the medicines from his mother. Mwasalemba was much more coherent than Syungu herself, and his interpretation was confirmed by Kakune and numerous other informants. Again I give the interpretation of the two principal informants without any editing other than placing consecutively statements made on different occasions.

i. *Mwasalemba's interpretation.* (Recorded by G. W. and translated by him soon afterwards.)

MWASALEMBA: Perhaps a youth, perhaps a girl, runs mad; he runs about naked so that we say: 'He's mad, why doesn't he cover himself?' He goes to the place of defaecation and takes filth and eats it: he goes into people's houses and takes things, he might even take some things from you, from a European, without fear; he knows not what he does. Sometimes, after a visit to a doctor, he recovers altogether and never has the fit again—that is the lesser kind of madness. But sometimes he recovers and then the fit takes him again later—that is the more serious

---

[1] The loft (*pijulu*) consists of horizontal beams running at wall level across a portion of the hut. Here every married woman keeps a supply of dry firewood. It is her private store-place which may not be touched without her permission.

kind. We take such a one [either type] to a doctor, tying a rope round his waist on the way. For if we leave him free he goes and drowns himself in the lake. So then the doctor says 'His heart has suddenly turned over', and gives him a powdered medicine to eat from a bark-cloth. Then when he has eaten the medicine the doctor puts a finger at the back of his tongue to make him vomit, again and again. So then the filth comes out of him. Then the doctor says: 'Don't eat meat or fish until I give you other medicine later.' Then he ties some of the same medicine in two bark-cloths and ties one round his neck, one round his loins. . . .

Sometimes a man in the mad fit finds a woman, then he takes the leaves off his waist, catches hold of her and, forcing her to the ground, has intercourse with her. Then when the woman returns home she complains that a man in the mad fit has caught and raped her. Then her husband says: 'Well, it's all over now. If he'd been in normal health I'd have sued him for a cow for adultery before the chief, but seeing he is mad there's no point in my doing so, it's all over now!' . . .

Sometimes madness comes by itself, although no ritual has been omitted, sometimes because they have not performed a ritual. The symptoms of the two kinds are exactly the same, their cause is different. The one connected with ritual comes because the shades are angry: 'Why have you left that child untreated, without putting stones on its head . . . ? It seems it is of no account.' And then the child goes mad.

When madness comes of itself the doctor takes the patient to a waterfall and lets the water tumble on his head; then he makes him vomit, and the vomit is carried away in the water. But that which comes from ritual they don't treat in this way; they make him vomit at home, and then perform the ritual for him.

Sometimes madness brings visions (injosi)—the man lets everything come in his speech and says of people: 'What sort are they? They are witches!' And if there is a gathering he speaks out: 'You are a witch—you bewitch your neighbour's cows!' So then people ask what he means by letting everything come in his speech like this, and they are told he has the mad fit on him. The madness gives him power to see the witches, he sees them surely. And of old if a madman with the fit on him accused you of witchcraft you would go at once to drink the ordeal. And if the ordeal accused you too then your house was burnt over you!

QUESTION: Why the washing and eating porridge?

MWASALEMBA: If we don't do this then the children will vomit a watery fluid.

I put a direct question to him about the sausages of porridge and he admitted with a smile, rather an embarrassed one: 'Yes, well, you have understood it; yes, it is a symbol of eating excrement . . . we do it at night.'

QUESTION: The water dripping from the little hut?

MWASALEMBA: If we omit this then the children when young don't go mad, but they vomit a watery fluid, and people say that we have not performed the ritual of water for them.

QUESTION: The meaning of leaves and fruit of bananas?

MWASALEMBA: Yes, it is because those who run mad throw away their clothes and wear leaves. So in the ritual we make them wear leaves; we think that if we don't do this they will have the madness and throw away their clothes. The leaves of plantain belong to the man (the father), those of sweet banana to the woman (the mother). They signify the completion of the ritual, both of their father and of their mother. We make them wear both kinds of leaf, even if one parent is still alive, because they begot them together, their blood is one, the man's blood and the woman's blood. The plantain fruit which they insert in the leaves in front is the procreative power of the father, it is like his penis; the sweet banana which they insert behind is the fertility of the mother, it is like a bark-cloth. We throw them away in the water so that they may float away, it is a sign of death; the blood of our parents which was one is finished now!

QUESTION: The leaves on the neck?

MWASALEMBA: When they run mad people do this, they wear leaves on head and neck.

QUESTION: The stones on the head, in ears, mouth and fingers?

MWASALEMBA: That is a symbol of death. Does not the corpse resemble a stone? It neither speaks nor hears; it does not hoe, or work with its hands at all. He whom we have buried is like a stone. We throw his death away into the stream.

QUESTION: The little hut?

MWASALEMBA: That is for cooking food in; we don't cook for him [the dead man] in the house because we did not bury him there but outside, so we cook for him outside. . . . We grind millet in the doorway because the doorway belongs to the shade. We say: 'Receive us, oh shade, since a person has died, receive us!' Because if we enter into the house we are with the shade, and when we come out we are with him, the doorway is the shade's (*ikifigo kya nsyuka*). It is like the pouring of water on the thatch; when we have come from bathing, we enter and come out again, the doorway is the shade's. And at other times, if someone is ill and the shade has been brooding over him, he stands in the doorway and prays to the shade (*ikumputa unsyuka*). Yes, when a man dies the shade broods over (*ikutobatela*) us living.

QUESTION: Does death come from the shades?

MWASALEMBA: Yes, when I have lain down at night, in the morning I tell my children: 'So-and-so and so-and-so came to me, I have eaten their food, they came to carry me off.' Then there is sickness and they say: 'The shades have brooded over you, you will die.' It is death in-

F

deed. We wash at the eating of millet to say: 'You shade, this millet which we eat comes to you because you brooded over us.' We wash our hands and mouths.

QUESTION: Why do you eat millet?

MWASALEMBA: The millet belongs to the shade. When we brew beer we put some in a calabash cup, but it is not drunk, it is left for five days and becomes lees [i.e. the liquid dries up], then we say: 'The shade has drunk it.'[1] We pray to him and say: 'He is angry.' We brew beer and pour it out in the banana grove, and say: 'You shade, what are you angry about, why have you brooded over the beer?' (They go first to divine.) We speak in the evening in the banana grove and all the children listen, and my wife in the house.

Similarly, if a cow calves and then does not take to its calf, does not lick it, then doctors say: 'The shades have caught hold of the cow, they have brooded over it. Then I pray with water only [in the other case there is both blowing out water and pouring of beer], and I speak as before. Then in the evening the cow takes to its calf and we say: 'The shades refused to let it recognize its calf.' That beer stays for two days —it's not strong!

QUESTION: The licking porridge off the mid-rib of the banana leaf?

MWASALEMBA: We eat porridge and he [the shade] eats. We eat off the mid-rib of the banana leaf because the banana grove is the shade's. When someone has died we cut the banana grove, and in the banana grove we pray. It is the shade's own.

QUESTION: Throwing beans into the pot?

MWASALEMBA: We say: 'You shade! We are eating these beans. Since you have brooded over our fellow who has died, receive him.' For we do not pray to him who has died now, but to that first one who died first. If we do not give him beans then the beans dry up, they shrivel in the fields and people say: 'The shade is angry. We have made a mistake in not giving him beans, we have not taken care of our fellow, his child.' Because the shade creates the beans. Yes, he, the shade, creates all foods, millet and maize and all.

QUESTION: The stealing of bananas?

MWASALEMBA: The millet and beans used are those of the house, but the stem of bananas must come from the house of a friend because bananas belong to the shade. Do you pray to him in the hoed fields? In the millet? You pray to him in the banana grove! Because of this you seek another's banana stem!

QUESTION: Circling round the fire to the harp and singing?

MWASALEMBA: The first shade who has died we have within us, he has brooded over us, we make him circle round, we are with him.

[1] At the drinking of the beer of inheritance in the Ndali ritual the shades are called upon. 'If the beer froths up that means the shades have heard', and the calabash cup is dashed to pieces on the hearth.

QUESTION: Where is the one who has just died?

MWASALEMBA: It is him the shade has brooded over. We say: 'You shade, look after this child of yours, care for him and don't abandon him. He also should be a shade, let the others speak to him in the future.' When we sing 'Farewell . . .' we lament him who has died.

QUESTION: And the trampling dance (*ukukanya inganya*)?

MWASALEMBA: We say: 'You shade, care for your fellow, don't desert him, may he be with you in your body.' We trample the ground because the shade is in the ground, he is within the body, he is underground, everywhere.

QUESTION: What do you mean by 'in your body'?

MWASALEMBA: Because the shade has created us, we came from him, we die, we go there to him; not to others, but to him.

QUESTION: The two leaves and beating and saying: '*Syeku, syeku* of father, *syeku, syeku* of mother'?

MWASALEMBA: Syeku is the name we have been given for the shade. We say: 'The shade, the shade of father, the shade, the shade of mother!' because since a woman has died we speak to the shade as if the husband was 'father' (*tata*) who brooded over his wife. He has brooded over all us living, both me and my wife. That is what these leaves are [i.e. the husband and wife]. We speak to that man who was first buried, saying: 'Perhaps you are within, perhaps you are beneath, oh shade!' We speak to that first man who was the first to die.

Sweeping the house is that it may be clean (*mwelu*). Before that it is dirty. . . .

The shade brooded both over the dead and over me, the living; he brooded over the dead who is with him and over me who am alive; I am in him—we all are. . . .

QUESTION: Why the water on the roof?

MWASALEMBA: If we neglect this then a child will go mad, he runs off to the water and the water comes into his nose [i.e. he drowns] because we have not given him water in the doorway of the little hut there. If we neglect something then the child goes mad and runs off and catches hold of faeces, he smears faeces on his body and urinates into his hands and washes with the urine.

QUESTION: Why does the shade want him to do these filthy things?

MWASAMELMA: Because if we do not perform the ritual for him and do not care for him we do not remember him, then he says: 'Since you do not remember me this child will also get dirty, because I have got dirty underground, I am dead. See, you buried me! The earth has entered my mouth and eyes, why do you not care for me?'

QUESTION: But even if you do treat him ritually, still the earth is in his mouth! How is he satisfied?

MWASALEMBA: Because this shadow (*isyungulu*) [pointing in explanation to the shadows of the banana trees] is what we care for, it is the shade (*jonsyuka*)! That (which was buried) is just earth, the body has rotted, it is the shade that we care for.

QUESTION: And the necklace of banana bark?

MWASALEMBA: We sleep with them. In the morning we bathe again and throw them in the water. . . . Yes, indeed, some throw them away in the little hut. It is the shade, we perform the ritual and throw him away. . . . If we do not perform the ritual we do not sleep, then we pray in the banana grove and are startled.

QUESTION: Why the banana bark?

MWASALEMBA: It is with the banana that we perform the ritual: the plantain is what we steal and the sweet banana what we cut at home, and in the banana grove we pray.

When a man dies his wives sit in a row on a bark-cloth. It's at the shaving of the hair, the doctor shaves them on the bark-cloth. It's a new one because we say: 'You must throw away the bark-cloths which your husband who has died caught hold of, and wear other cloths.' So they sit on a new one.

QUESTION: What do they do with it?

MWASALEMBA: They throw it away on the litter.

QUESTION: Where?

MWASALEMBA: In the little hut. It means: 'Here we have mourned; let us throw away everything, let us wear others.' If a woman has died we men do not sit on the bark-cloth, but if I have died then my wife sits on the bark-cloth and throws away her old ones, and also when a son has died the mother throws away her old bark-cloths, but she does not sit on the bark-cloth! No! And she does not throw away her bark-cloth for the death of a small son, nor for a daughter, even though she be grown up. No! See, she is also a woman and wears a bark-cloth in front. But for a grown son a mother throws away her bark-cloths, saying: 'Because he was my child, I bore him, he sucked my breasts, so I throw away the bark-cloths.' Only for a grown son who has wives in his house does the mother throw away her bark-cloth, not for a bachelor.

QUESTION: The stones between the fingers?

MWASALEMBA: We throw him away. It is the shade.

QUESTION: Is the first intercourse after a death a ritual or not?

MWASALEMBA: No, it is not a ritual; we begin to have intercourse when the ritual is finished. But among the Penja when someone has died and the ritual has been performed and is finished, the husband takes a cow and gives it to the father of his wife, saying: 'I take the woman.' Then he has intercourse with her. But we do not, except in the case of twins.

QUESTION: And ordinary intercourse?

MWASALEMBA: The shade is together with the heart (*alinajo indumbula*); it is he who is roused and goes to a woman, it is he who stiffens us in front, we men, and the woman is also roused. If you have not the shade in you (*ukanajo unsyuka*)[1], then you are sterile, you are impotent, you do not copulate with women; we say that the shades have brooded over you. Why do they not rouse him to go to women? He just looks at them. Because the shade rouses within a man and says: 'Ha!' It rouses a man to copulate with a woman. If it has brooded on him then it does not rouse him; it is within him, it does not wish to come out.

QUESTION: Why do you let the hair grow in the death ritual?
MWASALEMBA: The hair is very important, it's very important.

Mwasalemba identified growing hair after spearing a man, and after the birth of twins and later shaving, with growing hair and shaving in the death ritual.

QUESTION: So letting the hair grow at an ordinary death is part of the ritual?
MWASALEMBA: It [the hair] is the corpse's. We have not yet driven him away. At the shaving we drive him off.

Syungu (wife of Mwasalemba) told me that stones were placed between the toes, not only of the participants in the death ritual, but also of a bride (*unsungu*)[2] and that the stones are children (*amabwe bo bana*). The girl should bear six or ten children to her husband.

'But', I said, 'at the death ritual you throw away the corpse, the shade.'

Syungu answered: 'Yes, it is so, children are born by the power of the shades (*mmaka ga basyuka*).'

Mwasalemba himself, when asked about this, said: 'The stones are the shade, we throw him away so that when he has gone the girl may bear children.'

SYUNGU: When a girl does not bear children we say: 'Perhaps the shades are angry, the husband has not finished giving marriage-cattle.'
QUESTION: And madness?
SYUNGU: If she goes mad we say, if we have not treated her: 'We have neglected the ritual, we have not treated her!' The girl runs about aimlessly, she smears herself with filth. But when we have treated her and she goes mad then we say: 'Perhaps Kyala has deserted me, see nothing remains, we have treated her.'

[1] He used both the phrases *ukusita kuja nunsyuka* (to be without the shade) and *unsyuka ikummobatela* (the shade broods on him) for the same phenomenon.
[2] *Unsungu*: a girl who has reached puberty but has not yet borne a child; one undergoing the puberty-marriage ritual (*ubusungu*).

QUESTION: What are the stones in the clefts of hands and toes?

MWASALEMBA: Kyala when he created men said: 'At the death ritual do this, it is the shade, it is the body.'

Mwasalemba went on to discuss the puberty ritual and attributed sexual desire and diarrhœa to the shades. He explained that faeces (which are buried) 'go below to the land of the shades' (*vide* p. 127; 210 ff.).

SYUNGU: If we leave out something a child runs off to Mwibonde [wild pasture-land] and catches hold of that which is bad and pants with madness (*ikigili*). Some go to Mwibonde and gather faggots and put them on their heads then throw them away again.

QUESTION: How is it that people ever omit a ritual?

SYUNGU: Some omit some of it. They make mistakes out of ignorance.

QUESTION: But do any omit it altogether?

SYUNGU: No, only the Christians. No pagan neglects it altogether.

QUESTION: But those who have run away and are not there (e.g. women who have eloped with lovers)?

SYUNGU: Yes, indeed, it is they who neglect it, but those who are at home perform the ritual.

QUESTION: How about stealing the banana bunch?

SYUNGU: Yes, we steal it, but we tell the owner beforehand, and when we eat the mash we mix the stolen with the home-grown, that which is stolen is always a plantain and that from home is a sweet banana. The plantain is the man's and the sweet banana the woman's. And when we bathe we wear a plantain leaf, which has been stolen, in front, and a sweet banana leaf, which comes from home, behind.

MWASALEMBA:[1] The girl brought the spear of her husband and stuck it in the ground. At the end Losi (my eldest son and her full brother) pulled it up and it will always be on my wall. The spear is an essential part of the ritual; without it the ritual would go wrong. If she came with no spear we should send her back again to fetch one.

We drink the medicine because, when our son-in-law has died and our daughter lies with another who has not been our son-in-law before, if she comes and gives us food with the filth (*indafu*) on her then we gasp and cough with *ingotolo*. It is quite different if she runs away from her husband when he is alive. Then we drink no medicine. Yes, then she comes, with *indafu* on her, and gives us food and nothing happens. I don't know why. Kyala made us black people like this. It is when her husband dies that we drink. We drink as soon as she lies with her new husband, not after she becomes pregnant. If we see that she is pregnant before she comes we are angry. She should come first to the ritual and then conceive. She does not wait until her periods stop before coming

---

[1] Referring to the *ingotolo* ritual for his daughter described on p. 66.

for the ritual. We think that when she has slept with her new husband she is full (*nsito*) and if she gives us food it will make us ill.

MWANGWANDA: The new husband gives us relatives a disease by impregnating the girl, he who is no relative of ours, the new husband. *Ingotolo* is an illness.

ii. *Kakune's interpretation.* (Recorded by G. W.)

KAKUNE: Yes, if we do not perform the ritual the children run mad. They speak foolishly and deliriously, they run about wildly wearing leaves, they eat filth. But they do not fight with their fellows—that is what those do who have the madness of Kyala. It is these of whom we say: 'Perhaps Kyala loved them.'

QUESTION: Why the first washing?

KAKUNE: That is to get rid of the disease, the filth, for they held the corpse in their hands. They do not eat the ritual food until they have washed.

QUESTION: Why the eating of porridge?

KAKUNE: Because of the tears we have wept. We have mourned him; now let us eat and strengthen our bodies again.

QUESTION: Why are beans thrown into the pot in the evening?

KAKUNE: These beans, which we throw into the pot, saying: 'This is my father's death', are an ending of the ritual. They remain all night in the house after they have been cooked, and the shades come and eat. In the morning the doctor [*unganga*, i.e. the officiant] washes us again with powdered medicine and we eat the beans and finish them. We use beans in the ritual for that is the food which our father hoed. We think: 'Our father has died, he will never hoe for us again', and so we say: 'This is the death of my father.' So then the shade of our father comes at night and tastes the food and says to us: 'I, your father, have died, you have mourned for me; live you yet awhile, do not come quickly to death; and may you hoe plenty of food and have no hunger.' If we leave out this ritual with the beans the fertility of our gardens disappears and we have great hunger, we eat nothing.

QUESTION: Why the circling to the harp and crumbling oil-seeds?

KAKUNE: The ointment (made from the oil-seeds) is to finish the ritual. The song (*ukalende*) is to say good-bye, to the shade, it means 'farewell', it is to drive him away. We circle round because our father was an active man, he walked round seeing his friends, he danced; that is why we circle round the fire. [In Kakune's family they do not cry the war shout of triumph, they only dance to the harp.]

QUESTION: Why the pebbles? [I told him what Mwasalemba had said and he agreed heartily.]

KAKUNE: Yes, that's it! We throw them away, this means 'We have driven you away now.'

QUESTION: Why the leaves and bananas?

KAKUNE: If you do not wear these and throw them away your own children [i.e. children of the participant] will die soon after birth; you beget a daughter and she dies, a son and he dies, then people say: 'See, you did not perform the ritual.' . . .

QUESTION: What is the meaning of the death ritual?

KAKUNE: Because the deceased has died on us (*atufwelile mumbeli*), if we do not treat him, he looks on us, we are together with him, he does not move away at all, so then, we drive him off.

He then described the acts of the ritual in great detail exactly checking what Mwaikambo and I saw when Kalata's mother died (cf. pp. 238–44) except that he did not mention grinding ointment at the circling round. I asked about this and he thought it was not done in his lineage but was not sure.

QUESTION: The stones between the toes?

KAKUNE: It is to make a separation, it is our separation, we are driving him off; we go into the water with pebbles and throw them away, they are the deceased, we drive him off.

QUESTION: And what about running through the house letting the water drip on you after bathing?

KAKUNE: Yes, indeed, we come from the stream carrying water which we have drawn, and flowers in our hands, and we throw the flowers on the thatch.

QUESTION: What does it mean?

KAKUNE: It is because we have come from the stream, we have driven him away in the stream, but we bring back water we have drawn and flowers—they are the deceased. It means we are with him for he has not moved (*akasama*); let us drive him out again. We throw away the flowers on the thatch and we pour water on the thatch and it trickles down on the body. It is he [the deceased] whom we receive. If we drive him away altogether at the water what will he say to us?

QUESTION: You receive him and drive him off again?

KAKUNE: We drive him off so that his whole body should not be seen, because we fear to see the dead . . . and at the same time we do *not* drive him away, he will come in dreams to tell us of misdeeds (*ukutubula inongwa*).

When we receive him we drive him away again at the anointing with ointment. The doctor anoints us on the toe, knee, elbow, stomach, and forehead, and says: 'I have finished them, anoint yourselves.' Then we anoint ourselves and say: 'You have moved to another village.' But at the same time we do not throw him away altogether, we pray to him and say: 'You, Father, stand by me.' We bring him back when we have bathed. He also bathed there, he is present![1]

QUESTION: The meaning of the shaving?

KAKUNE: The doctor takes a bunch of *ikisajelo* grass and a little millet beer and then makes two cross lines in the hair before shaving, and he shaves us.

QUESTION: Why?

KAKUNE: It is the ritual, we drive him off.

Being unable to get any more I then suggested that the *ikisajelo* and beer represented the shade and that they took him on to their bodies in order to throw him off.

Kakune: 'Yes, that's it, you are very intelligent for you understand it! That's it!'

QUESTION: And is the *ikisajelo* grass the shade's which the seers uproot?

KAKUNE: Yes, we have heard that long ago there were three seers (*abakunguluka*), X and Y and Z [I missed the names], who went with two village headmen to look; one seer uprooted the *ikisajelo* grass to look beneath at the land of the shades and he called the village headmen to look. When they shrank back and said 'He!' he said it was a homestead such as those above.

QUESTION: Did this happen in the day-time?

KAKUNE: It happened in the day-time, in the open, not in a dream. But later on, when one village headman had gone he said: 'Let me look again.' He tried to uproot it but the *ikisajelo* grass was stuck, it would not come up. But all that happened a long time ago; seers are not seen nowadays. And when we have finished everything, at the time of destroying the ritual house, the doctor touches us all with the razor, that is the tuft (*itemelo*).

QUESTION: Is this before the beer of inheritance?

KAKUNE: Yes, before the beer, on the day of bathing. It means that letting the 'hair of the corpse' grow is finished, we have finished. You may drink freely. And have we written about the roasted chicken and the bananas?[2]

G. W.: No.

KAKUNE: What? No? But we all eat these with our fellow villagers—and a bull if we have killed one, for we kill a bull if we have it—at the bathing in the stream. And in the evening the doctor prepares the

---

[1] The statement above was not made quite so straightforwardly as it is written down; at certain points Kakune stopped and I prompted him either with: 'And then?' or 'What does that mean?' There were no leading questions and I took down his words exactly.

[2] Our best informants often asked whether what they told us was properly recorded.

porridge—sausages of porridge are buried in the ground and bitten off by the principals who stoop down to do it.

QUESTION: What does it mean?

KAKUNE: It means that we are about to honour them; they eat, and he whom we have buried also remains below, he also eats, we bury the sausage in the earth and we say we are burying him also, then he will fear to come to the house.

QUESTION: And this porridge is a symbol of the filth which those who run mad eat?

KAKUNE (laughing): Yes, because if we omit to do these things the children become feeble, their hearts say 'He! he!' [panting and excited] and they rush off to the road and eat dirt (*imindo*).

QUESTION: Why should the shades do this to them? How are they interested in dirt (*imindo*)?

KAKUNE: I don't know. We say it is because we have not accompanied them on the road and on account of this the shade is very angry and says: 'We shall see whether their children flourish!' He has bewitched them (*abalogile*).

QUESTION: And what about the circling round with the harp and the trampling at the fire?

KAKUNE: That is not very important, Mwaipaja [G. W.], it is because he cultivated food and danced at beer drinks when he was alive, so we dance for him now that he is dead. . . . A widow must lie with her husband the night before she comes to do the (*ingotolo*) ritual, and she comes with his filth on her, she does not wash. If she comes without having lain with him the night before then we all get the disease. The disease comes from the new husband, it comes from his seed, the seed that begets us men. When his seed enters her womb then she is heavy (*nsito*) and if she eats or drinks out of our dishes and pots while we are empty (*bwasi*), before we have stopped ourselves with medicines, then she gives us the disease. She has not given us the protective medicine (*imbosyo*).

If a woman changes from one husband to another and both are alive, there is no danger and no ritual. It is death that brings the danger, because that man [her first husband] has died; he has died and rotted below, and from that disease comes. The disease only comes from this situation. If no relative has died there is no *ingotolo*. But if my wife has run off with another man and then comes back to me with his semen in her, then I take some powdered medicine and eat some and throw a little on the fire, and if I do not do this then my legs will hurt, I shall be unable to walk properly, and my body will become weak. Neither she nor her relatives take medicine, nor does her new husband, if she goes to him and he pays for her and takes her. He just marries her.

If the widow is left with a sucking child and is empty [*bwasi*: i.e. her new husband has not been sleeping with her], then at first, before she lies with him, we (her relatives) eat with her. But when the child leaves the breast and her husband begets another then she comes to perform the ritual. Otherwise we cannot eat with her. And so with a pregnant widow—at first we eat with her but when the child is born and has been weaned and her new husband begets another she comes to perform the ritual.

The new husband must send a bull or a sheep with his spear, and we who drink the beer divide the meat, saying: 'Thank you, you have nourished us.' Yesterday he sent 30s., and I, the doctor, got 1s. If it had been a bull I would have got some meat. The husband does not come himself, but he sends a friend to bring the woman. This friend does not eat or drink the medicine, but he drinks the beer without medicine and the cassava we cook. [In the ritual just completed] Mwasalemba provided three pots of beer—we drank one before and two after the ceremony. That was what the men were waiting for.

No, it never happens that one who has drunk the medicine of *ingotolo* falls sick of it afterwards, never.

The spear is taken and kept by the girl's brother at the command of her father, who says: 'Take this spear, your sister has brought it.' It is a symbol (*ikimanyilo*) of kinship, it is like the spear with which a girl was betrothed in the old days. At the betrothal the lover would stick the spear in the ground, the girl pulled it up and took it to her father, sticking it into the ground before him, and he, if he agreed, told her brother to take it up. And if there is any dispute later about cattle then the spear is proof of agreement. It has the same significance at betrothal and at the *ingotolo* ritual. Sometimes the heir has to bring cattle that have not yet been paid by the dead man. When the woman's brother takes the spear into the house at the *ingotolo* ritual, that means: 'Now you[1] have entered into the house—your house—so we bring you in.' And then she can go in.

The calling out of 'Thief' is a custom in the ritual, but it is like a song, it's not important. The firewood is shown to the woman and a bean and a grain of maize are put into a crack of the wood. That means that the ritual is complete.

No, there is no extra safety in coming to the ceremony; those who drink at home are equally protected!

iii. *Evidence of other informants*

CURRENT TALK: Some people have been told by those who have run mad, that they see a man who comes to them sometimes. When that man is with them then they lose the sense of what they are doing. The

---

[1] It was not clear from the context whether 'you' referred to groom or bride. The symbolism suggests the act of marriage but of this we have no direct evidence.

man tells them 'Go there', and then the victim goes; perhaps he says 'Run', and then he runs where he is told. Some say that smoke comes out of the ground, rises, and goes to the bush, and that they run to the bush where the smoke ended. They say that the smoke rises from the ground and goes with great speed to the place at which it comes to an end.

And those who run mad say: 'When you fellows catch hold of me and I overcome you though you are many, it is not that I fight alone by myself with my own strength, but there are four men with me who help me. And when you tie me up they help me to loose the rope.'

MWAIKAMBO: A boy of my own age ran mad; when he recovered he told us some of what he had seen in his madness (*mumbepo syake sya kigili*). He said he had seen lots of black cows, all entering the ground, going one by one into a hole; and that he had thereupon become unconscious and run wildly about.

A Christian told me that he had a relative (a non-Christian) who ran mad and who constantly told them how the fit started in him. He said that it was when he saw in the spirit (*mumbepo syake*) a very old person wearing ragged clothes, then he ran mad. The Christian who old me this added that he thought himself that perhaps it was Satan that his kinsman saw.

Those who run mad eat filthy things—mud, cowdung, human faeces, all kinds of frogs and so on. When you ask them about this they say they do not know what they are doing. And they often run about naked.

MWASANILA AND MWALIPOSA (two old men).

Madness takes two forms: one comes from Kyala, one from the ritual. When a man has the madness from Kyala his actions are filthy. He eats filthy things without discrimination, he loses his own sense of humanity and the sense of his friends' humanity also, he loses the sense of his own actions. This is one way of telling that a man has the madness from Kyala. Another way is this: they catch the madman and go to a doctor to treat him with medicines; well, when the doctor gives him the emetic the patient vomits butterflies. When they have made him vomit and given him another medicine too he either recovers altogether or perhaps he goes mad again later. But even if he recovers, his body is different from that of other men, and when he is angry his heart seems to be full of madness again. The madness of Kyala s the most serious.

The madness of ritual is the less serious kind; people who have it do not act in a filthy way. Their madness is like a passionate anger (*ilyojo*), that is all. When you catch such a man and take him to a doctor for the emetic we find no butterflies in the vomit. Again, if he has taken the medicine and recovered, his body is perfectly healthy and it seems as if he never was mad at all; not like those with the madness of Kyala, their bodies are changed i.e. the internal state of the body, the heart.

Another way of diagnosing the madness of ritual is this: people catch it from the food of other people's ritual; if a man who has not completed the ritual of his family [who has not been through the ritual at the deaths of both his father and his mother] eats the ritual food of another family, then madness falls on him or on his children, and the victim speaks like an idiot.

Then if the man's children die the doctors see signs of the madness of ritual; it may be due to infection from other people's ritual food or from omitting the ritual of their own family. They give the surviving children medicines to drink which look towards the ritual and also they begin to perform the ritual.

The actions of those with the madness of Kyala are these: they eat filth, run about unconscious of what they are doing, and speak foolish things. In their mad state (*mombepo syabo*) they tell us that they lose the sense of being people and of the humanity of others also. If it is madness of ritual, the cure is to perform the ritual and also to give them the medicine of the ritual. If it is of Kyala, to give them the medicine of madness.

ASOMBWILE (a doctor): Madness (*ikigili*) is of two sorts: one comes from Kyala and one from ritual. The symptoms are alike; all eat filth and throw off their clothes. But when a patient is brought to a doctor, he knows, when he has made him vomit, whether they have neglected a ritual or not.

MWAMBWIGA: Madness is of two sorts: one comes from we know not where, the other from the ritual. When a man has the first sort he throws off his clothes and eats filth; but the sort which comes from the ritual does not make him eat filth and he does not throw off his clothes; but he just talks nonsense.

ANGOMBWIKE: There are two sorts of madness: one is from Kyala, in which no one eats filth, they just run about wildly; and the other from the ritual, in which all eat faeces and filth.

UMBOKEGE AND HIS WIFE, JENALA (Christians): In the state of madness the man's head seems to himself to be empty. When he sits or stands there is a giddy whirling before his eyes; he seems to see people and they speak with him and then, when he answers them, we others think he is talking to himself. Sometimes these people seem to be a long way off, then they call out his name, he answers, and then he begins to be mad.

Mad people see a man, very terrible, and when he comes to them they flee from him. They say he is Mbasi. This about Mbasi and about the empty head and giddiness is common report; we heard it from no particular madman.

Another way of knowing the madness of ritual is this: if a man runs and fashions earth with his fingers, tying some up in leaves and rolling some up between his palms, if he does things which they do in the ritual, then they perform the whole ritual. Saga, Jenala's grand-mother, did these things, but then they began to perform the ritual and at once she recovered. She just talked to herself and went on moulding earth. She could not throw her clothes away for she was sick, her death was very near. As soon as they had done the ritual and she had recovered, she died. The reason they had not performed a complete ritual for her was because she had been away at the time it was performed. She had run off with a lover. It was the ritual of her mother which was not performed for her.

It is clear that, though informants were not agreed about the distinguishing features of the two types of madness, they were agreed about its general characteristics, and that one form was connected with neglect of rituals.

QUESTION: Why the little hut?

MWAMULENGA (an old chief): When performing the ritual they build a little hut in which to carry it out. This hut tells us of the man's be-haviour when alive, he lived in a house. So that now he is dead we kill his home too, and that is why they destroy the hut at the end of the rit-ual. They perform the ritual in a house because he lived in a house.

QUESTION: Why the stealing of the stem of plantains?

MWAMULENGA: This tells us about driving the disease away, that the disease which killed him should leave our homestead. The stem of bananas is a symbol (*ikimanyilo*) of the disease. We do not know where the disease came from. When we steal the bananas we think that the disease came from some other place and killed him, it has not always been in our house. That is why we go to another homestead to steal the stem of bananas. But when we are driven away with the bananas that is a symbol of driving the disease away again, we drive the disease away. Sometimes the householders come out and drive us away, some-times they stay still, and we who have come with the thief drive him away. We arrange with the householder beforehand. The meaning is the same in either case.

QUESTION: Why the food?

MWAMULENGA: The salted and unsalted food, the mash, the beans and bananas which they take out separately, the chicken, the roast bananas, those in which they put lentils and pumpkin-seeds—all these they eat, for they are afraid that if they do not, but leave one of them out, then when they eat, in the ritual of other people, some of those they omitted, the ritual will infect them. So that is why they eat everything. If a man doesn't eat any chicken he will catch the disease afterwards from the very smell of a ritual chicken!

QUESTION: Why the sitting on a bark-cloth?

MWAMULENGA: The bark-cloth shows death, particularly the death of the woman, it is a sign of grief.

QUESTION: Why drawing lines and mocking?

MWAMULENGA: Sometimes people in a mad fit do the most laughable things. They do not attend to their bodies at all, or perhaps they shave their hair in a most ugly way so that people laugh at them. In the ritual we laugh at the participants and say: 'Poor fool, it found its father dead, went stealing and they speared it on the head!' And then we think that he, as it were, has run mad after his father's death.

QUESTION: Why the flowers?

MWAMULENGA: The holding of a flower (and grass) also shows the actions of madmen. For sometimes the madman goes into the grassland and plays games with the flowers and grass and then, coming home, throws them on the thatch.

MWAIKAMBO: People talk about what madmen do, but I have never seen a mad person, I have only heard what people say. They say a mad person talks to himself like someone in a passion of grief, or anger, or fear, and moulds earth!

Mwafula (the village headman) does the Sangu ritual and did not know why the banana is stolen, though he understood the main function of the ritual. His wife, a Kukwe, did not know, nor did either of the two others. 'The old people have always told us: "If you leave something out of the ritual you will go mad, or perhaps someone will die. You will find the ritual (*ubunyago*) in the belly [at the autopsy]." But they never explained all the details, saying: "This means such and such, and that such and such." We do not know all the ramifications. As for finding the ritual in the stomach of a dead child, they find half-digested food and say: "It is the ritual (*bunyago*)." '

QUESTION: Why do you go and steal another's banana in the ritual?

NSYANI: It means that if your comrade's father has also died he [your comrade] may eat because they have mocked him, he can eat because he has finished; we say: 'Are you not going to take someone else's sickness on you (*utisakukombela ifya bangi*)?'[1] Because those who have not been treated do not eat.

QUESTION: So you act stealing and eating the food in another's ritual?

NSYANI: Yes, indeed [with a gesture of emphatic assent]. So here we mock the mourners, saying: 'That's a thief!' and we steal someone

[1] *Ukukombela*: to catch someone else's sickness, or to take another's quarrel on oneself.

else's stem of bananas symbolizing that we may eat other people's food, we have finished the ritual. Because during the ritual those who have not completed it eat apart. If they eat ordinarily we say of them: 'You so-and-so, you!' And at the last beer of the death ritual, when they have mixed the beer, we . . . say to the women: 'Where will you go?' 'We will find his cattle.' 'Very well.' Then we drink. But if the widows agree, according to custom, then we give them to our comrade, saying: 'These are your wives.' He sleeps with them in the house and we drink.

QUESTION: What does circling with the harp mean?

NSYANI: We spoke of that before. He who plays the harp is just someone who makes us go in line, they have finished him, he was brooded over. He says: 'Let me help my friend and play the harp for him and make him circle round.'

QUESTION: And what does the stamping dance (*ukukanya inganya*) mean?

NSYANI: It is to drive away sickness, to drive him away, to say: 'Go away with your sickness'.

QUESTION: But how exactly?

NSYANI: Because he who has died trampled the ground long ago when his father died, and we trample now that he has died, and his father trampled for his grandfather, and his grandfather for an ancestor. It means: 'We have finished with you, go away.' And at the bathing we put pebbles between our fingers and let them fall into the stream... [He performed a dramatic pantomime of sitting down in the water and falling first one way and then the other, and pushing his hands away so that they let the stones fall out. As he let them fall he said: 'We have driven you away, we have finished with you!']. . .

QUESTION: Why the shelling oil-seeds during the circling round?

NSYANI AND MWANGWANDA: We do not do it, we differ in our rituals. But we do the stealing of the banana bunch and throwing things in the pot at the fire, and hitting the ground and saying: '*Syeku, syeku.*'

QUESTION: Why?

NSYANI AND MWANGWANDA: Because if we don't do it our children run into the pasturage and make balls of rubbish (*ifisaka fya mindu*) and eat; then they become weak and foolish; but if we perform the ritual then they are fine children.

QUESTION: Why the throwing into the pot?

NSYANI AND MWANGWANDA: It means that we have finished with him [with a gesture of throwing away].

QUESTION: Why the washing at first?

MWAFULA: If we do not wash them they become weak and foolish, so we treat them and wash them and give them porridge, and then they recover. If we leave them they go off to the rubbish heap and make dirt (*bipelile mindo*); they take the dirt from the rubbish heap, they

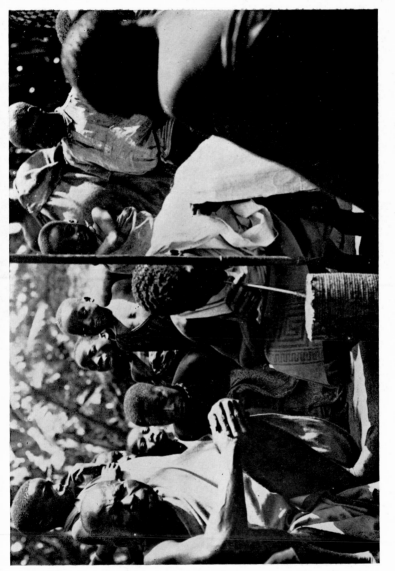

3. *The beer of the 'gasping cough'. Mwasalemba on the left*

4. *The bride washes with ikipiki in the doorway of her mother's hut*

even defaecate in the house. And at the inheritance, when I have inherited the women, they go to their own homes with a bull if I am
wealthy, or perhaps three shillings. They go back to their fathers with
the dirt on them—*ingotolo*!

QUESTION: Where does the *ingotolo* come from when you do not treat
them?

MWAFULA: Kyala is startled and you gasp with *ingotolo*, your breath
is short.

QUESTION: Does the husband also go to his place?

MWAFULA: Yes, he always returns to his father's.

QUESTION: Why the two leaves representing a man and a woman at
the hitting the ground and saying: '*Syeku, syeku*'?

MWAFULA: Because we are two [holding up two fingers], a man
and a woman. Formerly when someone died as a bachelor they took a
leaf of the sweet banana and said: 'It is your wife.' They buried it with
him, saying: 'Go to the land of the shades because you were never
married.'

QUESTION: What does the mocking at shaving mean?

MWAFULA: It is one with stealing the plantain stem. We mock them
meaning, may they escape, and not take rubbish from the rubbish
heap. And at the shaving of the hair we drive him away, saying: 'Go
to your fellows.' He has been alone, he was on the road, may he go.

Porokoto the Chief admitted that the wearing of leaves and
bananas in the rituals of death and of puberty were symbols of
fertility (*ifimanyilo fya mbapo*); the plantain represents the penis, the
sweet banana represents the clitoris, 'for in the old days they wore
leaves only, no cloths'. In the puberty ritual the wearing of leaves
and bananas is the same. It is a sign of fertility: 'the ritual is now
finished and the girl is someone's wife.'

Mwaijumba, who provided the beer of inheritance for the ritual
of Njobe Nani, explained to us as he drank: 'We drink beer to
drive away our friend. It means that everything is finished:
"Come to your house frequently now. It is finished! May the
fathers [i.e. the other shades] receive him! May he not return!
We have poured out this beer for you, it is finished." '

G

CHAPTER IV

THE RITUAL OF PUBERTY AND MARRIAGE

I. IN SELYA AND MUNGONDE

(a) *The events*

THE puberty ritual for girls among the Nyakyusa is fused with the marriage ritual. Girls are usually betrothed well before puberty and they may live with their 'husbands' for some time before they grow up, for the view of most Nyakyusa is that a girl should become accustomed to her husband gradually and that it is good for her to visit him from time to time, sweeping his house, cleaning the byre, drawing water and cooking for him, and learning the art of love-making with him and no one else. While she is still very immature it is insisted that he should only have intercourse with her *inter crura*, but when she is approaching puberty he often has full intercourse with her. No legal case can be brought against him in court if he does so, provided that he has not forced or frightened her, but his friends may tell him he is foolish, and is 'teaching his wife adultery', since now he can have no proof, in the physical examination at puberty, that she has not slept with other men. No stigma attaches to the girl; if it is her husband who has deflowered her she is acclaimed in the ritual as a virgin. In some pagan families, however, notably those of chiefs, girls are not allowed to visit their husbands before puberty. The girl's father has the right to refuse it, for before the ritual a wife is only 'borrowed'. Unlike the neighbouring Bemba, the Nyakyusa are not anxious lest the girl should conceive before her first menstruation—if she should do so the ritual is performed in the ordinary way—but many fathers dislike letting their daughters go before the main bulk of the marriage cattle have been handed over. Opposition on the part of the missions and the Administration to early marriage also influences the more sophisticated. The period of betrothal is long, for pagan girls are commonly engaged from about 8 years old onwards, and the average age of puberty appears to be between 15 and 16.[1]

With the onset of first menstruation the ritual (*ubunyago bwa-busungu*) starts immediately: it is begun even for a girl not yet betrothed, though for her it cannot be completed. The main acts are a treatment of the 'bride' (*unsungu*) with medicines to fortify her against the dangers of menstruation and intercourse; seclusion at her father's homestead and a driving of the shades of his lineage from her body that she may conceive by her husband; instruction in the duties of a wife; examination for virginity; and the exchange of feasts between her husband's family and her own to celebrate her maturity and virginity.

The first treatment is with a medicine called *undumila*. 'If the girl grows up at her father's place we, her mothers, treat her at once; if at her husband's she is sent home to us, if it is near, but if it is far away, her husband's mothers treat her there.' She must take the medicine before she tastes any food after the onset of menstruation. A pungent-tasting root is pushed through the tip of a funnel or 'cup' made of a leaf of the bark-cloth tree, and salt is poured into the cup. The girl takes the tip of the root in her mouth and pulls it inward with her teeth, thus causing the salt to trickle into her mouth. Her mother also makes millet porridge and adds to it a medicine, *ikipiki*, and gives a little to her, burying the rest under the hearth of the hut.

She is then secluded in her mother's hut. Her girl friends who have not yet reached puberty prepare a litter of banana leaves for her to sit and sleep upon, and they keep her company (*ukupanja*), hence their name, *abapanji*. They come 'to cheer their fellow that she should not be left alone'. They sleep with her on the litter, and spend the greater part of their days there, learning to depilate and adorn themselves and, some say, to stretch the vagina by manual manipulation. Food for them is provided by the bride's mother, and on the litter they entertain the young men of neighbouring boys' villages, singing and dancing, and cuddling. In a bride's hut intercourse *inter crura* is permitted, and no 'husband' can claim damages if his betrothed wife lies with another young man there, unless penetration has taken place. On moonlight nights the girls

---

[1] Information from Christian women who knew the exact ages of their daughters and of pagan contemporaries of their daughters. Cases of first menstruation ranging from the ages of 12 to 18 were cited, but those under 14 years old were regarded as unusually young. The mothers' information was confirmed by a woman missionary who ran a school for Christian adolescent girls in the district.

play special games in the courtyard, such as 'Knock, knock, little man'; they put bits of banana leaves in the forks of the fingers and toes and sing: 'Knock, knock, little man; knock, knock, little woman!' Then they spread wide their arms and legs and fingers and toes and knock them together. The leaves that fall out when they do so are collected and hidden some distance away. Then they all separate and hunt for them, singing:

> 'We look for our fellow the barren one.
> I don't know where she is, the barren one.'

When they find the leaves they pile them up and then each snatches one, singing:

> 'Here she is, here she is!'

Then the game ends.

Another traditional song goes:

'Little mouth, little mouth, She-who-makes-her-friends-quarrel.'

But many of the songs the maids sing with the young men are just current popular songs.

'The maids are friends for the bride to amuse herself with. They amuse themselves with young men, singing, and if some other bride is secluded at the same time, they go and compete against her and her maids in singing.' At the seclusion of Mwaihojo's daughter described below, a dozen girls, all a little younger than herself, kept her company. Five were her own half-sisters, one was a wife of her father who had not yet reached puberty, one a daughter of her father's sister, and four were daughters of her father's neighbours.

Although a bride's hut is the centre for sex play, women who are sleeping with their husbands and are therefore 'heavy' (*nsito*) with semen, do not enter it and may not cook for her, for any contact with them is felt to be dangerous to her. Her own mother refrains from intercourse until her daughter has gone to her husband.

The bride is not confined to the hut (as among many other African peoples) but is free to move about the immediate neighbourhood. Her movements are, however, limited by the taboo on crossing a stream, the need to avoid sexually active women, and the avoidance of her father and other men of his village, as well as her in-laws. When she leaves her hut she is accompanied by her maids and always carries a mat or cloth to screen her face from her father and his contemporaries, her father's full sisters, her older brothers,[1] and her 'mothers-in-law' (*abakamwana*).[2] These she must fear and respect (*ukutila*) and so avoid. Her father-in-law and his brothers she avoids altogether from the time of her engagement, or at least after she has reached the age of 8 or 9. Her companions do not *ukutila* with her, though those of them who are already betrothed will, of course, avoid their own fathers-in-law.

During the period of seclusion the girls have two specific tasks: to weave the fine mats used as beds, and to fetch firewood. Every bride should take to her husband's home at least one fine mat (*ubunyasa*) which she has made herself, as well as several coarse ones (*imitefu*),[3] and weaving a fine mat is a lengthy task, occupying a skilful woman a month. Each girl weaves for herself, but the firewood that each must fetch is stacked in the bride's mother's loft. The bride also occupies herself hammering out bark-cloth, pleating it for the strip worn between the legs, and decorating bark-cloth belts (*vide* plate 5), so that she may have the fresh ones required during the ritual, and a supply to take with her to her husband's; but this work is not emphasized as an obligation: rather it is a recreation. Women take great pride in the decoration of their belts—we watched several brides making them and handing them round for the admiration of their fellows. The maids may work in the fields if required to do so, but the bride herself does not, and 'she gets fat because she does not have much work to do'. The whole ritual normally lasts about three months, but if, for some reason such as a pressing need to go out to work, the husband is in a hurry for its completion, various acts may be telescoped. The time-table depends primarily on when the marriage-cattle and food for the various feasts are ready.

From the time of first menstruation until she does it ritually, a bride should neither wash nor oil herself. The prohibition is felt to be a very onerous one and some girls now break it, but women said 'in the old days we did not wash'. 'Girls nowadays are more cunning. We were afraid.'

---

[1] Some informants denied that she avoided father's sisters or brothers. Others insisted that she must avoid them because 'brothers are fathers, and father's full sisters are father'.

[2] i.e. her husband's own mother and other women he calls mother. In this account the plural 'mothers' indicates own and classificatory mothers.

[3] Nyakyusa beds are made of layers of mats laid on rollers between two logs at head and foot. One chief's bed we noted was made up of sixty-eight mats.

If a bride is her husband's first or second wife[1] (but not if she is a junior wife) she washes with him ritually at his homestead. The officiant (*unyago*), who may be her husband's own mother or some other mature woman chosen by her, pours out medicated water, and groom and bride wash together, his hands being above and hers below. This usually takes place about a month after her seclusion, but neither it nor the following events are timed to coincide with periods.

In one ritual we watched, that of the daughter of Chief Mwaihojo, the go-between in the marriage and the brother of the groom came to fetch the bride for the ritual washing (*ukusukusula*), bringing her a small gift of 10 cents, four weeks after her first menstruation. She washed in medicated water with her husband at his house and returned to her father's the same night (May 19). Next day, about 3 p.m., the groom's 'mothers' (*abakamwana*), twelve of them, and one girl, arrived carrying six stems of bananas and four enormous pots of curds for the ritual of *ukwingesia*, 'putting her in'. They approached, singing two of the ritual songs:

> *Litubuke, litubuke,*
> *Tubuke mwailugula.*
> Let us go, let us go,
> Let us go for ever and never return.

and

> *Akasyunguti kambagila*
> *Paliti po pabuko bwangu.*
> The *syunguti* tree suited me,
> The place is like that of my own in-laws.

The bride was carried first by one and then by another of her 'mothers' (*abanna*)[2] while a compact group of mothers and maids, with the bride raised high in their midst, danced to and fro. And all the time she held a mat to shield her head and face. After five minutes or so the dancing stopped and the 'mother-in-law' sat down in the shade, as Kyobwe (a senior wife of Mwaihojo who acted in place of the bride's own mother who was divorced) came to greet them formally and receive their gifts of food. Meanwhile the bride herself knelt on the ground beside Kyobwe's hut, her head covered with a mat, and surrounded by her maids. Presently

---

[1] Informants differed on this point. Some maintained that chiefs alone washed with two wives, commoners with one only. Others insisted that commoners also washed with two.

[2] i.e. her father's wives, and wives of his brothers and neighbours.

the groom's mothers began to dance again. They approached the group of girls and the groom's own mother took the mat off the kneeling bride and spread a large scarlet cloth over her. Then she lifted her on to her shoulders and danced with her. The two parties coalesced and danced together, singing the ritual song *Tukulelela akela* (We sing a dirge). Everyone was smiling and joyful despite the song. By 3.40 the dancing was over and a large mat was spread for the 'mothers-in-law' to sit down in the shade. The bride knelt again with bent head covered by her mat and surrounded by her maids.

At this point Mwaihojo, her father, began scolding angrily because the groom's party had not brought a bull. 'Always when people come to marry my daughters they bring a bull, always. It looks as if the girl had been to visit her husband and you had found fault with her and did not like her.' The groom's mothers replied: 'We are poor.'

Mwaihojo: 'How can you say you are poor? You can find the marriage-cattle, you say. Why didn't you bring some of them? Then I would have killed one to eat now. See, I have killed a bull already. If I had known that you were not going to bring one I'd have killed another.'

The groom's mothers sat with downcast heads. For a commoner's daughter bananas and milk are adequate for the *ukwingesia* feast, but a chief has the right to expect a bull.

Presently the groom's own mother and one of her companions entered Kyobwe's hut to roast bananas and grind some of the bark of a tree they had brought for medicine. The powder was put into a small calabash with water. The bride knelt in the doorway of Kyobwe's hut and, as her mother-in-law poured out the medicated water, she washed her hands and wrists and mouth in it. The bride's half-brother, a lad of 15 or 16 years, was washed also, standing by the doorway of Kyobwe's hut, though he was most reluctant to co-operate. He kept looking towards his elder brother Lazarus, a Christian, and did not submit until Lazarus said: 'All right, go ahead!' Kyobwe, seeing his reluctance, said: 'You need not wash if you don't wish to, it doesn't matter. Perhaps we'll leave it out as it's European times now.' Then finally she said: 'Well, just hold out one hand,' and she washed it. Had the bride been the eldest daughter of either of her father's two senior wives he would have washed in place of her brother, and had her own mother not been divorced she would have washed also.

One of the women of the groom's party then fetched two banana leaves, one of sweet banana and one of plantain, and put them down in Kyobwe's hut. Meantime the mother of the groom changed the bride's belt and the bark-cloth worn between the legs, dressing her in new ones, and burying the old cloth, soiled by first menstruation, in a bundle of dry banana leaves. These she placed on top of the fresh leaves already mentioned, covered the pile with a small rough mat, and sprinkled it with powdered medicine. The bride knelt on the mat and, with head bent, ate roast bananas also sprinkled with the powdered medicine, which her mother-in-law handed to her. Her young brother who had washed with her also shared the bananas. After this the bride is free to wash, but not yet to oil herself.

The groom's mothers were feasted on meat and bananas—two large and two small basketfuls—and returned home. The atmosphere all through the ritual was one of rejoicing, and it was markedly a women's affair. The chief and several other men were present but, apart from his scolding of the women for not bringing a bull, the chief played no part at all.

According to strict custom the groom's mothers should have come a second time with gifts of food (*ukusumbulela*)[1] to cement the friendship, but since the groom was in a hurry to get to work on the Lupa gold-fields this act was omitted. 'They brought the two lots of food together,' we were told, 'some of the milk and bananas were for the *ukwingesia* and some for the *ukusumbulela*.'

Three weeks later (June 14) the groom, with his go-between and other friends, brought the main body of marriage-cattle (*ukukwa*), and they danced the stamping dance (*ukukanya nganya*) in the bride's father's courtyard and on the litter of the seclusion hut, brandishing their spears as they stamped to the war rhythm. The bride's companions and mothers danced in a separate group, one mother carrying the bride on her shoulders. A lavish feast of cooked food was set before the groom and his friends, and they in their turn scattered pieces of meat and cents which the bride's maids and 'mothers' scrambled for. Meantime a quarrel broke out between the bride's father and her brothers over the distribution of the marriage-cattle.

Six weeks after the *ukwingesia* (July 29) the bride, accompanied by two of her father's wives, two of her maids, and a third girl invited because she was a good singer, went to wash ritually again

---

[1] *Ukusumbulela*: to give a present for the first time to a new friend.

at the groom's home (*ukusukusula*). The party was given a hen when they arrived and a second the next morning. The groom and some of his friends spent the night with the bride and her friends. (He and she lie together on this occasion but do not yet have full intercourse.)[1] In the morning the mother-in-law shaved the bride's head, eyebrows, and eyelashes, leaving only a small tuft on the nape of her neck. Then she mixed water with powdered medicine and poured it for groom and bride to wash. The groom washed his hands and mouth only, the bride her hands and mouth and whole body. During her seclusion she might not use oil or the red powder favoured as a cosmetic by Nyakyusa women,[2] but after this third washing she was free to do so, and she oiled herself meticulously. Meantime the groom was shaved by one of his friends.

On the same day the bride returned to her father's homestead with her own party and seven 'mothers' of the groom who brought five stems of bananas, a pot of water, and a small bull for the ritual of 'clearing out the litter' (*ukusosya ulufumbo*). She herself was wearing the skin of a bull over her head—'she wears any skin she can get hold of'. One of the groom's party shaved off the last tuft of her hair and buried it carefully in the *ulufumbo*, the litter of banana leaves on which she had slept and sat during her seclusion. Had her own mother been present she would have shaved also and so should the brother, but he did not do so. The groom's mother and Kyobwe (representing the bride's mother) carried out the litter to the edge of the banana plantation surrounding the homestead. As they did so they whispered to each other. Kyobwe said the bride was a little liar. Her husband had offered her 1s. to take to her mothers and she had refused it saying: 'No, they swear at me and grudge me food.' 'She's your child,' said the mother-in-law. 'No,' said Kyobwe, 'she's another woman's child, she's a foolish child.' Every scrap of litter in the hut was carefully collected and a little of the soil below it scraped off and carried out with the leaves. All who had helped with the clearing washed their hands carefully.

Then the groom's mother made a basin of two banana leaves close to the pile of litter. Into it she poured the water her party had brought with them, and sprinkled in powdered medicine in

---

[1] One or two informants maintained that 'she must not refuse him now or he will refuse to wash with her, saying: "She is not my wife." ' But others were insistent that according to strict custom only intercourse *inter crura* was allowed. Full intercourse at this time would make nonsense of the *ilibalaga* ritual which follows.

[2] Formerly also by men: cf. V. Giraud, *Les Lacs de l'Afrique Equatoriale* (1890), p. 176.

the form of a cross. The bride knelt down and carefully washed her whole body. When she had done so the groom's mother told one of her party to light the pile of litter. As it blazed up, the bride leapt across it. Three of her maids and a married half-sister had plucked banana suckers, of the sort used for propagating bananas, and they struck her with them as she leapt back and forth over the fire. She was nervous, though the jump was easy, and her maids jeered at her. Then she returned to Kyobwe's hut and dried herself in the sun. Now that the litter was burnt she had come out of her seclusion and was free to sleep on ordinary mats; from the entering of seclusion to the coming out, she could only sleep on the litter, except for the night preceding the burning which she spent with her husband.

The mothers of the groom were feasted on sweet potatoes and curds provided by the bride's family, and there was a discussion as to whether the bull the groom's party had brought was 'milk to eat with the bananas' for the bride's family, or 'the bull of virginity'. The bride's father insisted that it was only a relish for the feast and he did not prepare the beer for the final act of the ritual. Two weeks later the bride eloped with her husband because he had not got another bull to bring her father, and the final rites were never performed for her.

On the night before the ritual of 'clearing the litter' the bride's father should put millet to soak for beer, and when it is ready the groom's mothers come for the *ilitemelo* and *ulufundo*, that is, to 'shave the sprouting hair' and instruct the bride; but for the daughter of Mwasofu, for whom we watched it performed, it was long delayed. She had reached puberty seven months previously and before that had lived for three months with the man who had first betrothed her, but he had been unable to find sufficient cattle for the marriage, and the ritual was completed with another man.

The groom's 'mothers' arrived about one-thirty, by which time everyone was getting impatient. The men had nearly finished their beer and grumbled that the groom's party was late, and the bride herself was begging her mother to be allowed to go and bathe. Her mother replied emphatically: 'No, no, how can you go? The mothers-in-law will wash you and dress you in brass body-rings. That's the ritual.' Six women came in the groom's party— his own mother, his sister, two 'village mothers', and two young married women of the groom's village. A large mat was spread for

them and polite greetings were exchanged. The bride herself
crouched down with her head covered with a cloth, but after the
greetings were completed she sat up and chatted with them. Then
one of the groom's 'village mothers', who was the officiant in
the ritual, his sister, and two young women from his village,
took the bride to the stream to wash. The officiant told the young
women to carry her, which they did for a few yards, then they put
her down. Her maids sang and she herself danced a few steps.
Women came out of the houses as we passed, dancing and clapping.
At the stream the bride took off her old bark-cloth and bathed
with her maids. As she finished she stepped into a flat winnowing
basket (*uluselo*) for a minute, then stepped out, and her husband's
sister decked her with four brass body-rings (*vide* plate 7) and a
folded cloth (*umpepe*) hanging down from the rings behind like a
tail. The bride shook the 'tail' and the others laughed and cried:
'*Kipetule*[1] *tukunsepeka*[2] (It is turned over! We clothe her with the
male genital covering!)' They walked back again laughing, and
when they reached the first houses one of the party said: 'We
should carry her now.' Another demurred: 'Let's go a little further,
she's heavy.' Then a woman of the village came along and called:
'Carry her! Carry her!' They arrived at her mother's house
singing: '*Nisya, Nisya, Nisya!* (Put me down!)' The groom's
'mothers', the bride herself, and her maids, all sang this. The rest
of the groom's party joined in and they walked up and down the
courtyard carrying her and singing '*Nisya, Nisya.*' The groom's
own mother carried a winnowing basket on her head and the
bride's 'mothers' rushed out and threw into it small bowlfuls of
millet, maize, pumpkin-seeds and lentils.[3] This grain goes to the
groom's 'mothers': 'The mother-in-law drinks beer made from the
millet.' Then the bride was made to sit down in the doorway of
her mother's hut; the officiant sat behind her, shaved a little of the
sprouting hair from the front of her head, and smeared her head,
arms, legs, and stomach with ointment and red powder supplied
by her own mother. Powdered medicine supplied by the groom's
mother was added to the shaving water.

When her toilet was completed, the women called the men to
come and give their gifts. The bride and her maids crouched
down and the cloth removed from her buttocks was spread

---

[1] *Okopetula*: to turn over.
[2] *Okosepeka*: to clothe, from *ikisepe*: male genital covering.
[3] Beans, cowpeas and ground-nuts are also mentioned as being given at this time.

over her and the maids closest to her. Her father, Mwasofu, and four or five other men, his village mates, came to give her gifts to break the taboo (*ukubonola*). Her father came first and asked: 'Which is she?' She was pointed out to him and he gave her 10 cents, greeted her with the words 'Good morning, my child', and shook hands. At the same time he admonished her saying: 'If you ever go away from your husband who has married you, then you have a case against you, you have a great case against you.'

The other men followed: 'Good morning, good morning, you have recovered.' They gave some cents and shook hands and repeated her father's warning. One, having no cents, brought a spearhead which he said he would redeem later for 50 cents.

Then over the girl's head the father spoke to the officiant: 'Where are the bull and the other cow?'

Officiant: 'I am poor. Thank you for giving us your daughter, thank you.'

Father: 'Pay a bull. See, my child has stayed at home a long time. It is seven months since she grew up and it is not right that she should stay here always. Bring the bull!'

Officiant: 'Yes, we all regret that, but I am very poor.'

A mother: 'You know very well that our child is pure [i.e. a virgin].'

Father: 'See, she is the eldest daughter, and there is someone here with a case against him. My brother has expectations from her, he is claiming cattle. If her husband comes to carry her off we will beat him, we will beat him, we will take cattle.'

Then the men went away and the women, 'mothers' and 'mothers-in-law', together began to admonish (*ukufunda*) her. 'Yesterday evening she was a child, now she has grown up, she is a woman, let us tell her about womanhood.' Her father's second wife, and an elderly woman of her father's village, talked most, but advice was shouted at her by several women at once and it was impossible to take it down verbatim. The following points were mentioned: She must cook for her children. (This was repeated with emphasis.) She must cook for her husband; she must be gentle (*mololo*) to her children; she must welcome and cook for her mothers when they come to see her.

One mother said: 'If your husband has built in a boys' village and his fellows come wanting water to drink don't say: "There is no water." Don't let your in-laws say to us: "You did not bring her up properly, she behaves proudly." '

Another whispered: 'When your husband comes to lie with you do not fight him, but accept him. If you avoid him you have a case against you,' and she laughed as she said it.

There was also whispered advice about menstruation: 'You wait three or four days. . . . When a child appears look after yourself.' During the instruction the bride sat with her maids crouching round her, their heads covered by cloths, all giggling a little. None of the mothers made any attempt to hit the bride, though in discussing the ritual a number of informants insisted that 'the mothers do not teach her by word of mouth only, they also beat her' and 'they scold her for all the things which she has hitherto done wrong at her husband's house'. Old Kasitile explained that: 'If the girl is a good wife, then the husband tells the mothers, saying: "You must not swear at my wife, she always listens to me." Then no one beats her. . . . But if she is proud at her husband's then they beat her.' 'The mother who bore her husband says: "She has been proud towards me, she's a harsh (nkali) girl," and they hit her with their fists.'

The teaching as described by a number of women may be summed up thus: the bride is told to fetch relish from the fields, draw water, sweep the house, tend the fire, fetch firewood ('if you do not draw water or fetch firewood you are a fool') and prepare food for her husband when he comes in from hoeing at midday and again in the evening; she must never be proud (namatingo) when her husband calls for water or anything else, but always answer with the submissive taa and not just say eh; she must be hospitable to her husband's friends and her own mothers when they come to visit; she must cook for children and be gentle to them. She must look towards her mother-in-law now—her own mothers are 'just people'. 'We have sent you to your husband's house and if we hear of quarrels there you are no child of ours.' She is told to wipe her husband after intercourse, to wash her own body often and to be careful to attend to herself properly when she is menstruating and to wash her hands frequently and not allow her husband to approach her then. She is told not to reject her husband at other times ('if you refuse him he will demand his cattle back'), and she is warned not to flirt with other men. Most instruction in the art of love-making (including demonstration of the correct body movements) comes informally from girl friends a little older than herself, rather than at the formal admonition by her mothers, though a little is given then also.[1] She is especially warned to depilate herself regularly. 'If she is hairy her husband will complain to the mothers and they will beat her.' The maids listen to the instruction along with the bride, and since every girl keeps several of her immediate seniors company before she grows up herself, no young woman can be left in doubt as to her duties as a wife.

At the shaving of the sprouting hair the 'bull of puberty' (*ingambako jabusungu*) should be killed if the bride is found, on examination by her mothers and those of the groom, to be a virgin, or if the husband has told the women that he himself has deflowered her. Mwasofu's complaint at the ceremony just described was that the groom's party had not brought the bull though his daughter was a virgin, and he insisted that the bride could not go to her husband until it had been provided.

At another puberty ritual which we attended, the bull was duly brought and, after examining the girl, the mothers announced her virginity with the cry of triumph (*akalulu*), and shouted: 'It is ours, it is ours.' They rushed through the courtyard dancing and applauding. Before the examination the bull had been tied up near the mothers, and immediately the joyful announcement was made it was killed. The meat of this bull is divided between the bride's mothers, her father's kinsmen with whom he exchanges cattle, and his immediate neighbours. The ritual portion, the *ijammapa*, cut from the top of the right foreleg, is taken by her father to his ritual grove of bananas and there he prays, saying: 'You, so-and-so (naming his father), since I have eaten the food of others (non-relatives) may she flourish at her husband's.' Another informant's version of the prayer was: 'I am eating the bull for my daughter, may she bear children!' A third said: 'Here is the meat! I have eaten the food of others, come out a little, may she bear a child at her husband's!'

If the bride is not a virgin the bull is not killed. It must be returned. Informants repeatedly implied, in talking of the ritual, that everyone knew beforehand whether the bride was virgin or not. 'If she is not a virgin we only do a little ritual, there is but one

---

[1] Our informants maintained that clay images were not used as a medium of instruction, as among the Bemba, though Nyakyusa girls mould stylized dolls out of clay almost identical with one shown for the Kisi in F. Fülleborn, *Deutsch Ost-Afrika*, Band IX, Atlas, plate no. 28, 30, 31, 72.

vessel of milk and two stems of bananas. We do not carry her in triumph. The mothers-in-law do not bring the powdered medicine.' One informant maintained that the bride was always examined before she washed with her husband (if she was a chief wife) and we once saw the bride examined at the *ukwingesia* ritual, but the examination before handing over the bull is the only one mentioned by most people. What is certain is that virginity must be publicly demonstrated in the ritual and that it is honoured.

After the shaving and instruction, the bride goes round her father's village visiting the men who have not already given her a gift. She is accompanied by the wife of the go-between who represented her father in the marriage negotiations. Each of her father's fellow villagers (as well as her elder brothers and her father's full sisters) should give her something—a bark-cloth, a chicken, a calabash, a spearhead, or some coins, as he greets her. These the bride divides between her maids, the officiant who treated her in the ritual, her husband, and herself; to the wife of the go-between is due one pot of the beer brewed for the shaving ritual, to take home to her husband.

If the agreed number of marriage-cattle have been handed over, the bride's father puts millet to soak for beer immediately after the rite of instruction has been completed and the bull of puberty eaten. When the brewing is ready the bride is formally taken to her husband's house (*ukumbeka*) by a 'mother' and one or two of her maids. Her own mother never goes—the woman of the party is usually a junior wife of the bride's father or the wife of the go-between. They take with them one or two pots of beer, a basketful of plantains to roast for her husband, two or three cooking pots, a log of firewood, a calabash of light ointment (*inyemba*), and a little pot of brown ointment (*imbale*) for anointing her husband and his friends in the village. 'What the wife brings when she comes for the first time is for all the men of the village to use to anoint themselves. They come every day to use it until it is finished.' These ointments are brought by every wife but they are especially important if the bride is her husband's first wife, and it is his bachelor neighbours who mostly use them. The bride also brings the fine mat and several coarse ones which she has woven during her seclusion, bark-cloths she has made for herself, and three hearth bricks (*amafiga*) carefully moulded for her by her mother out of clay and manure mixed with medicines. These are set up in her new home, and her mother-in-law provides her with fire and a pot.

After the bride has had full intercourse with her husband she cannot return home, or see her own parents, until she has taken them the ritual *ilibalaga*. After sexual intercourse she wipes her husband's genitals with her hands, then wipes them on a fowl and some millet: these together form the *ilibalaga*. In the morning she goes off without washing—'with the filth of intercourse on her'— to her parents' house, taking the fowl and millet with her. The fowl is killed on a path and cooked with *ikipiki* medicine and, if the bride is the eldest daughter of one of the father's first two wives, her father and mother eat it together. Her mother eats alone if she is a younger daughter, or the mother is a junior wife. If the father is a chief the husband may kill a young bull and beef is sent in place of the hen.

After eating the *ilibalaga* her parents resume intercourse[1] which has been taboo from the time the girl first menstruated. If no hen is brought because the husband is poor, the parents still resume sexual intercourse, but the bride, when she visits her home, must not take water from her mother's pot. Someone else draws for her and she drinks it outside from a separate calabash. If she drinks inside, or if her mother uses the calabash she has used, it is believed that her mother will get diarrhœa. She also avoids her father's bed and stool.

With the ritual of marriage must be included the negative ritual of avoidance between a woman and her husband's father and between those identified with him or her. The taboo applies from the time of betrothal or, if the girl has been betrothed as an infant, from well before she reaches puberty, and forbids father-in-law and daughter-in-law ever to look at one another or meet face to face on the pathway, or enter the same house, much less speak to-gether. As we have seen, a similar taboo applies between the bride and her own father during her seclusion, but is relaxed when he has given her a gift. Between a woman and her father-in-law, how-ever, it is never relaxed, except among the more sophisticated Christians. A myth of origin tells of a case of incest between father-in-law and daughter-in-law which led to the establishment of the

---

[1] Kasitile maintained that if the mother has not reached the menopause the parents do not lie together until the daughter's pregnancy is apparent. 'For the mother to conceive before the daughter is forbidden, but old women are fruits sucked dry.' Mwakionde denied any danger in mother conceiving before daughter.

5. *Shaving the bride*

6. *The groomsmen dance the stamping dance*

taboo, and the practical difficulties of observing the taboo if fathers and sons live in the same village is cited as a reason for the age-village organization.[1]

The marriage ritual may be said to finish with the eating of the *ilibalaga*, but avoidance of father-in-law and daughter-in-law continues until death and no clear line can be drawn between the marriage ritual proper and the rituals of pregnancy and birth which follow.

It is plain from the events described that the *ubunyago bwa-busungu* is a marriage as well as a puberty ritual and that the husband and his family play an essential part in it, but if a girl is not betrothed before puberty a curtailed ritual is still performed for her when she grows up. She drinks the *undumila* medicine, she washes with a brother, and her mothers put her formally into the hut of seclusion. They cook for the various feasts, and they tell her brothers to call their friends to help dance the stamping dance. The litter is cleared by her mothers in due course, and she is shaved and instructed. When she is eventually married, only the rites of slaughtering the bull of virginity, taking her to her husband, and returning with the *ilibalaga* are performed. She does not wash with him ritually.

(b) *The overt purpose and symbolism*

The avowed purpose of the *ubusungu* ritual is to protect the physical and mental health of the girl and to ensure her fertility. 'If the ritual is not performed the girl will fall ill, go mad, or not bear children.' Numerous informants were agreed on this point. Angombwike expanded it, saying: 'It is said that if they do not perform the ritual of *ubusungu* the bride will go mad. When she is sick of the madness they perform the ritual. If the doctor says: "Those below are angry," then the father of the girl takes water and prays in the banana grove saying: "My father and my grand-father, let the child recover from her sickness." Sometimes the doctor says: "The so-and-so's (naming a village) have cursed her"; then the father seeks a bull and they eat it. It is the curse which comes from the mouths of people when many whisper saying: "Why have they not performed the ritual? Why have they not performed it?" It comes from their evil breath.' Neglect of the puberty ritual is therefore thought both to anger the shades and to shock the neighbours, who expect to feast on this occasion.

[1] cf. Monica Wilson, *Good Company*, pp. 82–6.

H

The first act of the ritual, the giving of the *undumila*[1] medicine to the girl, is a symbol of sexual intercourse, and it is thought to be a prophylactic against pain in intercourse, frequent or painful periods, and injury from contact with those who are 'heavy'. 'It is given so that her belly may not be painful,' said Mwaisumo's mother, an elderly woman. Kasitile's wife explained: 'The pungent root is the penis of the husband, the cup is her vagina, the salt, also pungent, is the semen of her husband. Biting the root and eating the salt is copulation.' Mwakionde's wife gave a similar interpretation:

The *undum'la* is put through the leaf of a bark-cloth tree, shaped into a cup, and it is a sign of man and woman, the penis in the vagina. It is similar to the plantains which we give her when we wash her. The plantains are a symbol of the husband. If we do not give her the *ikipiki* medicine the blood never dries up, and it is the same with the *undumila*. If it is not given she constantly has periods and is barren. Yes, some have a period twice in one month—those who have rotted. Only a few are like this, not many. . . . The *undumila* is given to the girl at once, in the mouth as soon as she grows up, so that she can go about without fear; otherwise, if she washes without having had it, then a heavy one may walk over her footprints, that is overstep her, and she will not bear a child, she menstruates continually.

Kasitile's wife said much the same: 'If the heavy ones have overstepped her, her body rots. The man is not sterile, but the woman is; the man's semen is fertile, but the woman has painful periods. It is the pain of periods we symbolize in the sharpness of the *undumila* and salt.'

The heavy ones (*abasito*), feared both during the puberty ritual and by a mother with a new-born child, are those who sleep with their husbands. They include women both before and after conception. 'When the pregnancy is advanced and the husband has left off sleeping with his wife, then she is not heavy and she can keep a mother with a new-born baby company and hold the baby. A man who is sleeping with a woman is also heavy. They say: "He will overstep us." ' This was the statement of Mwakionde's wife and Kasitile, questioned separately, confirmed every point. We then asked Kasitile: 'How is the heaviness (*ubusito*) from lying with a man dangerous to those going through puberty and childbirth?'

Kasitile: 'Because those who are with their husbands are heavy, they are strong, their fellow the bride (*unsungu*) is empty, light in

---

[1] *Undumila* is derived from *ukulumila*: to bite, to be painful.

front. See, the man ejects semen! Does it not go inside? The woman becomes heavy and oversteps the bride.'

Even after she has been treated, the bride avoids any close contact with those who are 'heavy'; in particular they are excluded from her hut. Her own mother 'does not sleep with the father at all from the time the girl grows up until she goes to her husband, and begins intercourse with him. It is taboo. She says to her husband: "See, I am keeping my child company." ' But the 'play' of her companions does not matter, for intercourse *inter crura* does not make anyone heavy; it is the semen of a man in a woman's belly which makes her heavy, and her husband also, through contact with her.

The second medicine used at the puberty ritual is the *ikipiki*,[1] made from the bark of certain small-leafed forest trees. The same species is used by many Nyakyusa families, but the identity of the person who provides it is very important, for it is identified with the blood (*ililopa*) of the family. In the puberty-marriage ritual the groom's mother provides the *ikipiki* with which the bride washes at her husband's (if she is a senior wife), at the rite of 'putting her in' (*ukwingesia*), at the second washing with her husband, at the shaving, and at the washing before jumping over fire. The same medicine is used each time. It is also sprinkled on the bananas she eats at the *ukwingesia*. The bride's own mother, however, provides the *ikipiki* which is added to her porridge and buried under the hearth the day she first menstruates, and that used for washing her father, or brother, and mother at the *ukwingesia*. Also, should it be known that the bride is not a virgin, the mother-in-law will refuse to bring her *ikipiki* and it must be provided for each rite by her mother. The medicine is in itself awesome (*nsisya*). Kasitile's wife remarked one day that the bride slept with one of her maids in front of her, 'at her stomach', and one behind. We asked why. She replied: 'That *ikipiki* medicine! It's awesome. She fears to be alone.' 'If someone has not given her the *ikipiki* to drink and heavy ones cook food and give it to her she goes bad, she has periods without cessation.' 'The mother gives porridge with *ikipiki* to the girl and buries some under the hearth. That means may she be heavy in her stomach, for if heavy ones warm themselves at the fire in the house, she is in danger of going bad, she will have a continuous issue of blood.' 'If the *ikipiki* were not given, her period

---

[1] *Um-piki*: a tree of any species. *Iki-piki*: medicine made from the bark of certain species (one is a Mussaenda) and used in the rituals of death, puberty, and birth.

would never dry up.' Kasitile said: 'The work of the *undumila* and *ikipiki* are the same, they are together. The heavy ones will over-step the girl, they are going to injure her so that she is barren, constantly menstruating, with painful periods.' Lyandileko, a woman doctor, and exceptionally intelligent, said: 'The bride uses the *ikipiki* medicine because she is empty (*bwasi*). So she washes and eats bananas with *ikipiki*. If she does not wash with it she will have diarrhœa.'

The *ikipiki* is also said to make a bride 'patient and polite'. 'If the girl did not wash with the powdered medicine (*ikipiki*) she might be rude and proud when she went to her husband's home and insult men there.' This was the statement of Mwakwelebeja, an old commoner particularly well versed in matters of ritual, and it was separately confirmed both by his wife and by Lyandileko, the woman doctor, but not everyone knew the connection. Mwai-hojo, the chief, who was present when Mwakwelebeja gave his explanation, said: 'Really! I never knew that!' and his wives, when applied to, said: 'We don't know. The mothers have died' (this though some of them were past middle age).

Angombwike identified the *ikipiki* medicine with the blood of a lineage and a bride's treatment with it with the union in marriage. He said:

As soon as a girl grows up people begin to think about her bearing children. They say: 'The molten iron is discharged, the blood for bearing children has come.' When they grind and brew beer in her honour, they do it in honour of her 'iron' [i.e. menstrual blood]. They give her medicines for disciplining her in the lineage of her husband. When the mothers hear they cry: 'Ours, ours, it has fruited! (*Ifyeto, ifyeto, fipele*).' The girl is given a bundle of the medicine, powdered, and is made to wear a belt of bark-cloth with the powder in it; the medicine is brought from the husband's home by his mothers. The husband, as it were, says: 'That is my blood [or semen] which I have sent to her.' The little bundle is the symbol (*ikimanyilo*) of the child she will bear, the belt with medicine on it means that the molten 'iron' belongs to the blood of that husband. The powdered medicine is brought by the husband's mother. A man's chief wife always has a bamboo flask or a pot full of medicine of their lineage (*ja kikololo kyabo*), powdered ready for use. If she dies it goes to the second wife, if the husband dies to the first wife of the eldest son, and by her it is distributed at need. The powdered medicine is the blood (*imbondanya*[1] *lyo ilopa*).

---

[1] i.e. the powder made from the *ikipiki*.

The bundle of medicine and the belt are burnt with the litter at the coming out. And whenever a child is born, every time, not only at the birth of the first or second, it is washed by the husband's mother with this same powdered medicine from the store in her pot. If this is not done they fear that perhaps the child will go mad or something dreadful will happen. They say of the powdered medicine: 'It is our kinship, it is our blood (*Bo bukamu bwetu, lyo ilopa lyetu*).' And if a girl runs off with a lover in the veld they mock her and say: 'Who has given you powdered medicine? You are no relative.' They say: 'She is not our relative, she has not got our blood. . . .' The medicine is to create relationship (*ubukamu*). Using it means that the bride is now of my lineage (*ikikolo*). You know that burial customs differ. When they have used the medicine they will bury my wives as they bury me, either sitting up or lying down, as the case may be. We Christians do not do this because we have another way. We take hands before the priest and say: 'This is my relative (*unkamu gwangu*).'

Another informant (a pagan), questioned separately, gave a similar interpretation. He said: 'Washing with the medicine means, "my wife has come. She is now my relative (*nkamu gwangu*)."'

As already indicated, the act of washing with her husband proclaims the seniority of a wife. Washing with her own mother and her father or young brother, is to proclaim kinship. 'The girl washes with a brother to show that she has brothers and sisters. If she does not do so it shows that she is a poor person without relatives.' 'She has washed at her husband's place, then she comes home and her father honours her by looking for a boy, not an old one but a young one, to wash with her. Then the girl thinks: "I have fathers, I am no bastard." But if she washed alone she would think: "Perhaps I am not their child, perhaps I have no relatives."' Kasitile said: 'If she washes with me, her father, it means: "She is my child, I begot her myself, she is my first-born."' Mwakionde, after discussing the circumstances under which a father washes, said: 'To wash is to admit that I have lived and borne a child and grown up.' 'And if a brother does it?' we asked. 'It means: "You young man, you are her father." If they ever quarrel the brother says: "Why do you not respect me, your father? We washed together in water."' A young brother is chosen 'because the grown-up boys are going about. They want one who has not made love to girls.'

Standing in the doorway of her mother's hut (or of the woman acting in place of her mother if the latter is dead or divorced) is again an acknowledgment of kinship. 'If she washed outside it would mean that she was not the daughter of her father.'

The two fresh leaves of plantain and sweet banana on which the officiant places her soiled bark-cloth, and on top of which she kneels to eat bananas are, as already stated, symbols of male and female. Everyone understood this. Fewer people were aware of the symbolism of eating the banana, but Kasitile and one or two others were fully conscious of it and forthright in discussion. He said:

At the 'putting her in' (*ukwingesia*) the mothers-in-law bring a new bark-cloth and dress her in it; the old one is thrown away on the litter. They mix together bananas and *ikipiki* medicine which she receives. Don't you understand? They treat her. The plantain is the symbol of the man, of his penis, we are treating her, may she 'cook well' for her husband [i.e. be proficient in intercourse], may she bear children. She eats on that bark-cloth which means may the blood go to make children, this is your husband. Eating is a symbol (*ikimanyilo*) of sexual intercourse. She eats the plantain, meaning she has intercourse with her husband.

He connected this with the admonition at the end of the ritual. When she eats the banana nothing is said, it is only implied, but 'at the drinking of beer they teach her, saying: "Look after your husband well; if you are sweeping the house and he catches hold of you don't be startled, accept him, and catch hold of him also. . . . Men when they do this beget children." '

The second washing at the groom's, which is performed for every wife and not only for a senior one, is interpreted as a cleansing ritual. In the morning the officiant calls the husband and wife and says: 'Come and wash now and clean off the filth.'

Shaving is both a purification and a sign of the completion of the ritual. 'The hair of a girl who has reached puberty is the filthiness of puberty, of the menstrual blood which she produces then. She throws it away.' Mwakwelebeja and his wife said: 'The shaving is to show that she has awakened to puberty (*alembwike ubusungu*). During the ritual she did not shave. We perform the rite of shaving that she may begin to shave again, and to let her smear herself with brown ointment. It is like a burial. If a man's close relative dies he does not shave or wash.' Mwaihojo said: 'The shaving is to show that the *ubusungu* ritual is finished.'

Clearing the litter which is 'filthy', contaminated with the menstrual blood of the girl, is also a symbol of purification. The washing in a leaf basin into which *ikipiki* medicine had been sprinkled in the form of a cross was interpreted by Lyandileko (the woman doctor already quoted) as the means by which the taboo on a bride crossing a stream was removed. 'We give her *ikipiki* to wash with that she may not fear streams. It is taboo to cross water while she is in the puberty ritual. Here I give her the *ikipiki* so that she may cross. If she crosses before she has been treated she grows thin. She will be like a stream [i.e. her periods will be very heavy].' Another informant remarked that if a bride crossed water before she was treated, the flow of menstrual blood would be excessive. Kasitile interpreted this rite rather differently. He said: 'It is to tell her not to break the commandment with the man. . . . "Do not break the commandment, do not step over him. When you lie down, let the man get up first." It is taboo (*mwiko*) for the woman to get up first and step over (*ukukilanya*) me, the man. My legs would swell up immediately. Sprinkling medicine thus [in a vertical line] is the man. He must get up first. Sprinkling thus [in a horizontal line] is the woman. She must follow.' Probably there is a double symbolism, as in several other rites. Both Lyandileko and Kasitile were experts on ritual and open in conversation with us.

Lyandileko explained the jumping over fire in a whisper: 'It means, Kagile (M. W.), that she will never begin again. She is going to do this at her husband's.' Angombwike said:

It is to give the girl fire, to say: 'Do not burn there at your husband's.' It means: 'Now you have grown up, you are a woman. I have made fire for you (*ngupele umoto*).' For when a girl has run off as a child and been defloured, then her mothers say: 'When shall we make fire for you? We cannot give it to you properly.' And at cooking she burns her hands, perhaps the water for the porridge spills over her hands and burns them. We hear that formerly they gave her fire, a torch of burning grass, to take to her husband's and kindle fire there, but they have left that. She jumps over fire, that is to give it to her.

The rite was also interpreted as a test of virginity. 'If a bride clears the fire she is virgin, if she falls in she has been foolish with men.'

The symbolism here is doubtless complex, but of the various informants Lyandileko, by reason of her status and personality, carries most weight, and I think it is probably correct to regard the jumping over fire both as a *rite de passage* and as a symbol of intercourse.

'The cloth put on the bride like a tail after she has washed at the stream comes from the girl's father.[1] He spits on it and gives it to her mothers to dress her in at the stream.' (Kasitile.) Angombwike explained further:

Dressing her in it means her father has made her grow up. It means: 'Now she is a woman let her act like a woman.' They symbolize the genitals (*ikisepe*) of the man, because among us, according to Nyakyusa custom, in front is a woman and behind a man. They tell her, saying: 'You have grown up, you have work [i.e. intercourse] with a man.'

QUESTION: *Kipetule?*

AGOMBWIKE: *Kipetule* is very old. It's to bless her and say: 'You have grown up. When you go to your husband it will not be painful. Have intercourse.' If the woman is no longer a virgin they do not speak of it. They say she knows already, she has learnt on the veld.

Kipetule, like *undumila*, is a word not used in mixed company. Once Kasitile whispered, when inquiry had been made, unwittingly, before other people: 'No, Mwaipaja (G. W.), there are children present, and my senior, that is bad. But when there are only cross-cousins (*batani*), then . . .' So the conversation changed.

The washing at the stream is a final purification. Lyandileko said:

We give the bride brass body-rings because she was not wearing good things (*inunu*), she was filthy during the puberty ritual. We wash her and put on body-rings and a cloth, and she stands in the winnowing basket, because now she must not step on dirt (*ububibi*).

The earth, it will be remembered, is associated with faeces, corpses, and the shades. Then comes the triumphal return to her father's house, the girl carried high, and the women dancing. 'Crying "*Nisya*" and carrying the girl, on return from bathing, is for display.' Lyandileko, asked the reason for throwing millet in the winnowing basket, replied:

It's to say it [the food, i.e. the meat of the bull of puberty] is ours. We examine the girl at the river. If she is rubbish (*lenga lindu*) we do not rejoice. The mothers of the girl give gifts (*ukubonola*). It's a rejoicing because it's ours, it's ours, the girl is virgin.

Nisya, the word the women repeat as they carry and dance with the bride on the return from the stream, was interpreted by Angombwike as meaning: 'Put me down.'[2] 'It is traditional and

---

[1] Mwakionde denied this, *vide infra*, p. 109.

[2] *Ukwisya*: to put down behind (as opposed to in front).

means: Since you have carried me, put me down, mother, I am a woman,' i.e. this is the symbolic ending of childhood.

Mwakwelebeja's wife interpreted stepping into the winnowing basket as being 'in order that she may cook well for her husband and serve his food nicely'. Kasitile, when asked about it, replied:

They honour the fearful ones (*abipasya*) themselves, saying: 'This is your child, she is Kyala, we are performing the ritual for her.' If they honour an *umwipasya* on the ground Kyala is startled, the child runs mad, she is ill. . . . In these customs we come together to teach the child. Kyala said: 'Shake the winnowing basket for a daughter and say: "We have sent you to your husband; if we hear of cases at your husband's you are no child of ours." ' The mothers of the village instruct the girl. She ought to look towards her mothers-in-law (as they do so) and, if she does not, they beat her again, saying: 'Those are your mothers there, we are not relatives, look to them over there.'

Mwakionde, a doctor, interpreted most of the events in the same way. Asked about the cloth hung over the bride's buttocks, he replied:

It is because during the puberty ritual she does not wear iron [i.e. metal] or a good bark-cloth. . . . Then the cloth comes from the husband [*sic*.] with the three body-rings. It is a way of saying: 'She's my wife.' They carry her and say: *Nisya*.

QUESTION: Why?

MWAKIONDE: Because she has grown up. Until now she was a child. A while ago we bore and begot her, now she has grown up herself and is honoured, she herself begins to bear a child. It is to finish and say: 'Go to your husband and bear your own children.' Her mothers and the women of her father's village throw millet and maize and pumpkin-seeds. It is a rejoicing. Our child has flourished, she has grown up. They give the seed to her mother-in-law, the mother of the groom, and she takes it away.

QUESTION: Is it not a ritual?

MWAKIONDE: No, it is only a rejoicing.

Mwaihojo's daughter, asked why millet was thrown into the basket, replied simply: 'It is shaken, we are rejoicing greatly,' and indeed the basket is shaken in time to the dance, almost like a tambourine.

The theme of rejoicing recurs again and again in the course of the ritual. At the 'putting her in' her mothers dance with her on their shoulders 'to honour her because my child has grown up';

her mother-in-law covers her head with a red cloth 'for display'. 'We are rejoicing because our child has grown up,' and she too takes her on her shoulders and dances with her. When the 'husbands' come to dance the stamping dance: 'It too is a rejoicing. It shows I have married a wife now.' All through there is rejoicing over the fine food, and the celebration and feasting is primarily among the women. The culmination comes when the girl is publicly shown to be a virgin and the mothers can claim the bull crying in exultation: 'It's ours, it's ours.'

An interesting sidelight on the attitude of girls towards the ritual came from a young man, a Christian, who was betrothed to a pagan girl and had forbidden her to go through the ritual. He said:

Once my wife, when she had reached puberty, asked me why I objected to her undergoing the puberty ritual. I said it was forbidden for us Christians to participate in it, and I asked her if she wished to do so. She said 'Yes', and I asked why. She said: 'When the ritual is performed for us we are famed. People tell each other that so-and-so's daughter has grown up and people from far away come to sing songs, so we become very well known. See, now I have grown up, but no one sees that I have done so. Only you know.' Then I said: 'We Christians also have the custom of celebrating growing up at the handing over of marriage-cattle to the father (*ukukwa*). We do not hand over cattle when girls are still small, so everyone sees that a girl has grown up when we do so.' She agreed and said: 'I, also, have seen a little of the handing over of cattle among Christians.'

In fact, the *ukukwa* is the occasion for a great feast among Christians to which many young men and girls come to sing and dance.

The giving of presents to the bride by her father and his contemporaries is interpreted as part of the rejoicing.

To give presents (*ukubonola*) is to rejoice. It's an occasion for display and rejoicing, because the girl has grown up. The father gives her a present because he rejoices that she has grown up. He says to her: 'Congratulations, you have grown up, you are going away to your husband, you are going away to gain a child!'

During the period of seclusion the girl's father is spoken of as her father-in-law (*unkamwana*). She must *ukutila* (respect and avoid) him:

Because he is her father who begot her. She thinks: 'I must respect my father-in-law, father.'[1] She says: 'I have grown up finally, I am a woman.' 'As I have grown up, I am a daughter-in-law (*unkamwana*).' 'If a girl looks at her father (during the ritual) she is proud (*namatingo*).' 'She used to be beaten if she looked at her father's friends. She is proud if she does. Her mothers will beat her.' She also fears ridicule—'We *ukutila* because we laugh at one another'—and mystical sanctions. 'If she does not *ukutila* (her father) she gets thin and brown. Since she has grown up she must avoid people.' 'She would become light in colour if she did not *ukutila* during the ritual.' 'She will grow thin and her body will be brown instead of black. We think that ugly.'

Mwandisi (the old blind chief), asked why a bride should *ukutila* her father, replied:

She avoids him and he gives her a gift to break the taboo. During puberty it is taboo. Kyala has created us so. Because if her father looks at her she grows thin, those below [i.e. the shades] are angry.
QUESTION: And those above?
MWANDISI: Yes! Do they not injure them? Do they not give those who throw out the litter a bull that they may eat?

Mwakionde (the doctor), asked the same question, replied:

It is because of the in-law relationship (*ubukamwana*). If I, the father, look at her she will grow thin and waste away, but at the beer we give her gifts of bark-cloth to break the taboo and say: 'You have come out (*usokile*). You have come out, my child. I am sorry about the fire, I am sorry.' Then she looks at us. She avoids me, the father, and my younger brothers and my fellows in the age-village who are all, according to our custom, her fathers.

Ukutila of her mother-in-law (shielding her face with a mat or skin) was interpreted by Mwakionde in this way:

It is on account of the dignity of her mother-in-law who says: 'She is my child, see, she respects and avoids me, saying: "She bore my husband." I am her superior. She acknowledges my dignity. She is wise, she respects me, her mother.'

Everyone was agreed that 'the bull of puberty' (*ingambako jabu-sungu*) is both a sacrifice to the shades, who are asked to bless the girl and make her fertile, and a feast for the mothers and that, strictly, it is only brought if the girl is virgin. 'We throw the *ija mmapa* meat in the banana grove and put a stone on top of it so that those below may eat, and we pray that the girl may bear a

[1] Some aspects of father-in-law and daughter-in-law avoidance are discussed in *Good Company*, pp. 83–6.

child at her husband's.' Neglect to kill the bull may result in sterility. Mwaseba, a middle-aged man, said:

If the officiants, the mothers of the girl, have not eaten, and the father also, the girl will not bear a child, these people are angry and the shades are angry, they (the shades) help them (the living). And if you do not perform the other customs of the litter the shades are angry, the fathers and the mothers. They say: 'What! Have you not treated the child?'

Mwakionde, the doctor, explained:

When a woman conceives and has a miscarriage, it is *mindu*, the shades are angry. Perhaps if we have not killed the bull of puberty we buy one. The shades are angry, saying: 'Why have we not received a libation of blood poured on the ground for our grandchild? They have done wrong towards us, we who created them.' The girl does not bear a child because pouring out the blood of a beast (bull or cow) is to pray (*ukona ililopa lya nombe ko kwiputa*).

Mwakobela, our neighbour, said:

If we have not eaten the bull of puberty, they bewitch us (*bikundoga*), the child does not bear a child. Our fellows in the lineage bewitch us, they say: 'We have not eaten the puberty meat.' Then, later on, the husband brings the bull and we eat, and the *ija mmapa* meat we throw in the banana grove, and we pray and pray and the girl conceives.

The fertility of the girl is believed to depend upon driving away the shade of her father's lineage from her body. We have already quoted (p. 98) the prayer: 'Here is the meat! I have eaten the food of others, *come out a little*, may she bear a child at her husband's.' Mwaisilage explained this conception:

Those of old said: 'We drive away Kyala and the shades, may she bear at her husband's.' She moves to others, to a different lineage. May that lineage rise up from the dead (*kisyukege ikikolo kila*). If we do not treat the girl she will not bear a child at her husband's.

To understand this it is necessary to understand the Nyakyusa theory of conception. It is held that sexual desire in both men and women comes from Kyala and the shades, and without their support a man is impotent, a woman barren. Kasitile was quite explicit on the matter:

Kyala is in the belly. He causes the blood of a woman which forms a child to flow and the blood of the man also. We say that Kyala is in the belly; he watches over us at the conception of a child. But our fathers,

Mwakanjoki and his fellows, said that Lwembe is there (in the belly), they did not speak of Kyala. Did you not hear at Lubaga?[1] What did I ask for?

G. W.: You asked for a child!

KASITILE: Yes, I asked for a child. The menstrual blood is that which we discharge when lying together. I, the man, discharge, and the woman also discharges. If Kyala does not support us, then that blood degenerates, it becomes blood which flows out at the period.

G. W.: But the girl has periods before intercourse?

KASITILE: Yes, indeed, that is her blood. Does a woman not discharge? If she sleeps alone, as a bachelor, her blood just flows out, it does not create a child. In intercourse we try to discharge together. If I see that the woman is gasping I try to discharge with her. If I am gasping and wish to discharge, I wait for the woman. Yes, there is choice. We are all like that. But our fathers feared that if the woman discharges first she will bear a girl, and if I, the man, discharge first she will bear a boy! The shades of her fathers are there in the body of a girl, and we drive them away. It is like the case of a widow; the situations are just alike. We treat the girl and say: 'Now the woman is free.' At the eating of the bull we seem to say: 'You shade, be present and look upon us. This meat is for you to go away a little. May she bear children.'

G. W.: So if the shade is in the girl she cannot bear children?

KASITILE: What can the shade go away with if you do not pray?

QUESTION: What happens if she washes and performs all the ritual with a man, a husband, and then leaves him, without having had full intercourse, for another man?

KASITILE: It does not matter. She is freed from the lineage of her father, she has moved to another lineage, so they do not treat her again. (*Sika mbombo, abwike nkikolo kya gwise, asamile nkikolo ikingi, popapo batikuntendekesya kangi.*)

On another occasion Kasitile said that intercourse took place 'when Kyala and the shades have gathered there. They come out in the woman and her belly sprouts [i.e. she conceives].'

Kasitile was not offering a personal interpretation when he talked about conception. Conversation with a number of people showed that the ideas he put forward were generally held. Mwandisi, the old blind chief, when asked where the blood to beget children came from, replied:

It is from him who makes us all do things, Kyala and the shades together.

---

[1] Rituals are performed on behalf of the country at Lubaga. Kasitile was a hereditary priest. See *Communal Rituals among the Nyakyusa* (forthcoming).

QUESTION: And menses?

MWANDISI: When the shades are angry a woman is constantly men-struating and does not bear a child; if they are not angry she conceives.

And on another occasion he said:

Lust comes from the shades; if they are angry with you you are im-potent; you cannot beget a child.

His wife added: 'My husband says in his heart: "Let me go to my wife." It is the shade that makes him.'

One informant after another mentioned *both* Kyala (or Lwembe) *and* the shades as being present in intercourse. Mwakionde, after talking of miscarriages being due to the anger of the shades, went on:

Kyala has created the bowel of desire. If a man is impotent we say Kyala has not given him breath to beget a child.

KAKUJU: If my child runs off with a man, whether a stranger or her husband, before she has reached puberty and I continue angry, if Kyala has helped me she does not bear a child. Then it is said 'her father was angry'. They come to me bringing the remaining marriage-cattle and I pray and she bears a child.

QUESTION: If the husband asked for her properly and deflowered her before puberty?

KAKUJU: There is no case, it was all right, even long ago. I said: 'Finish paying the cattle.' Perhaps he begged me, saying: 'I am poor, Father,' and I was satisfied.

No pagan questions the power of the shades over fertility, and this power is believed to be exercised by the mother's lineage, as well as that of the father. Angombwike, the Christian, said:

The pagans fear that if they do not perform the puberty ritual when a girl reaches puberty, she will dry up. The blood will not come again even though she is not pregnant. Then, if her periods do not come for two or three months, like this, she will never bear a child. They say the shades are angry and have bound her fertility. And if she does not reach puberty at all, if menstruation does not begin, her father prays in the banana grove, saying: 'You, fathers, what are you angry about?' And if the girl's mother's brother is angry on account of cattle—perhaps her father has not given marriage-cattle properly for her mother—he, the mother's brother, binds a wisp of the litter (*ulufumbo*) from her puberty ritual in the loft, then the girl will not bear a child. Inquiry is made of a diviner who says: 'The mother's brother has bound her.' The father takes a cow to him and says: 'I am sorry, I have done wrong, I have thought of it now, this is the cow.' Then, in the evening, the mother's brother blows out water in the banana grove and prays much to the fathers. And when he has prayed he says: 'Send the girl to a doctor to drink medicine.' Then the girl bears a child. The pagans say of us Christians when we have children without performing the ritual: 'You have a medicine, you are baptized with a medicine.'

Mwakobela confirmed that the mother's brother, like the father, may prevent a girl bearing a child.

Yes, it is so, if I do not give marriage-cattle for my wife our child will not bear. We go to divine and the oracle catches hold of my wife saying that the fathers are angry. We ask what they are angry about, and the answer is 'cattle'. Then I, the father of the girl, go with a cow and leave it and return. My wife and daughter remain there. They pray and pray and the girl conceives.

It is clear, therefore, that the shades are present in intercourse and control conception. At marriage the shade of her father must 'move aside a little' so that the bride may conceive, and she herself becomes dangerous to her mother (and in a lesser degree to her father) because she has mingled her blood with that of another lineage. Mingling the blood of different lineages is dangerous and a bride can safely meet her mother only after performing a ritual in which her parents, as well as herself, become 'one flesh' with her husband. 'When a bride brings a hen and millet to her mother it is to say: "Mother, I have wiped my husband's genitals, I have grown up." ' All our informants were agreed that this *ilibalaga* or *ilibuko* (both words are used) is to safeguard the mother's health, particularly to prevent her suffering from diarrhœa. Mwandisi's statement was clear:

In the puberty ritual, when a bride has come from her husband, having lain with him, she catches hold of a little millet and a fowl without washing herself and carries them to her mother. The mother eats it with the fowl that her belly may be firm. If the daughter does not bring these things, then, when she drinks from the same calabash as her mother, she oversteps her mother, who has diarrhœa. Yes, the illness comes from the shades because she has come hot from the bed. . . . This diarrhœa comes from the belly when those below are angry and those above also. They say: 'The mother has overstepped the child' or 'The child has overstepped the mother'. If a girl has reached puberty we, the parents, do not come together until she has gone to her husband and lain with him. If we have intercourse we overstep our child, she will be barren and not bear children, but when she has lain with her husband then we two lie together again.

Kasitile identified the hen with the body of the girl, the millet with the seed of her husband, and a daughter going to the back of her mother's hut (*kosofu*), or drinking out of the common calabash, as meeting with her mother.

If she does this before she has brought a fowl she soils her mother. Her mother develops diarrhœa. That is getting rid of the dirt (*kokusosya ubunyali*). . . . The mother's diarrhœa is like that from adultery. If my wife lies with a man in the bush, and I lie with her also, she soils the food which I eat with her, it is dirty, and I have diarrhœa, it is to get rid of the filth. . . . Yes, even though we do not lie together, I get a little diarrhœa, the filth of my wife.

QUESTION: Is the *ilibalaga* to drive away the shade again?

KASITILE: No, it is something else. It is to save the mother that she may not have diarrhœa and may not become weak.

The explanation given of the Kukwe *ilibuko* rite makes clear that it is a symbolic mingling of 'the blood' of son-in-law and mother-in-law, which makes contact between them (through the bride) safe.

Failure to bring the *ilibalaga* is thought sometimes to result in very serious illness. One of the wives of our neighbour, Mwakobela, was delirious. We asked what the cause was. He replied:

Her daughter reached puberty and went to her husband, but refused to drink with her mother. She just came and took water in the calabash cup, she brought nothing from her husband. . . . If the husband is poor a girl brings a fowl for drinking with her mother. . . . The divination said: 'It's the girl.'

QUESTION: Why did she not bring a hen from her husband?

MWAKOBELA: He is not a man of wisdom, he's very harsh, and a fool.

After the *ilibalaga* has been eaten by her parents a bride is no longer dangerous to them, and she, fortified by the various treatments with *undumila* and *ikipiki* medicines, no longer fears the 'heavy ones'. The critical periods of first menstruation and first intercourse are past. But the rule of avoidance between her and her father-in-law (and those identified with him) continues through life and is directly associated by the Nyakyusa with the danger of incest. They account for the rule by a myth which tells how a certain chief looked on his son's wife and saw that she was beautiful and took her, and men were shocked, and forbade a father-in-law and daughter-in-law ever to see one another again. And this taboo, they say, is the reason why fathers and sons must live in separate villages. To avoid (*ukutila*) is 'to fear, to show respect'. Avoidance occurs between women in a limited degree— a girl shows respect to her father's sister, a daughter-in-law to her mother-in-law and her husband's father's sister by not looking at them directly or touching their backs; but these women are in some measure identified with father and father-in-law, and the taboos are most stringent regarding things or actions which are associated with sexual activity. The behaviour of Nyakyusa women suggests very strongly that the fundamental idea in *ukutila* is avoidance of incest.[1] Avoidance between father-in-law and daughter-in-law is the primary rule of good manners and morals in domestic relations, and is constantly expressed in everyday activities.

Besides being a celebration of the change from childhood to womanhood, and of movement from the lineage of her father to that of her husband, the puberty—marriage ritual includes a legal contract. Either at the betrothal, or when the bulk of the marriage-cattle are handed over, the groom's go-between thrusts a spear into the earth of the swept courtyard and there, publicly, before her kinsfolk and neighbours, the bride must pluck it out and hand it to her father, in token of her consent to the marriage. 'It means: "With this spear you may slay me if I run away from my husband." And her father keeps the spear and may kill her if she does—some fathers did so in the old days.'

After taking the spear the father plucks a banana leaf and hands his daughter the mid-rib with which she strikes one of the cows brought by her husband, and all the women of the homestead acclaim her. Thus her acceptance of the marriage is demonstrated. And each time an instalment of the marriage-cattle is handed over, the go-between of her father and the go-between of the husband must both be present as witnesses; and they notify their sons of the contracts they have so witnessed so that the sons may give evidence after the death of their fathers if necessary.

[1] cf. Monica Wilson, *Good Company*, pp. 83–6, 106, 123, 160–2; 'Nyakyusa Kinship' in *African Systems of Kinship and Marriage*, edited by A. R. Radcliffe-Brown and Daryll Forde, p. 127–8.

I

2. IN KUKWE COUNTRY

(a) The events

The puberty and marriage ritual performed by the Kukwe differs in detail from that performed by the Nyakyusa proper, but the main elements—the seclusion of the bride and avoidance of her fathers and brothers, the laying of a ritual litter, the meeting of maids and young men on the litter, the avoidance of water, the treatment with *ikipiki* medicine, shaving and ceremonial purification, the instruction, the celebration of maturity and virginity by the exchange of feasts between the bride's parents and those of the groom, the slaughter of the bull of virginity provided by her husband, and the taking of a fowl to her mother after first intercourse —all these recur. And the overt purpose of the ritual is again that the girl may be fertile, and healthy in mind and body. The main differences are in the symbols used for intercourse and purification, and in the location of the rites. Among the Nyakyusa proper most of the ritual is performed at the bride's home, whereas among the Kukwe most of it is performed at the groom's home.

When a Kukwe girl first menstruates her father sends his go-between in the marriage (*umfusya*) to inform her husband that she has grown up. If she has been visiting her husband, and is at his house when the first period begins, she runs home to her father's, and the formal message is despatched to her husband. He sends back a hen with the message: 'Thank you, you have nourished my wife,' and some time later sends a second hen by his go-between summoning her to come and wash. A party of two or three 'mothers' (her own mother does not go) and ten or a dozen maids takes her to her husband's, and there (if she is a senior wife) she washes with him in water mixed with powdered *ikipiki* medicine. The officiant pours the water which the husband catches in his hands, and the wife holds her hands below his. Then they kindle fire together by friction (*ukupegesa ulupendo*), husband and wife both twirling the stick (his hands are again above hers) and the officiant holding the horizontal trough. On the fire they have kindled porridge is cooked, which they eat together. A junior wife washes and kindles fire and eats porridge, not with her husband, but with his younger brother.

After the ritual meal 'mothers-in-law' cut banana leaves and spread the litter for the bride at their homestead, not at her father's. The officiant sprinkles powdered medicine over the floor on one side of the hut and makes two girls lie down with the bride between them. These two remain with the bride all through the period of seclusion, never leaving her, but the other maids may come and go if called away to perform other duties.

From the onset of menstruation until the ritual washing a girl may neither cross a stream nor wash; after it she crosses streams and washes her hands and feet, but does not yet bathe her whole body. She sleeps on the litter with her companions for about a month and 'by day and by night the young men sing songs with the girls. . . . The play in the puberty hut resembles adultery—we call it love-making (*ukuganisya*).' 'The groom visits his bride on the litter.' 'Gifts of beer and firewood are brought by the bride's mothers (*ukusumbulela*) and, after her second period has passed, the rite of *ukusosya* (bringing out) is performed.'

The litter is swept out and burnt. Bride and groom are shaved and go separately to bathe. 'The women carry the girl and the man's fellows carry him.' The girl is examined to prove her virginity and the women return with her rejoicing, and make her and her husband run in and out of the doorway of a hut over which they pour water. Then follows the admonition.

At the *ukusosya* (bringing out) rite the officiants drink a special brewing of beer made in the following fashion: the chief officiant puts a little millet, mixed with powdered medicine, into a flat winnowing basket, makes the bride stand in it and, loosening her bark-cloth soiled by first menstruation, lets it fall into the millet.[1] Then she shreds and burns it, lest an enemy, wishing to prevent the bride conceiving, should get hold of it. The bride's fresh bark-cloth is sprinkled with medicines to make her 'heavy', the ashes of the old one are treated with medicines to ensure her fertility, and the millet is put to soak and brewed into beer in the hut in which she lies secluded on the litter.

We saw the Kukwe *ukusosya* rite performed only once. The girl, a daughter of a chief, was not yet married or betrothed, so there was no groom to play his part, and the whole ritual was carried out in her father's homestead, her own mother going through it with her. She herself appeared most reluctant, and there were various modifications due to the pressure of new ideas. We quote the account to show the manner of washing, and of entering and leaving the hut—rites which were described in detail by a number of informants, and which are characteristic of the Kukwe ritual cycle.

---

[1] It was not made clear by Kukwe informants exactly when this happened.

Record of M. W., 13 September 1936

I arrived at nine o'clock in the morning to find Syungu, the elderly wife of the chief's senior brother, who acts as officiant in all the rituals for the chief's family, grinding and cooking *inyemba* together with a powdered medicine and red pigment, to make an ointment. I asked the purpose of the medicine. She replied: 'It's *ikipiki* that she may be heavy, that she may bear children and not be barren.'

Some of the chief's wives gave me beer—ordinary beer. They themselves were drinking from a pot which had stood in the inner part of the house (*kusofo*) and to which medicine had been added. They explained that it might be drunk only by themselves, the chief's wives. A strange woman, a Penja, came along and, though warned that this pot was not for her, insisted on drinking some of it. She explained how Penja ritual differed from that of the Kukwe—they kill sheep for the puberty ritual. Usually this beer stands to brew in the seclusion hut 'on the litter'.

The women were preparing a dish of beans and bananas cooked together, and when it was ready a little was given to the officiant, some was put aside for the girl (*unsungu*),[1] and the remains were offered to the guests. One of the cooks threw away the central stem of the head of bananas used, but was told by the officiant to fetch it back, as all the rubbish must be cleared away together at the end of the rite.

After midday the officiant shaved some hair from the girl's temples and the back of her neck, and then she shaved the mother completely. I asked why the girl was not shaved completely and was told: 'Her fellows would laugh at her if she had no hair.' The officiant prepared four banana leaves, stripping each off on one side of the mid-rib and shredding the other half so as to make a rough fringe. Standing with her back to the girl, she touched herself over the genitals, breasts, and forehead, then handed the leaf back over her head, telling the girl to fasten it round her waist. She repeated the performance with the second leaf, telling the girl to fasten it round her neck. The girl complied with the first leaf but refused the second, saying: 'I have a cloth,' and she pulled her breast cloth round her shoulders. The officiant followed the same procedure with the girl's mother, who fastened both leaves round herself. Then one of the chief's wives took the mother on her shoulders and carried her round the corner of the house. The bride followed on foot, and three other wives of the chief, singing:

> Kyanalu
> > Kyatiko
> Kyanalwe
> > Kyatiko

---

[1] Usually we have translated *unsungu* by 'bride', but in this case she was not betrothed: cf. footnote 2, p. 73.

The words 'refer to the cries of the mother in labour'—'they symbolize the adolescence of the bride and the toil of the mother in labour.'

They went together to the stream, the girl's mother walking after they were past the homesteads. The girl and her mother sat down on the bed of the stream, facing down-stream. The other women made them hold out their hands, and between each finger and toe, and behind each ear, they placed a small pebble. Flowers and grass, twisted together, were placed on their heads, with stones on top. Then both were made to lie down in the water. The girl was pushed down and slapped gently. She protested a little and was told: 'You are proud.' The women and girls on the bank laughed. She was told to take off her clothes and wash herself and, looking rather embarrassed, she went a little way up-stream into the shelter of some bushes. The women said said she was shy of me. Her mother took off her cloth and washed it, and all the chief's wives present, a younger sister of the *unsungu*, and another little girl did so also. The *unsungu* slipped on a fresh dry cloth, her mother a fresh bark-cloth, and each was given a little bunch of ferns and flowers to carry. One woman filled a small calabash with water and the party returned to the mother's house. Mother and daughter were told by the officiant to throw their flowers on to the roof of the hut just above the doorway; she herself poured some of the water brought from the stream on to the thatch and made the girl enter the doorway as the water dripped down. Again she poured water and made the girl come out. The rite was repeated for the mother. Then the officiant took the red ointment she had prepared with medicine, and touched herself with it on the left toe, the left knee, the navel, the left temple, and left elbow. She touched the girl with it in the same places, smeared it on her legs, arms, shoulders, and head, and did the same for the mother, and for the small sister who had washed.

Next she cleared away the banana skins and bean-shells left by the women who had cooked earlier and, along with this refuse, she burnt a bark-cloth strap taken off the girl when she washed. There was no litter (*ulufumbo*), though the women said it was usual for there to be one. Then the girl ate some of the cooked bananas, beans, and mash of beans and bananas prepared, and drank some of the medicated beer with her mother, and the curtailed rite was at an end.

Usually, we were told, the mothers sing: 'Put me down, Mother, put me down,' as they carry the bride back from the stream after examining her, and throw gifts of grain into a winnowing basket, as they do in Selya, but there was no such rejoicing for this girl. It seemed likely, from the events omitted, that she was known not to be a virgin, but we had no proof of this. When the *unsungu* is betrothed, her husband also shaves and washes, is carried to the stream, runs in and out under the dripping water, is anointed with red ointment, shares the mash of beans and bananas, and drinks medicated beer with her from the same calabash. In the old days it was taboo for either bride or groom to set foot to the ground on their way to the stream.

For a senior wife, the mother-in-law moulds hearth-bricks with powdered medicine, and sets them up in the groom's hut. A mother goes through the ritual with her eldest daughter if the daughter is her first-born, or with her senior daughter-in-law if her eldest child is a boy. 'If they do not do this they go mad.'

As in Selya, an admonition of the bride by her 'mothers', in the presence of her in-laws, concludes the full 'bringing out' ritual. We never heard it in Kukwe country, but the points mentioned by informants were similar to those emphasized in Selya. Kajinga, Porokoto's second wife, summed up the teaching thus:

Obey your husband when he calls you. Fetch water and wood. Don't say: 'First let me fetch firewood' if your husband wants you to do something else. Do what your husband says first, then to-morrow go for wood. It is forbidden to refuse when your husband wants to sleep with you. In the morning get up and wash. Wash first, then light the fire and give your husband food. Don't say: 'There isn't any food.'

Next day, on her return home, the bride is given presents by the people of her home village (*ukugwa*), her father making the first gift. The groom brings the bull of puberty on which all the 'mothers' feast, but the meat from the top of the right foreleg (*ijamapa*) is reserved for the bride's own parents who sing as they eat it:

> *Kyatile, Kyatile, Kyatipwe*

Some days later a party of 'mothers' takes her formally to her husband's house (*ukumbeka*) with gifts of beer and food and firewood, and are feasted by the groom's people and given chickens and shillings.

When she is finally living with her husband, before she can visit or greet her parents, the bride must put milk and a fowl (some use a live fowl, others a cooked one) under her bed at night. After having had intercourse with her husband 'she takes the fowl and milk and gives them to her parents with the filth of intercourse still on her. This is called the *ilibuko*. If she does not do this her mother will fall ill and have diarrhœa.' 'When they take the food (from under the bed) in the morning it has the filth of intercourse on it, then the father and mother should eat it. If this is not done they will fall ill with diarrhœa. If the hen is taken alive some eat it and others do not.'

After discussing this rite Mwasalemba went on:

You know, also, that when a girl has gone through the puberty ritual at her husband's she must not take firewood from her mother's rafters (*kwijulu*) until she is obviously pregnant. Before then, while she is lying with her husband, she must not. We say: 'How can you take your mother's firewood when you are sleeping with your husband?' It is just the same whether the mother is old or young. If the bride goes through the ritual without sleeping with her husband that is all right; it is when she begins to sleep with him that she begins to avoid her mother's loft. At that time I, the father, may meet her mother and sleep with her, but with *coitus interruptus*. I must not make her pregnant. The daughter must begin. As soon as she is pregnant then we parents can begin to conceive a child again. If we do so before our daughter, then she will never bear a child at all, and others will say: 'How could you overstep your daughter?'

Avoidance between father-in-law and daughter-in-law is observed as in Selya, but is slightly less strict.

(b) The overt purpose and symbolism

As has already been indicated, the symbolism of the Kukwe ritual of puberty is similar to that of Selya. The same actions are interpreted in exactly the same way and, where actions differ somewhat, they are still interpreted as expressing the same general conceptions. For example, the Kukwe bride and groom make fire together by friction and eat porridge cooked on it, whereas a bride in Selya eats bananas with powdered medicine, but both actions are symbols of sexual intercourse. Both in Selya and in Kukwe country the bride is purified and, as part of the process of purification, the shade of her father's lineage is driven from her body; but only among the Kukwe is this symbolized by sitting in a running stream and allowing the water to wash away pebbles from between her fingers and toes.

That there may be no doubt about the interpretation of the Kukwe ritual we again quote a number of statements by Nyakyusa informants. These refer specifically to the Kukwe form of the puberty ritual.

Chief Porokoto's wives, discussing the ritual together, were emphatic that 'if the bride does not wash with powdered medicine she will go mad and she will bury children'.

Syungu, the officiant for all the rituals in Porokoto's lineage, said:

If a girl goes mad, we say, if we have not treated her: 'We neglected the ritual, let us treat her.' She runs about aimlessly and makes bundles of filth. But if we have treated her we say: 'Perhaps Kyala has gone away from me. See! Nothing has been omitted, we have treated her.' And if she does not bear a child at her husband's her in-laws say to her: 'Did your father and mother not treat you?'

MUNGASALWA (a middle-aged pagan): It is said that if she eats food with her fellows who sleep with their husbands they will harm (overstep) her, and she has diarrhœa. When she has been given powdered medicine, then she eats with them. . . . To lie on powdered medicine which has been sprinkled on the ground is to give the bride weight (*ubusito*), because if it is not done those who are with their husbands will overstep her and she will have diarrhœa.

POROKOTO'S WIVES: In the old days we put medicine in her porridge so that she would not run away from her husband . . . not now. It's European times now.

QUESTION: In Selya it is said that if she is not given powdered medicine she will be proud.

WIVES: Yes, here too. And if the girl is proud we beat her.

MUNGASALWA: Washing and catching in her hands the water that falls from her husband's hands has two meanings. In some families the husband and wife wash separately, in others they wash together. In either case the first meaning is present, in the second both meanings. It is said that when someone has not washed in the puberty ritual his or her children will die, for that water (with which he neglected to wash) will enter the child's stomach and kill it. The water is in the child's stomach but its symptoms are those of diarrhœa. The nubile girl catching water in her hands teaches us that the woman will receive everything. The man is like the upper grindstone, the woman like the nether grindstone (we speak of intercourse), which means that the women receives the semen which comes from the man.

Making fire by friction is a symbol of procreation.[1] If the fire does not kindle we say the couple are sterile. Two fire-sticks are used, one is the man the other the woman, and the fire is the child. The sawdust made by the rubbing is the semen.

KAJINGA: If the fire does not come the man is sterile and the girl will quarrel with her husband and perhaps run away. It does not mean she will be barren with other men.

---

[1] *Ukupegesa*: to make fire by friction; *ukwipegesa*: to masturbate.

MUNGASALWA: The bride does not cross water for it is said that the blood which began to flow when she reached puberty will not dry on her body if she does.

To sleep on the litter and to refuse to sleep on sleeping-mats is a sign of childhood (for during childhood girls do not think much about cleanliness, but are dirty); it means that they leave behind them [literally 'come out from'] childish things. The litter is burnt because if it has not been burnt the children take bits of it to make a fire and cook food, then, when they have eaten that food, their bodies are sick. We say the body becomes unhealthily fat (*ukujegejala*). Food is collected for a bride because if, later, a woman, who has not had food collected for her, eats food collected for another bride going through the puberty ritual, she will fall sick and her body will grow unhealthily fat. Bringing food for the *ukusumbulila* and giving gifts at the *ukugwa* are to congratulate the bride because she has grown up, she is now an adult.

X: The wearing of banana leaves [at the bringing out] is a sign of fertility. The ritual is finished, the girl is someone's wife now. . . . The plantain represents the penis, the sweet banana the clitoris.

Sitting in a stream and letting water carry away pebbles placed between fingers and toes is a symbol of purification and separation from the shade. The first element—purification—was mentioned by most informants: 'The rite means that the dirt is finished,' said Porokoto's wife; but the more self-conscious identified 'dirt' with the shade. Mwasalemba made the matter quite clear. When asked why pebbles were placed in the clefts of fingers and toes, he replied: 'Kyala, when he created men, said: "At death throw it away, it is the shade, it is the body." '

QUESTION: In the puberty ritual?
MWASALEMBA: It is to say that the shade has brooded over the child, since he created blood we throw him away. May the shade go with these stones, then may she bear children; if he does not go, if you do not treat the girl, then Kyala broods over her and she does not bear children.

QUESTION: Why does she avoid her father at this time?
MWASALEMBA: Because I, the father, and her mother, perform the ritual for our child. Our shade has entered into her, has brooded over her, therefore we do not come together on the mat until we have finished treating our child; when we have finished, and have treated her, then we do what we will on the mat. If I want to lie with my wife [during the ritual] she refuses, saying: 'Our child has not yet finished, she is still undergoing the puberty ritual.' But if she agrees and we lie together, then our child will never bear. When we have finished the

ritual I come together with my wife again, but if our child is unmarried it is taboo to procreate a child, we practise *coitus interruptus*, the semen falls on the mat. . . . This is until the girl goes to her husband, until she is married. If my wife wears a bark-cloth I say to her during our daughter's puberty ritual: 'Arrange your bark-cloth carefully lest I, the man, desire you, I shall catch hold of you and we will cause the shade to make our child barren.' When she has gone to her husband we say our shade has finished, he has gone away in the water. Our child has gone to another shade. Yes, she also has intercourse with her husband at his home, but that does not matter, I have intercourse with my wife.

He was emphatic that the parents begin full intercourse as soon as the girl goes to her husband, it is not necessary to wait for her to become pregnant.

QUESTION: What do the spirits do in intercourse?

MWASALEMBA: The shade causes my penis to stand up and says: 'Go to the woman, there.' And also the woman's shade says: 'Your husband comes into you.' It is the shades which create desire, then we have intercourse, the shades meet together, hers—the woman's— and mine. If I do not go to my wife the shade says: 'Why, what's wrong with my place? Are there thorns? Why do you not enter?' They brood over (*bikobatela*) us both, both me and my wife.

QUESTION: What do they want?

MWASALEMBA: They want to create a child.

QUESTION: Why then do men desire masturbation and sodomy? [At first when I asked this he said: 'No, the shade is a woman,' but then he corrected himself].

MWASALEMBA: It is the shade which creates this desire, we have it within. A youth masturbates, the semen falls on the ground—perhaps two youths; it's also the shade. And a woman also masturbates. . .

QUESTION: You perform the rituals for many reasons?

MWASALEMBA: Yes, if we do not perform the rituals the shade broods on us and we do not bear children. Perhaps he broods on the crops, and they do not grow well but poorly, perhaps we run mad.

On another occasion Mwasalemba said:

The shade is in the heart. It is the shade which desires to go to a woman, which causes us men to have erections and excites desire in women. If you have not got the shade you are impotent, you do not go to women. We say: 'The shade has brooded over this man, why do they not rouse him to go to women?' He just looks at women. Then the shade rouses up in the belly and says: 'Ha!' It rouses up and the man has intercourse with a woman. If it has brooded over him, it does not rouse him, it does not wish to come out. And although the faeces are firm they are the corpse. Because we bury a corpse underground, and faeces also go underground to the shades. They disappear by night, that is the shade. If someone excretes faeces and finds it in the grass we say: 'The shade has caught hold of him.'

QUESTION: Are faeces associated with sexual intercourse?

MWASALEMBA: Yes, the shade does both things, he causes diarrhœa and sexual intercourse. If you defaecate firm stools that is not the shade, that is the food we eat, but watery diarrhœa which troubles you repeatedly at night—that is the shade. If you have diarrhœa for three days people say: 'The shades have hammered you' or 'The shade has caught hold of you.'

QUESTION: Madness?

MWASAMEMBA: That is the shade because it says: 'Since you have me in your belly, and they have not treated you, I cause this—these faeces are the corpse. A madman defaecates and catches hold of his faeces, perhaps he eats them, perhaps he binds it up in the grass and catches hold of it. It is the corpse.'

Kakune, the doctor, also interpreted the puberty ritual as being, in one aspect, the transference of a girl from her father's group to her husband's and, like Kasitile and Mwasalemba, he identified sexual desire and potency with the shades. He said:

At puberty a girl has left her father's and has gone to others; if she dies he to whom she has gone buries her.

QUESTION: Where does the blood of a woman come from?

KAKUNE: If the girl is unmarried, from her shades; they create her blood, but in the ritual we treat her so that she moves to my place, she comes to my shades; the blood of a married woman is created by my shades and hers together. And the 'blood' of a man [i.e. semen] also comes from the shades.

QUESTION: Do the shades reveal themselves at birth?

KAKUNE: Yes, because if I am angry or my father is angry I do not beget a child, but when he has prayed I do so. If I am angry with the woman and she has caught hold of me and injured me, then we do not have a child. The ordeal (umwafi) convicts the woman. She goes to her father who prays. Then we have a child.

QUESTION: Where does the power to bear and beget children come from?

KAKUNE: From the shades, you have the shades in your belly. If they are not there you are all like women in the house, you cannot have an erection, but when the shades work, you have an erection.

QUESTION: Whose shades are present at intercourse?

KAKUNE: Mine, the man's and the woman's, we both have them,

they both work in us, they are not only in one partner. They work in the woman and in the man, they work in both of us.

Mwangwanda, an elderly pagan, explained the symbolism of the new hearth-brick at some length:

We take a new hearth-brick and plant it by the hearth in the bride's house. It means: 'You have grown up, you are a woman, you must always cook a pot,' and she cooks on that hearth-brick. . . . It means: 'You have grown up, the food that your mother sent will come no more, you must cook for your husband yourself.' It is planted for the senior wife only, not for others. If I find that my first wife is not a virgin we do not plant a brick for her—she has lain with another. But if she has a younger sister and she brings her as a junior wife and she is a virgin and I deflower her myself, then the first sister is still the senior wife and we plant a brick for her and her child will inherit as the senior son, for another shut up her womb [i.e. made her virgin again]. If she has no younger sister I may marry her, but she will not be my chief wife. The next one I marry will be my senior wife and for her the brick will be planted and her son will inherit.

There is also an association, not made explicit by our informants, between a log of firewood and a marriageable woman. One of the tasks of the bride and her maids is to fetch heavy logs of firewood which are stored in her mother's loft. At least one log goes with her when she is taken by her 'mothers' to her husband, and this she keeps all her life, taking it with her if she moves. From it the shades are said to chip splinters when they wish to warm themselves at the dying fire at night. After she has gone to her husband and before she conceives, a bride is forbidden to touch the firewood in her mother's loft, and in the funeral ritual, when a widow returns home for the *ingotolo* she steals a log of firewood from her mother's loft and takes it to her husband's. Into the cracks of this log the officiants press seeds. It seems probable that the reddish log represents a woman in her reproductive capacity, which is formally transferred to her husband and segregated from the reproductive activities of her mother. This, we repeat, is our own interpretation, not formulated by any Nyakyusa.

The taboo on a bride who has slept with her husband approaching her mother until she has brought the ritual *ilibuko* is associated with the danger of mixing the bloods of different lineages.

A bride avoids dipping water out of a pot and drinking from a calabash belonging to her relatives for the following reasons: A girl is of one blood (*ililopa*) with her mother, and when she goes to her husband, the blood of another lineage mingles with hers, but it has not reached her mother because they have not met. To drink water together from one calabash is to meet. Then the mother has diarrhœa because her body is not accustomed to the blood of another lineage. To have diarrhœa is to go bad, to expel (*ukusosya*) the filth. The *ilibuko* of the fowl is the body of the groom which mingles with the body of the girl's parents that they may be one blood with him.

Thus, not only husband and wife, but also parents and son-in-law become one flesh.

As in Selya, a direct connection is made between the parents receiving a bull for the bride's virginity, and her bearing a child to her husband. Mwasalemba explained: 'Kyala together with the shades have made the girl grow up. If the girl runs off with her husband and I, the father, have not received cattle, then the earth is angry, the shades say: "We shall see if she will flourish there." Then the girl does not conceive, and the diviner says: "The shades are angry." The groom's people bring cattle, then I, the father, pray for my child and she conceives, her belly swells.'

CHAPTER V

THE RITUAL OF BIRTH[1]

KYALA (or Lwembe) and the shades create desire in men and women and control conception; when the shades are angry women do not conceive—this is one of the main tenets of pagan Nyakyusa cosmology, and it is combined with a limited knowledge of physiology. It is clearly understood that conception cannot take place without intercourse, and that gestation in humans lasts for nine months, but it is believed that repeated intercourse is necessary for conception, and formerly, if a man found his wife pregnant after having lain with her only once, he accused her of adultery.

(a) Taboos of procreation

The procreation of children is an ultimate value of Nyakyusa society and the accepted end of marriage, but it is regarded as dangerous under certain conditions and is hedged about with taboos. These are enforced so that both parents and children may be healthy; a breach of them is thought to result in violent diarrhœa, as well as monstrously swollen legs and weakness in men, general debility in children, and miscarriage or an excessive menstrual flow in women. The onus of observing them falls primarily on women, though their husbands must also co-operate, and a breach of taboo is treated as immoral, for it is believed to endanger the life, or health, or property of others.

Certain general conceptions underlie the taboos. The first is that of *ubunyali*, filth, which is held to come from the sex fluids, menstruation, and childbirth, as well as from a corpse, and the blood of a slain enemy. All these are felt to be both disgusting and dangerous, and the sex fluids are held to be particularly dangerous to an infant, hence the taboo on husband and wife resuming intercourse very soon after childbirth.

At first, when the child is very young, we think it very bad for the parents to sleep together at all, because when the child is very young

[1] This account came from a score or more women not cited individually, as well as from our regular informants on ritual whose names are mentioned.

the women has constantly to handle it and if, just after intercourse, she has to do this without time to wash first, then the child, we think, will get diarrhœa or grow thin. Women[1] always wash very carefully in the mornings after intercourse, both for the sake of the children and the husband. If the woman touches food unwashed after intercourse we think it will make her husband sick, and he will get unhealthily fat. If a child is old enough to play by itself . . . so that the wife can wash properly before attending to it, then it is all right for the couple to have intercourse, but not for the woman to become pregnant again yet. She should not do that until the child is weaned![2]

Contact with menstrual blood or a menstruating woman is held to be dangerous to a man, more particularly to a warrior, hence there is an absolute taboo on intercourse during menstruation (for five to eight days) and restrictions on cooking for a man. A menstruating woman does not blow up the fire on which her husband's food is cooking, or squeeze the food to test whether it is ready, or scrape ash off bananas or sweet potatoes she has roasted, or serve food, for 'her breath comes from her belly and it is dirty; her belly is dirty on account of the menstrual blood. All her body is dirty. She does not wash. When she washes, you, the husband, think that the flow has dried up and catch hold of her!' So a woman who is menstruating fans the fire instead of blowing it, and calls a co-wife or a child to serve the food she has cooked. She does not even crouch over the fire to warm herself, lest she contaminate it; and she neither uses the common calabash cup for drinking nor scoops water from the household water jar with her hand, but fashions a cup for herself from a leaf, or has her own little water-pot. She avoids passing behind or shaking hands with a man; she avoids a new-born infant; she keeps well away from cattle, neither passing behind them when they are in the homestead nor clearing out dung from the byre; she avoids touching medicines or entering the house of a doctor; and she avoids eating pumpkin or pumpkin leaves, or picking them. These taboos are enforced lest she injure men or infants or cattle or medicines, for 'she is dirty' and her 'dirt' is thought to cause purging and to rot medicines, and she,

---

[1] The 'filth' is on the wife because she cleanses her husband with her hands.

[2] *Coitus interruptus* is practised until the mother is ready to conceive again. 'Formerly it was taboo to make a woman pregnant before her previous child was four or five years old. Her husband's sisters made a great case about it. The child must know how to run before a younger brother was born. We said: "How can a woman carry two children?" Now she becomes pregnant again when the elder is two. Of those who bear again before that it is said: "They kill the elder child." ' (Statement of Nsajigwa, an elderly man.)

for her part, fears lest the medicines with which men protect themselves and their cattle may injure her, causing her menstrual flow to 'last a whole month'. She avoids pumpkins lest she suffer from a small growth in the vagina called a 'pumpkin' and bear sickly children. 'It is said that this disease is due to women picking or eating pumpkins when they are menstruating . . . the menstrual blood resembles the pumpkin and they fight together.'

If a wife fails to warn her husband that she is menstruating and permits him to have intercourse with her, he will be furiously angry and may even divorce her saying: 'You are soiling me, get out!'

Any contact with a menstruating woman is believed to cause him suffering. 'His legs become swollen and painful and he is very tired.' 'Strength leaves the man.' 'He sits back weakly; he has no speed in running.' Kasitile explained:

The danger of menstrual blood is that it is filthy; it is an illness. Formerly, if a foolhardy man took his wife when she was menstruating, when he went to war, he fell. We others said: 'Why were you vanquished? Did you enter when your wife was unwell? Do you not know that it is a very serious illness?'

Angombwike added:

Formerly, the fear was greater than it is to-day. If a man made love to a menstruating woman they said he would fall ill of *imbela*, an illness for which there was no remedy. His belly ached and his body grew red; he just lay down. His face swelled and his legs ached. Now pagans are not so much afraid of menstruation; they have listened to the Christians.

Asked why sleeping with a menstruating woman should make a man weary, informants linked the danger from menstrual blood with the danger that besets a husband when his wife commits adultery, and the 'blood' of two men mixes in the woman's womb. Menstrual blood is not so dangerous to a husband as the 'blood' of another man, but yet it is 'filthy'. One of Mwakionde's wives said:

My husband gets tired if he sleeps with me when I am menstruating because he has given us our menstrual blood; it is that which has entered into me; there are two bloods, his and mine.

Mwambuputa, a village headman, elaborated further:

If my wife has committed adultery and cooks my food or draws water for me, then my legs are weary and I also have diarrhœa. If she scrapes bananas when she is menstruating, or conceals that she is menstruating and we have intercourse, then my legs are tired, but I do not have diarrhœa, because it is my blood; she is my relative (*nkamu gwangu*), she is my wife, her blood and mine are one. But when she has lain with a man in the bush there is his blood; I have diarrhœa to get rid of it; the food which she cooks for me is dirty, she has made it filthy, I have diarrhœa and get rid of it, she oversteps me. And also if she has concealed that she is menstruating and we have intercourse, I am overstepped. To overstep is to insult—but since the blood is mine I do not get rid of it. That menstrual blood is very dirty!

If I have always been all right and strong, and I find that I get tired walking and hoeing, I think: 'What is it? See, always I was all right, and now I am very tired.' My friends say: 'It is women, you have lain with one who was menstruating.' And if I eat food and start diarrhœa they say: 'It's women, they have committed adultery.' My wives deny it. We go to divine, and one is caught; if she agrees that's that, but if she denied it, formerly we went to the poison ordeal. The woman drank alone, not I. If she vomited then I was defeated, the woman was good, but if it caught her then her father paid one cow.

What we feared greatly in the old days, Mwaipaja, was war. We feared to die. For if my fellow in the village committed adultery with my wife then, when we went to war, we both died; if we went to fight at Mwangomo's [a neighbouring chiefdom], both he and I would be speared. Then people were astonished and said: 'Why, have so-and-so and so-and-so died? Perhaps they both lay with the same woman.' For this reason we drove adulterers from the village, and for this reason the chief was angry with an adulterer, saying: "This is my place! Why do you kill my people?" '

Others confirmed Mwambuputa's statement that adultery led to death in battle:

Formerly, when there was war, if your fellow made love to your wife in secret and you all went to fight, you died on one day on account of the woman.

Mwandisi linked the disquiet in a man's belly with the anger of the shades seated there.

If a woman has gone behind the house with another man and comes and cooks food for her husband, blowing up the fire and cooking for him, then the food turns round in his stomach and says: 'Is this my kinsman?' She made friends with others behind the house and cooked for them [i.e. committed adultery]. So then the man develops diarrhœa because the food turned round in his stomach. He falls down on the road, he falls down in battle.

K

QUESTION: The spirits are angry?

MWANDISI: Yes, they say: 'That woman for whom we gave marriage-cattle has overstepped her husband.' Yes, it is the shades who are angry in his belly.

Kakune, a doctor, made it clear that the danger to the husband when his wife committed adultery came from the semen of another man entering her.

If your wife commits adultery you get very tired on a journey, you suffer from diarrhœa; in the old days we fell in war.

QUESTION: What if the adulterer practises *coitus interruptus*?

KAKUNE: Yes, if the man is clean he withdraws and the semen falls to the ground. If he always withdraws when he has intercourse with my wife, then I escape, nothing happens. The woman is like a child. See, when your wife who has not yet reached puberty plays with young men on the veld it is no matter. Do they create a child with her? No! But if she is an adulteress he is there in her, and I am there in her, and Kyala says: 'Ha! Are there two?' And he spears you, the owner of the woman. You are soiled by going to the woman; that is filth. But if I catch an adulterer with my wife, even if he has practised *coitus interruptus*, I am angry and kill him—there is jealousy! But as for diarrhœa, I do not suffer from it.

The most dangerous adultery of all, according to the Nyakyusa, is that of a man with his father's wife. Angombwike explained:

If a man dies and his son has been lying with his wives in secret, whether with or without his permission, the son is very much afraid to approach his father's place. If he goes near or touches the corpse he will himself die, for he is one flesh with his father; their blood has mingled in the woman's belly. He keeps a long way away and so do the wives with whom he has lain. The leading men of the village are told about it and a doctor is fetched and the son and the wives involved are taken to a waterfall and treated there. If he is the eldest son a younger brother kills the cows meanwhile. Then he comes back to the homestead and kills a cow himself. While you were away in Europe I saw a case of this with my own eyes. A man died whose son had been lying with his wives. As soon as the son approached his father's place he fell down sick to death. People picked him up and rushed him away to a distance. Then he began to breathe a little easier. They took him to a waterfall and treated him and he recovered, more or less. He is still unwell from time to time. It is not madness, just illness. And if, before the father's death, such a son approaches his father, the old man gets very ill indeed and the elder wives turn the son out of the house. There is none of this trouble if a brother [either a full brother or a half-brother] has lain with the dead man's wives. A brother will approach the corpse without fear. But there is another trouble: if a man seduces his brother's wife the husband may have diarrhœa perhaps with bloody stools. Many people do not come to their fathers' funerals before the burial. And also if the father is ill, and they see he is near death, they run away, returning when he has been buried. Because it is said that a man will die if he has slept with his mother, his father's wife, and sees his father or sees the corpse, as did Jones, the son of Kisokora. He slept with his mothers in secret. When his father died (in a different village from that in which Jones lived) Jones seized his father's cattle and ran away with them. When they had buried his father he came to mourn. The women with whom he had slept told on him because he had given them syphilis.

A wife who commits adultery with her husband's son is held to be in great danger also. Mwandisi said:

If they conceal it and approach the grave both the son and the wife will die. Both are washed naked, under a waterfall. The officiant washes them together with a fowl.

QUESTION: Why the waterfall and the nakedness?

MWANDISI: The water is to take away the sickness. Being naked is so that the case may go away and you, the man, may be empty (*bwasi*) and the woman may be empty. For if such a son looks into the grave and approaches to weep, the shades and Kyala are angry and say: 'Are you a relative? How can you look into the grave? It is you who have killed him, by causing him diarrhœa.' And if the woman approaches and holds her dead husband in her arms, then she dies. Those below are angry and say: 'Is she your relative?' And she dies. But if she has committed adultery with someone who is no relation she approaches and does not fear, and the adulterer does not fear either, but approaches.

For a woman, adultery is held to be dangerous also in childbirth:

If she has had lovers, she has a difficult delivery and the child refuses to come out until she confesses. Sometimes she confesses three, then the child comes, it comes out. . . . She confesses the name and takes a bit of stick and spits on it and throws it away, and you will be surprised to see that she gives birth at once. If she is very bad she will tell you three names and throw away three sticks.

Any contact with childbirth is held to be even more dangerous to men than contact with menstruation. It also is thought to cause weakness, and it is warriors who are most affected. Traditionally, no man entered the confinement hut in which a woman remained until the cord had dropped off the new-born child and she had purified herself, and she did not normally resume cooking for her husband for some weeks; but these taboos are less strictly observed than formerly, partly, our informants insisted, because the country has been pacified and men do not fear to die in battle if they neglect them.

The obvious interpretation here is that a man is felt to partake of the weakness of a menstruating or confined woman if he comes into association with her. 'His legs become swollen and painful and he is very tired'; 'strength leaves him'; 'he has no speed in running'; 'his belly aches and his body grows red'. . . . The picture is surely one of a *woman's* physical weakness: a man is identified with his wife during pregnancy, observing the taboos she observes, and during menstruation and confinement he must isolate himself as far as possible from her lest he share her weakness; but none of our informants make a connection between the weakness of the woman and the weakness of the man—the interpretation is ours. The Nyakyusa were obsessed with the idea of 'filth' emanating from menstruation and childbirth; indeed, the feeling that women, by reason of their physiology and the taboo on washing during menstruation, are dirty, is cited by men as one of the reasons for not eating with them or sitting to chat with them. Only in this limited sense is the conception of ritual impurity linked with social status. Here the contrast with a Hindu society, in which states of ritual impurity (basically very similar to those of the Nyakyusa) are linked with caste differences, is marked.[1]

The second general conception underlying the taboos of procreation is that of *ubusito*, heaviness, a condition associated with sexual intercourse, pregnancy, the python of witchcraft, and medicines.[2] A 'heavy' (*nsito*) person is dangerous to an 'empty' (*bwasi*) one, hence women sleeping with their husbands, and pregnant women avoid mothers with infants and brides in seclusion, who are 'empty'; and the 'empty' are treated to prevent diarrhœa and give them weight. Diarrhœa and 'emptiness' are closely associated.

The great specific against 'emptiness' is *ikipiki* medicine, used in the puberty, birth, and death rituals, and even used to protect cattle against a menstruating woman. 'If a woman is the only wife

---

[1] cf. M. N. Srinivas, *Religion and Society among the Coorgs of South India* (1952).
[2] cf. Monica Wilson, *Good Company*, p. 95.

her husband may give her *ikipiki* to rub on her hands and on a stick with which she touches each of the cattle. She gives them *ikipiki* that they may not be "empty". Then she can clean out the byre at any time.'

A third idea that recurs, again and again, is that of *ukukilanya*, overstepping, which is used in both a literal and a metaphorical sense. It is taboo for a woman to step over her husband in any way, hence there are explicit rules (taught during initiation) on posture in intercourse. It she should step over him it is said that 'his legs will swell' and he has grounds for divorcing her. It is taboo for an adult to step over a child and for a woman who is having intercourse to step over one who is not, though a child may step over an adult and a virgin or youth who is not having intercourse may step over a married person of the same sex who is not. In a society in which everyone sits on the ground, often with legs outstretched, observance of the taboo necessitates care.

In its metaphorical sense *ukukilyana* is used for a 'heavy' person coming into close contact with an 'empty' one, as, for example, a woman who is sleeping with her husband entering the hut of a woman with a new-born child, or the mother of a bride resuming intercourse before her daughter has had intercourse, or a bride who has not yet brought the *ilibalaga*, the symbol of her union with her husband, to her parents, drinking from her mother's calabash, or entering the inner part of her hut; or a wife who has committed adultery cooking for her husband. It is used, too, of a woman who continues to bear children after the marriage of her son for, it is said, if she does so the son's wife will never conceive at all, or will be long in conceiving, or her child will not walk, on account of a curse.

MWAIKAMBO: It is not customary for mother and son both to have infants. Women mostly begin to stop intercourse when their sons marry. They say it is not good that both mother and son should have small children, because the mother of the young man now thinks of helping her daughter-in-law in nourishing her children. If mother and son both have babies, people are much astonished and say it is not a good custom; they create a curse (*ikigune*) and the fertility of the son and his wife rots.

Mwaihojo's wife put it this way:

I leave off having children when my son is married for I should receive my grandchild in my arms, and care for my grandchildren, and be with them in the house.

Ukukinda means to pass, to surpass, and *ukukilanya* (overstepping), in its metaphorical use, implies that 'one has power and the other is weak, so the powerful one does some injury to the weak one'.

Fourthly, as was made apparent in the puberty ritual, it is held to be dangerous to 'mix bloods'. Adultery is not only an infringement of the exclusive rights of a husband, but it may injure him directly, causing him to have diarrhœa, which is a 'getting rid of the filth' due to contact with a strange 'blood'. It was implied that intercourse with a menstruating woman was in some sense 'mixing bloods' also, and the danger to parents of contact with a newly-married daughter before a precautionary ritual has been performed, stems from the same thing; the parents, through their daughter, are brought into contact with the blood of another lineage, that of the new son-in-law.

Besides being 'heavy' and therefore liable to 'overstep' others, a pregnant woman is thought to reduce the quantity of any grain she approaches, for the foetus within her is voracious and snatches it. Therefore neither she nor her husband (who participates in her condition) may approach other people's millet[1] or beans or oil-seeds spread out to dry, or speak to those who are reaping or grinding or stamping or brewing, without making a gesture of good-will by spitting on a pebble or knotting a leaf, and throwing it into the heap of grain. The sanction is fear of a miscarriage, for the owners of the food may have used medicines 'so that the food may be much and people be astonished'. Her own crops a pregnant woman may handle freely, and a chief's wife does not observe the taboo in her own village.

Two or three quotations will make these conceptions clearer:

ANGOMBWIKE: When my wife has conceived they say we are both 'heavy', both my wife and I. Then, if oil-seeds or millet are out drying in the sun, they tell us not to speak. 'You are heavy ones,' they say. So we are silent. They say that if there is talking we will catch hold of the oil-seeds or millet, and it will diminish. Yes, I must avoid the grain even though I am alone, because I am heavy.

KASITILE: Maize does not vanish but millet and beans. The child which is being made bewitches them; they disappear. . . . The child has opened its mouth wide, its jaws gape.[2] It is that child which is being

---

[1] Some held that millet was the only grain affected; others maintained that maize was also.

[2] *Umwana apambwile ulupambo nkanwa. Ulupambo* is used of the gaping jaws of a crocodile.

created in the belly which snatches millet and beans. These are the foods that Kyala said are important.

MWAIKAMBO: When a woman is pregnant she fears to pass people who are at work planting, smithing, milking, or brewing beer, because they say the child in the belly, the weight (*ubusito*), is like a witch, it will damage food like witchcraft; beer is spoiled and tastes nasty, food does not grow, the smith's iron is not easily worked, the milk is not good. If a pregnant woman comes across her fellows planting she stops them for a few minutes while she passes. If they are brewing they give her a little beer to taste.

ANGOMBWIKE: As for avoiding food, a woman avoids especially when she has been pregnant for one or two months. It is said that if she passes through the gardens, perhaps when people are planting, or when they have already planted but the seed has not yet sprouted, the child in the belly tries to snatch the millet, and it meets the medicine (for people plant millet with a medicine, saying: 'May my millet not rot in the ground'), then perhaps the mother has a miscarriage. If the child in her belly has sprouted then she does not fear much . . . and if the millet has sprouted she does not fear much, but when it has not yet sprouted then the medicine is fierce.

Besides the symbol of the foetus with 'jaws agape' snatching food, there is a symbol of 'seed within' fighting 'seed without'. Mwaikambo was careful to point out that this interpretation was a personal one, assented to, but not volunteered, by others he consulted; however, it was later confirmed by Kasitile.

MWAIKAMBO: A pregnant woman should avoid those planting beans and millet, or straining ointment, sunning millet, or brewing beer, because there is kinship (*ubukamu*) between the child in her belly and food, we call all of them seed (*mbeju*). The seed in her belly and that outside fight; that within is fierce and overcomes that outside. To help them plant is to make friends; to knot a leaf is to bind the anger of the human seed. All those with whom I have discussed the matter agreed that this is so, but they have agreed when I began to explain it to them; none of them understand the other symbols. I discussed it with about eleven men.

KASITILE: The taboo against a pregnant woman passing millet and other seed spread out to dry is because these seeds fight with the child inside. It is seed, it defeats them; it is seed, it is water, it is blood. To bind a leaf is to bind that blood within, that it may not kill the seeds out drying. If someone else's food is being planted and a pregnant woman approaches, and does not bind a leaf and throw it in the grain basket, then the seed is insufficient to plant.

A general principle of Nyakyusa thought is the opposition of like activities; things which are felt to be alike are often felt to be antagonistic. We have shown that certain of the pregnancy taboos are interpreted in terms of the opposition between seed in plants and seed in the womb, and between pumpkins in the field and pumpkins in the vagina, and we have touched on the opposition between procreation and war. Sexual intercourse, 'the war of the mats', is directly compared with war; the two are felt to be alike and therefore incompatible. Association with a menstruating or parturient woman is felt to be weakening to a warrior; continence of a warrior before battle is enjoined—'men feared to die quickly if they slept with their wives just before war.' Moreover, a menstruating wife never touches her husband's weapons lest they be weakened.

Hunting is classed with war and the same taboos apply. Added to them is the notion that, since a pregnant woman is often angry, the animals her husband hunts will be angry also, and he is in much greater danger than an ordinary hunter.

ANGOMBWIKE: If you go into the bush and you have left your wife heavy, at home, if you meet a lion it will not run off, but will injure you, maul you. And if you are many, a leopard or a lion will attack you, the heavy one, not the others.

QUESTION: Why?

ANGOMBWIKE: It is as if there was much anger. And we've noticed something else, if a lion attacks cattle it always attacks a cow in calf. And another thing. If a woman is heavy she is very bad-tempered (*nkali*), it's like a passion. Perhaps the woman is bad-tempered or perhaps good, and you, the husband, are bad-tempered. Pregnancy shows in many ways. . . .

A pregnant woman has a great fire in her body, she sweats a lot and is passionate (*nelyojo*), she is fierce (*nkali*). That fire is strong; we all flee from the woman, we all dislike her. And when pregnancy begins the animals in the bush wish to kill you, the husband. That fierceness [the fire] makes them hate you; you are like a twin. A first-born child is very fierce (*nkali*), so a woman is very passionate and sweats a great deal.

His wife's pregnancy puts a man in danger from wild animals, and so does a quarrel with her, quite apart from the pregnancy which tends to produce such quarrels. Mwaisumo said: 'If I go hunting after quarrelling with my wife it is very dangerous, I might be killed by a wild animal.'

Besides the idea that animals will *attack* the husband of a pregnant woman there is a notion that they will *flee* from him, and therefore he will be hopelessly unsuccessful in hunting. Isaiah, who persisted in hunting while his wife was pregnant and rarely brought in anything, was the laughing-stock of his neighbours. Lyandileko, the woman doctor, explained: 'The animals flee because the man smells. He smells because his wife is pregnant.'

Procreation and smithing are also felt to be in opposition because they are felt to be alike. A pregnant woman usually avoids a forge altogether, lest she miscarry, and her husband, if he approaches one, remains silent until he has picked up a piece of charcoal, spat on it, and thrown it into the fire. If he neglects to do so, the iron does not coalesce. Kasitile explained the taboo very clearly:

If a woman is pregnant she and her husband both fear to go near a forge lest either the iron or the foetus is spoiled. The foetus is spoiled only because medicines are used on the forge; that is to say, the medicine of the forge spoils the iron in the belly of a woman, and she has a miscarriage. But if there is no medicine then the iron is spoiled; it is difficult to work until the smith has sought a doctor to treat it with medicine; then the iron is all right again.

Kasitile speaks of 'the iron in the belly of the woman' and the details of this symbolism are instructive. Angombwike said:

When a smith forges a spear he does not sleep with his wives[1] because, we say, when a woman conceives the fire blazes within her to forge a person, and the woman's fire and the smith's fire fight. When a smith comes with the fire of his smithy on his body and lies with a woman, the woman has a miscarriage.

The iron of a woman is that within which receives the seed [i.e. the womb]. And we ordinary people who are not smiths, we fear the smith's fire. We do not fear to injure a woman, no, but we fear *ilipondelo*, the disease of the forge, in children. If a man sits talking with a smith at his forge and catches hold of the iron being forged there, if his wife at home bears a child, the child will cough: 'He, he.' It's like the cough of *ingotolo*, but we call it 'the forge'. Then people say: 'The forge! Indeed, you, the father, must have sat with a smith at the forge.' Then the father thinks, and he remembers, and takes the child to that smith with whom he sat, and the smith lets his bellows play on the child's body

---

[1] All informants were agreed that a forge is dangerous to a pregnant woman or her husband, but a smith consulted denied that he observed any sex taboos himself. 'The fire is mine.' 'But,' he said, 'if my wife is pregnant or has given birth to twins, when I go to someone else's forge I myself, with the wisdom of a smith, spit on a piece of charcoal and throw it in the fire.'

and that cures him. So, when a man comes to a smith's forge for the first time, he always takes a piece of charcoal from the fire and spits on it and throws it into the fire. This means: 'I have come to your forge, smith, may this fire not come on my body.'

And sometimes the smith's iron does not glow and sparkle well. Then he is angry, saying: 'Heavy ones are present. Some of you have pregnant wives, you are spoiling my fire.' We all pick up pieces of charcoal and spit on them and throw them into the fire again. Then the fire blazes up well and the iron glows and sparks.

Mwambuputa, the village headman, confirmed this:

When my wife is pregnant I fear the smithy. I spit on a piece of charcoal. Until she gives birth I fear, but when we just play together on the mat, and she has not yet conceived, I do not fear. . . . Only when it is seen that the 'iron' is there do I fear.

QUESTION: The iron?

MWAMBUPUTA: It's the blood of the man. The man is the smith. He forges iron there with the woman. The woman is the bellows. The smithing flourishes because of the sweat. Sometimes a woman conceives if I have lain with her two or three times—if Kyala gives us a child—but some delay, and I sleep with them a whole month.

QUESTION: The woman is a bellows?

MWAMBUPUTA: Yes, because when she is having intercourse she gasps: 'He, he, he!'

QUESTION: And the man?

MWAMBUPUTA: Yes, but where do we find the fire? In the body of the woman! It's a great fire. Hence we say the bellows is the woman. It's smithing. Women are the anvil. Is there not fire in their bodies? Therefore I hammer there.

The primary taboo is on the pregnant woman approaching the smithy lest she injure it, but it is also thought that, like grain and cattle, it may be treated with strong medicines which will cause her to miscarry if she breaks the taboo. Hence the Nyakyusa dictum: 'She who has a miscarriage is she who is proud (*namatingo*).'

The conception that like things are antagonistic, and that the sexual activities of different couples must not be mixed, is clearly shown in the taboos relating to fire and the calabash cup used for water. An elderly councillor of Ngonde, himself a Christian, explained it:

It is taboo for married people to blow up the fire in someone else's house, or to drink from the calabash cup; if they do they will bring a coughing disease to the owners of the house.... Pagans used to fear to let those who are sleeping together touch the hearth-bricks or blow up the fire in their house for, if they do so, then the owners of the house, both man and woman, fall sick coughing. They say it is the disease of fires (*myoto*). ... But when a woman has borne a child and is suckling it, and her husband is not with her, then it is not taboo.

Making fire by friction and, in more general terms, fire, are symbols of sexual intercourse, and 'the fire of the body and the fire of the house fight'. Drinking from a calabash cup is perhaps also a symbol of intercourse—the shape of the cup suggests it—but there is no direct evidence of such an association.

The taboo on mixing the sex activities of different couples is pushed to the point that women avoid for a day the milk of a cow that has been with the bull. 'They say: "We will harm the cow. It will abort." They compare it with themselves as women.'

Two last pregnancy taboos may be noted which turn, not on the feeling that like things are antagonistic, but that like produces like. Things felt to be alike are treated as causally related. We quote Mwambuputa, the village headman:

Women fear to stand in a doorway when they are pregnant. They say: 'How should the child stand in the doorway? It will refuse to come out.' Because if birth is delayed, it is as if the child refused to come out of the house. That is the symbol. And I, the husband, feared also [to stand in a doorway]. Now we men do not fear; it is finished; but women still fear.

And another thing, when a woman was pregnant we feared to sit close together, I, the husband, and my child. It was taboo. And for my wife and another woman to sit close together was taboo. It was said that she would bear twins, because we had sat together. Now we men do not fear, but women still do.

(b) The confinement

A first confinement, like first menstruation, is the occasion for elaborate ritual, and though at later confinements (as at later menstrual periods) certain taboos must be observed, they are less numerous and less strictly enforced than those connected with the birth of the first child, *umwana gwa busungu*.

A first child should be born at the husband's mother's house, 'and if the first child is a girl they will tell her to come again for the second, saying: "Come that we may treat our husband [i.e. grandson]." ' The woman lies, during labour, on a heap of leaves behind the huts, moving inside after delivery, on to a litter of banana leaves spread for her. Her mother-in-law attends her and treats her and the new-born child with *ikipiki* medicine. She washes them in a basin made of two banana leaves, one sweet banana, one plantain, and is particularly careful to wash the infant's mouth and the mother's vagina. Powdered *ikipiki* is sprinkled in the water in the form of a cross. This is done 'that the mother and child should not have diarrhœa'. The cross is a symbol of over-stepping (*kokukilyana kuno, kokukilanya kuno*, demonstrating a cross) and is made 'because heavy ones, those who are with their husbands on the bed, will come and overstep the mother and child if they are not treated'. Mother and child are also given a roasted banana with powdered *ikipiki* sprinkled on it. In bringing the *ikipiki* the husband's mother acknowledges the legitimacy of the child. 'If someone does not give a child *ikipiki* it is a bastard. It is as if the husband said: "Why do you insult your husband by committing adultery with others? Others have created this foetus; it is not mine!" '

The cord is tied with a shred of bark-cloth and then cut with a bamboo knife. 'An iron knife is taboo, it's a spear, other children will die from the spear disease (*ulukwego*); to use a spear is like killing someone.' The after-birth is buried in the banana planta-tion with a piece of the cord sticking up, and later the litter is burnt at the same place. 'Only officiants (*abanyago*) eat of these bananas growing over the burying place—no young person may do so for it's the banana grove of the litter.' The cord must be buried upright or 'the mother will not bear again'.

A delayed delivery is most commonly attributed to the woman's adultery,[1] and she is pressed by the midwife to confess the name of her lover or lovers, but it is also believed that it may be due to *imindu*, that is the shades. The husband consults a diviner who indicates whether the *imindu* is on his side or that of the woman's father and the one who is thus indicated should pray. 'Sometimes the woman herself tells of a quarrel which would lead to *imindu* and then her husband or father goes to pray.'

Mother and child remain in confinement until the navel cord drops off, sheltered from 'heavy ones', who should not enter or even greet the mother from the doorway, and from men, to whom both mother and child are dangerous. 'Men must not see a tiny

[1] Unlike certain other Central African peoples, the Nyakyusa do not attribute difficulty in childbirth to the adultery of the husband.

child, the beauty of the body, the blackness, has not yet come. It's dirty (*nyali*); even after it's come out it's dirty.' 'The confinement is not now feared by men, they just go in, because European times have come. There is no war now, but long ago they feared to enter, they feared to see the hair and the navel cord. They said: "We will get weary in the legs." ' 'When they went to war their legs became tied up.' During her seclusion the mother eats alone off leaves or out of special dishes, and even after she comes out of the hut she is careful not to eat with women who are 'heavy', or allow her dishes to be used by men. She has her own water-pot and calabash cup for several months.

To the Nyakyusa, the most dangerous point in the confinement is the loosening of the cord, and the baby is watched, day and night, to make sure that the cord does not fall between its mother's legs (*mmago*) for if that happens it is believed that the child will be sterile. As soon as the cord is safely off, mother and child are washed and shaved with *ikipiki* medicine 'to get rid of the filth', and anointed with ointment. They are given a millet porridge mixed with *ikipiki* which has been buried after dark at a cross-roads and left overnight. 'They say people will overstep the child. If they have not made porridge for him he will have diarrhœa.' The porridge is administered to the infant in the doorway of the hut. Then 'they throw out the rubbish (*ilindu*)', the litter is burnt, the hut smeared, and mother and child 'come out'. In some families the husband kills a bull, especially to make a carrying skin for the baby, but whether he kills specially or not the baby is slung in a skin which conceals it from men.

Angombwike made it perfectly clear that the use of *ikipiki* in the ritual of birth has a double significance: it is to 'close up' the bowels of the child and the womb of the woman, and it is to acknowledge kinship between the mother and the new-born baby on the one hand, and the father's lineage on the other.

When a child is in the belly it is said that 'it's a person (*mundu*, i.e. a non-relative)'. When it is newly-born and has not yet eaten the *ikipiki* it is called *kanenelo*, which means that it is not yet our relative, we do not know it. The child is called *kanenelo* until the umbilical cord falls off and it eats the *ikipiki*, and comes out of the house. If an infant (*kanenelo*) dies in the house people do not mourn, they just say: 'The woman had a miscarriage.' They come to her and say: 'Have you recovered?' They do not say a child has died, and they don't say anything to relatives at a distance. As for the ritual, the mother undergoes a ritual alone, or with her older child, only the two of them [i.e. the mother and the immediately preceding child]. Before a child has eaten the *ikipiki* they make it of no account, calling it *kanenelo*. . . .

When the child is born both mother and child are treated with *ikipiki*, and powdered *ikipiki* is sprinkled on the heap of leaves on which delivery took place. When it is a first child they wash the mother's breasts in the skin for carrying the baby, that is to put the child to the breast for the first time that they (the breasts) may participate in kinship (*gaje ga bukamu*). But for a second child they only wash off the dirt, they do not wash the breasts in the carrying skin, they say: 'We did it for the first child.'

Then they bring mother and child into the house (*bikubingesya*). To a visitor they say: 'Friend, you are a month pregnant, do not come in. You are heavy.' And if a woman is eight months pregnant she also does not come in, she is heavy. If a heavy one comes and wishes to enter, the mother of the newly-born child refuses at the doorway; the heavy one takes earth from her footprint and rubs it on the child on the litter. She receives him on her lap and the others say: 'Thank you, you have met with him.' Then the pregnant one can speak to or about the child without fear, she has met it.

When the cord has fallen off they bury *ikipiki* on the road; it remains overnight, and in the morning they dig it up and bring it and make millet porridge for the mother, not for the child. How can a tiny child eat? To the child they give powdered *ikipiki* in a little water. The woman and child eat together—it is as we, in our ritual, eat together the blood of Jesus, the *ikipiki* of the pagans is their blood. And when a child has eaten the *ikipiki* they say it is their relative now, 'it has entered into our *ikipiki* (*ingile nkipiki kyetu*)'. The mother when she eats the millet porridge closes herself up because much water and blood comes out of the womb. It is said heavy ones must not overstep her.

Then they shave the hair of the child. They anoint its head with *ikipiki* and shave it—not the mother. If she chooses she also shaves, it is customary, but they don't anoint her with medicine. If she does not choose she does not shave. They sprinkle fine ash from the fire on the child's head.

The *ikipiki* at puberty is one and the same, and at death, it is one and the same. If a woman had reached puberty and washed with a man, and then leaves him and comes to me, we do not give her *ikipiki*, we say: 'Let her eat the *ikipiki* of kinship in the birth ritual, when she has borne a child.'

Kasitile made the same points about the function of *ikipiki*:

Yes, the *ikipiki* of the birth, puberty, and death rituals is one; that of the twin ritual is different. When a child is born they spread a litter for him. They fear that if heavy ones come and speak, those who are pregnant, the child will suffer, it will become weak and exhausted on the litter, and will have constant diarrhœa. So they go to the cross-roads and mix millet flour and powdered *ikipiki* with the feather of a chicken, they give the child some in his mouth to make the motions firm, and close the bowels. They do this[1] at the cross-roads that those who pass may step over it and take the disease away. That medicine closes the bowel, it saves the stomach and bowel when heavy ones come, those who are pregnant. If we do not treat it the child becomes exhausted with diarrhœa, though the mother is all right.

It is taboo to give birth in the house, a woman bears a child outside on a pile of leaves; when she has borne the child they sprinkle powdered *ikipiki* on those leaves, but if I, the father, am angry about the child I refuse the *ikipiki*, saying: 'It's not my child, it's a bastard.' That is of old though. Now, in European times, they treat all children. Yes, now all are my children; formerly there were bastards. The *ikipiki* is our blood, it is kept in the senior wife's house.

There was some disagreement on this point. Nsyani, an elderly man who was already married before Europeans came to the country, when asked: 'Do you perform rituals for bastards?' replied: 'Yes, they are born with[2] my cattle (*Bapapigwe munombe syangu*).' Four other men who discussed the matter together, agreed that—

When a woman has borne an illegitimate child we know that the child is the child of her husband because it was born with his cattle (*munombe syake*). Whether the child is a boy or a girl, whether the genitor is known or unknown, and whether he has paid damages or not, the children belong to the woman's lord (*mwene nkikulu*). When an illegitimate child is born to an unmarried girl her fathers perform the ritual, for that 'man of the long grass' is like a bull. For an illegitimate child born to a married woman the rituals are performed by the husband, for the 'man of the long grass' is like a bull or a cock. Who is going to give a calf to a man alone, the bull who begot it?

But Lyandileko who, as a doctor and a grandmother, was intimately concerned in such matters, insisted:

If a woman has committed adultery and we do not know the man, we give her earth; it's just rubbish. If I give her medicine she and the child will die. If she has borne the child in the long grass and her father refuses to let her enter the house, non-relatives give it to her. If I, the mother, am there I give her this earth [touching the ground].

[1] The baby is not taken to the crossroads, only the *ikipiki* and millet flour.
[2] Literally *within*.

If a woman has difficulty in labour we officiants tell her: 'Speak! With whom did you commit adultery?' and the child comes down. When she has spoken it is born. We do not give her medicine. We give her earth.

QUESTION: What if an illegitimate boy dies, do you perform the ritual with *ikipiki*?

LYANDILEKO: No, because he was a child of the long grass [i.e. illegitimate], we only treat the mother. We do not perform the ritual with the *ikipiki* of the husband. If it is a girl, and she to whom we gave earth grows up, the father [i.e. her mother's husband or, if the mother was unmarried, her father] says: 'Let the husband perform the ritual, because the cattle are mine, she is my child, and that is the custom.' If they give a child of the long grass the medicine it will die, because it is not its medicine. . . . I know about it because I give children the medicine.

There is no question about the legal rights over an illegitimate child, and Nsyani and the other men held that ritual and legal control went together. Lyandileko and Kasitile, both specialists in this field, held that traditionally, at least, the *ikipiki* could only be used for a legitimate child: to do otherwise was dangerous.

So important is this acknowledgement of legitimacy that in many Christian families, where other traditional rituals are ignored, the husband's mother still brings *ikipiki* for his child.

As soon as the child is born a fowl—a cock for a boy, a hen for a girl—is sent to the young wife's parents, to notify them of the birth. Then her 'mothers' come 'to keep her company' (*ukumpanja*) during her confinement, and at the end of it they take her home with them for a visit of a month or more. They bring her back to her husband, formally, with gifts of beer, food, and mats (*ukumbeka*), just as they did after the puberty ritual. We met one party, taking back a young mother to her husband, in which there were twenty-one women carrying baskets with food or pots of beer. The grandmother was happy and excited and, dancing up to greet us, she said, breathlessly: '*That's* the owner of this beer [pointing to her daughter], all these pots!' The feast was unusually lavish on this occasion. Two pots of beer, two stems of bananas, a vessel of milk, and a mat, were taken by the daughter of Chief Mwaipopo when she returned to her husband after the birth of her first child, and that seems to be the ordinary standard. The husband kills a bull calf for meat for his guests, or gives them a shilling or two.

Even after her return a wife may delay before cooking or drawing water again for her husband. Mwaisumo said:

Some men do not let their wives cook for them until the child's body has gone black and it laughs. . . . This is mainly due to the mockery of friends, for some people refuse to come and eat with a man if the food is cooked by a woman who has recently borne a child, even though she has come out of confinement. They laugh at him and say: 'Why do you eat food prepared by a newly delivered woman? Have you no sense of disgust?' And her friends laugh at the woman, too, saying: 'Look you, the child has not yet grown at all!'

MWAMBUPUTA: Formerly a woman with a new-born child did not cook food. We said she was filthy. What food that she had overstepped would anyone eat? Until two months had passed she avoided cooking, then she cooked.[1] And she hid the child. Men should not see it for two months. It was taboo.

This is the full ritual performed for a first-born child and, some say, for the first-born of each sex. For others there is no sending a fowl to the girl's parents, or bringing her back with gifts, and it does not matter where the child is born; but still the seclusion of mother and infant, treatment with *ikipiki* medicine brought by the husband's mother, and shaving are felt to be important.

We did not find any significant differences between the rituals of birth in Selya and in Kukwe, but there is one rite peculiar to the Lugulu people and regarded by other Nyakyusa with somewhat shocked amusement, which is interesting because it expresses, in crude terms, a conflict between the groom and the bride's family repeatedly suggested in the ritual of Selya and Kukwe, but never openly acknowledged. We did not see this rite ourselves, but quote the account of Kakune, the doctor, whose mother was Lugulu. Though himself a Kukwe, he speaks in the first person as if he were Lugulu—a dramatic device common enough in Nyakyusa.

KAKUNE: When my daughter goes to her husband, and first becomes pregnant, they tell us: 'She is pregnant.' And we say: 'Oh, she is pregnant? She is pregnant! War has come!' When she has borne her child, the go-between in the marriage representing the husband comes to her parents with a hen to tell them. Then later they send the go-between a message, saying: 'Come'. Meanwhile they have prepared huge quantities of food: porridge, and curds, and beer. And then the girl's husband calls his friends of the age-village (he does not call his relatives, but his

---

[1] A monogamist eats with his friends in the age-village, or is provided for by his mother, like a bachelor.

L

brothers he will call if they are near) and they come with a bull. They arrive at nightfall.

The girl's parents meanwhile have called all their relatives (but it does not matter if some relatives do not come; it brings them no trouble) and friends of the age-village, and the boys come too. And they shut the door fast and start drinking the beer. 'They have come, they have come, let us close the door', they say. Then the go-between outside calls to us: 'We have come,' but we are silent. We answer never a word. At last we answer and ask: 'What have you brought?' And he answers: 'A bull.'

'What-sized bull?' 'A little bull.' 'He! What do you mean by bringing a little bull only?' 'Well, it's a nice big bull!'

Then they come and bang on the door and we hold it shut and they bang, and bang, and then we begin insulting one another. We accuse them of filthiness, saying: 'They defaecate, they urinate!' And of incest, saying: 'You have intercourse with your mother'; and of foolishness, and they accuse us likewise. At last they burst in and the insults continue inside. They actually defaecate in the house.[1]

But soon we call out: 'They have entered, let us make peace, friends,' and we all sit down. Then I (the father of the girl) call on the go-between, and he sits down opposite us. I and my wife, the girl's mother, sit by the fire. Then I ask him: 'What have you brought?' 'I have brought a bull!' 'Oh! Eh!' 'I am hungry, give me some food.'

Then we discuss this for a time and agree, and we give them the food to eat and some beer. They eat, the young men snatching food over there, and our young men here, and we, the elders, eating sedately at the back.

Then, when they have eaten, we begin to insult one another again over the cattle that have been paid, the laziness and slovenliness of the bride, the dirty cooking of her mother. They scold us and we scold them. Then after a time, with insults flying, and the young men stamping and stamping, we call out: 'Silence, silence,' and the noise subsides.

Then our son-in-law comes to the fire at the summons of the go-between, who says: 'Praise your father,' and he says: 'You of so-and-so, son of so-and-so (he mentions all my names), our true father.' Then the go-between says: 'Praise your mother!' and he praises her: 'You, so-and-so, daughter of so-and-so, our true mother!' and he goes back and sits down. Then the bride is called by the go-between and she is made to praise first her father and then her mother. And if there is any man who eloped with the bride from her husband's, but she later returned to her husband, the lover comes too. He fears to go blind

---

[1] Angombwike confirmed this asking, when the rite was mentioned, whether we had been told these details.

if he does not. He does not enter the home. There would be fighting if he did! But he stands outside, and when he hears them praising he praises the parents too. No one hears him, he does it to save his sight. He comes with two or three friends but gets no food.

Then we give them beer, and they drink and we drink till dawn. And dawn finds many in drunken sleep. Then the go-between says: 'Dawn has come, friends, let us go!' And they go off and we bid them farewell. And my son, the bride's brother, goes off with them. The husband goes home with his friends, and then the go-between and my son and daughter (these three only) come back. Then our go-between [representing the bride's father] who is on the look-out for them, says: 'They come!' and we go out and call: 'Why do you come here again?' And we throw clubs at them and drive them off. Then the go-between goes home and the two come back and we greet them and say: 'Have you slept?' And food is cooked and they eat. Then that same day the girl goes off to her husband, alone, with food that her mothers have cooked.

QUESTION: What is the reason for the custom?

KAKUNE: They have made the custom to gain wealth—that bull. The porridge (*ikyende*) and relish (*iliseke*) must be called *minyama*. If I, the father, or the mother, or the husband, call it porridge, then the one who does so will go blind. We Kukwe do not do this, but if one of us marries one of the people who observe it, that is, a daughter of the Lugulu, he must avoid or else he will lose his sight.

CHAPTER VI

THE RITUAL OF ABNORMAL BIRTH

Twin birth is a fearful event to the Nyakyusa. The parents of twins, and twins themselves, are *abipasya*,[1] 'the fearful ones', felt to be very dangerous to their relatives and immediate neighbours, and to cattle, causing them to suffer from diarrhœa or purging, and swollen legs, if any contact takes place. Therefore the parents are segregated and an elaborate ritual is performed, in which a wide circle of kinsmen and neighbours and the family cattle participate. The infants are naturally segregated with their mother, but it is the danger from the parents rather than from the twins themselves that is emphasized. *Ilipasa* is commonly used to mean 'twins', 'twin birth', but it is more accurately translated as 'abnormal birth', for it is used of a child born feet foremost (*unsolola*) as well as for any multiple birth, and the same ritual is performed whatever the type of *ilipasa*.[2]

(a) The events

The ritual has four phases: first the building of temporary huts or shelters, one for each parent of the twins, in which traditionally they lived and ate, each in isolation, never raising their voices above a whisper, and each speaking only to an attendant. The woman is attended by her mother, the man by a young son or daughter. The second stage is the 'induction' (*ukwingisia*) or 'washing' (*ukusukusula*), when a ritual litter is spread for the parents and kinsmen and immediate neighbours wash their hands

---

[1] *Ukupasya*: to be afraid.

[2] *Ilipasa* or *ipasa* (pl. *ama-*): twin, twin birth, abnormal birth.

Ukupasa: to bear or beget twins or an abnormally born child.

'*Ilipasa* is of two sorts, to have two children is *ipasa* and to have one child when it comes out at birth feet foremost is *ipasa* also; they say it is a fearful child born feet foremost (*umwana mwipasya ubusolola*), so in both cases they speak of *ukupasa ilipasa*.'

Abapasa ipasa: parents of twins; *ulupaso* or *ulwiho lwa ipasa*: twin ritual; *ukupasana*: to branch from one root.

We have no information on the incidence of twin births or breach delivery among the Nyakyusa, but even supposing it to be higher than in western Europe, it is still the exception, not the rule. cf. M. D. W. Jeffreys, 'Twin births among Africans', *S.A. Journal of Science*, v. 50, 4 (1953).

with medicines and have their legs splashed with a scalding con-
coction. Visitors to this ritual bring gifts of millet which is put to
soak for beer. When it is brewed the 'bringing out' (*ukusosya*) rite
is celebrated. The temporary huts are burnt and a new shelter is
erected in which the parents have ritual intercourse. Parents,
twins, and relatives are shaved and anointed with medicated
ointment, and together with their neighbours again have their legs
splashed with scalding medicine, this time by the father of the
twins. The children are given sausages of medicated porridge
which they must eat from the ground. The parents of the twins
burst out of their hut and rush towards the pasture land, the father
brandishing his spears. Then all the participants snatch some of
the meat of a sheep or small bull which has been killed. The rest
of the meat is reserved for the fourth, and final, stage of the ritual.
A mess of cooked bananas, meat, and medicine is taken by the
mother of the twins into her hands, immediately after the ritual
intercourse. Her husband takes some of this to bury in his father's
banana grove, or to throw in the direction of his father's grave;
the rest the woman takes to her own parents, to be buried in her
own father's grove. She drinks beer ritually with her parents, and
'steals' things from her mother's house, then returns to meet her
husband and drink beer ritually with him.

So far as our information goes[1] the form of the ritual among the
Kukwe scarcely differs from that of Selya and the plain and we
describe it as we saw it performed in Selya for our neighbours,
Mwakobela and his wife. Mwakobela was a junior half-brother of
the chief, Mwaipopo. (See Tables (a) and (b).)

12 May 1935

i. *The birth of twins*. (Record of G. and M. W.)

Twins were born about eight-thirty this morning. We visited
them at 5 p.m. in company with Mwaiswelo III (linked half-
brother of Mwakobela) and Kikuku, who was representing Mwaipopo. Mwaipopo is 'owner' of the ritual because he is their 'father'
(i.e. their senior brother). Mwaipopo did not go, though he
was quite near, at our place. We found the woman with the
two new-born infants sitting outside under the bananas, accompanied by the mother who bore her, and her mother's elder
sister. The men seated by the house were the father, Mwakobela
(Mwaiswelo II), his half-brother Mwakalendile and four friends
from near by.

[1] We did not see the full ritual in Kukwe country, but had several accounts of it.

'To-day there is no ritual, we have come to express sympathy (*ukuti ndaga*).'[1]

The two grown sons of Mwakobela were building a little hut of saplings and had finished the main structure, but had not yet thatched it. 'She will sleep there to-night. They will put leaves on top.' Kikuku brought a message from Mwaipopo, to whom they had previously sent to tell him of the twin birth: 'If the hut is not finished she may sleep in the house, I agree to that. But Mwakobela said:

No, the hut is finished, she can sleep there. [To me]: To-night she will just sleep there, then the doctor will come [it is Mwaipopo's business to find the doctor] and will induct her (*ukummwingisya*), and then we shall lay the litter. The woman and her mother sleep there for a month with the twins—no others—the mother alone keeps her company (*ikumpanja*); then the doctor will come again to bring her out (*ukunsosya*). The ritual is in two parts, the induction and the bringing out.

They tie up the cord of the first twin to be born with a shred of plantain bark, and of the second with a shred of sweet banana bark, the plantain bark is a sign of seniority.

The woman may not cook while she is in the hut—it's taboo. But the other wives cook food for her and bring it to prevent her dying of hunger. Also her friends of the village will come with food and firewood to greet her. The pot in which food is cooked for the parents of twins must not be covered when it is on the fire, and if plantains are cooked only the middle bunches on the stem are used, not the ends; those at the ends are thrown away. When they are eating the wife may not begin until the husband has received his and put some in his mouth, then she too may eat.

It is wholly taboo for the mother of twins to call for anything she wants. She knocks with a stick to summon the one who brings her food. . . . If her husband wants anything he calls to his wives, it is not taboo, but he does not shout loudly, he must be careful not to make too great a noise, for if he shouts his children's hearts are startled and, it is said, they will die.

Traditionally, when the mother had to leave the hut to relieve herself, she walked backwards and hid her face with a piece of mat, to prevent herself from looking at the front of anyone. She avoided cows at pasture, and if she caught sight of anyone in the distance she waved a hand to warn them to let her pass.

May 13

Mwaiswelo III (Mwakobela's brother) came to fetch us at ten-

---

[1] This phrase can imply either condolence or congratulation.

forty-five to come and eat. 'Yesterday we just conversed, you did not eat. Now we have come to fetch you.' The mother and infants were in the little hut. Mwakobela was sitting and eating with us. They explained that of old he would not have done so. 'The people in the old days were greatly afraid—the father of twins did not meet and converse with other people, no, they were much afraid. He waited in the bananas. But since the Europeans came we do not fear. The Europeans took the twins in their arms and said: "Don't be afraid." In the old days the father of twins would take a spear and shield and dance the war-dance, and cry the war-cry, but we have dropped this custom nowadays.'

May 14

We visited Mwakobela and found him sitting alone making a hoe-handle. His wife was in the hut with the infants, attended by her mother.

May 22

We found Mwakobela hoeing a garden for beans. He told us that the elder of the twins had died two nights ago and had been buried early yesterday morning. . . .

No one came to the infant's burial; we buried him ourselves. But had he been a big child then people would have come. The doctor has not come yet [for the induction]. I have not got the millet yet.

July 7

ii. *The induction (ukwingisia)*

We arrived about 11 a.m. and found Mwakobela and his brother sitting outside the house with several guests. They were cutting a hide to make thongs for tying up cattle. By noon there were present twelve men, twenty-two married women, three adolescent girls, six 'daughters-in-law' sitting apart, and a crowd of children.[1] The doctor, a middle-aged woman and a distant connection of Mwakobela, arrived about noon. With the help of Mwakobela's wives she built a fire outside and cooked a pot of medicines. The women sat round this fire chatting; the little girls built themselves a separate fire, and the small boys yet another. Tiny children were with their mothers. At two-fifteen the doctor started the washing. She took a little powdered medicine from a bamboo flask and put it into a calabash of cold water. She made

---

[1] The identity and kinship connections of those who participated are discussed in Chapter VIII.

the boys form a queue and bend forward, holding out their hands while she poured water over the hands of each of them. After washing, each took a mouthful of water and spat it out. They were warned not to spill it on their legs as they washed and spat. Some young men washed with the boys, and women watching shouted advice, but a number of the boys went off without taking a mouthful of water or without spitting. After the boys came the girls, and then the women and babies and some more small boys who had arrived late. We counted twenty-six boys and young men, twenty-six girls and babies, and twenty-four women washing.

Then came the splashing of legs. The doctor shredded a banana sucker to make a tail. All the company gathered round the boiling pot of medicine, and the doctor, dipping the tail into the pot, splashed the boiling liquid on to their legs. Children screamed; women hopped with the pain, but shouted to their children to come and be treated. Frightened small children were hauled back by men, women, and elder children—a full sister of the twins, about 9 years old, was dragged in yelling. Mothers were especially careful to see that their babies were splashed, and pulled up the cloths binding them to their backs, so that their legs might be exposed. Mwakobela and his brother came to be splashed but some of the young men hurried away immediately after washing, disregarding the women who shouted to them that it was taboo for them to leave before they had been splashed. The women took the whole ritual much more seriously than the men, and they were very particular to see that their children were treated. One old woman who had helped a child to wash, holding its hands, came back again to wash herself. The doctor and other women shouted that she had already washed. She replied: 'Oh, I just helped the child. Have I really finished?' The mother and re-maining twin did not stir from the hut—she looked dirty and dishevelled. The doctor was elegant; she wore five brass body-rings and her body was well oiled and rouged. She organized everyone with great confidence and was treated with respect, a mat being spread for her to sit upon (no other woman had a mat), and her assistant fetching and carrying everything she required.

Many of the women relatives had brought gifts of millet and after the treatment was over they tipped their small basketfuls into a big grain basket. Then they had a snack of roasted plantains (Mwakobela provided three stems) and went home.

23 July 1935

iii. *The bringing out (ukusosya)*

Seventeen days after the induction the 'bringing out' took place.[1] The hut had been burnt last night and a new one built in a new place. Mwakobela was inside it and when we went to greet him he only put his head out, saying: 'I am not coming out.' The doctor had slept at the homestead and a small bull had been killed yesterday evening. Mwakobela had provided it because the sheep which Mwaiteteja (his brother) had got from the hills had died. Twenty-one men were present and there were two pots of beer, of which we were given one. Mwaisumo (our clerk) left (as we had told him to do if he wished) and the men remarked: 'He is baptized, he only looks on, it's taboo for him to participate, it's taboo for him to drink the ritual beer.'

The meat was being cooked by Mwakobela's wives and the doctor was preparing the medicine. There were two lots of medicine: a fine powder (*imbondanya*) made of *kabombelo* and *ikipiki*, and a rough sort (*unkota*) made of *kajenja*[2] and *nkunguni*. The doctor explained: 'The powder is used for smearing on the forehead to enable people to meet the parents of the twins; it is not very important, it prevents the belly swelling. It is also drunk in beer at midday, for the same purpose, by the parents of the twins, and then by all their relatives. The second medicine is used for splashing on the legs with hot water; it prevents the legs from swelling. If anyone does not come to-day and his legs or belly swell, he will come to me, the doctor, and I will put hot medicines on his legs and give him powder to drink in beer. I will not smear his forehead then, no. . . . The non-relatives have their legs splashed but do not anoint their faces or drink the medicated beer.' Mwanyoso remarked: 'Our wives often do not come. Then we take home a little of the lees of the beer for them to drink.' Thirty-six people who had not washed at the induction washed now.

From the time we arrived at 7.30 a.m. the women were busy shaving each other and all the small girls except one. She was not shaved for she was in mourning—her mother had died recently. After shaving, the women and girls washed and anointed and rouged themselves. The mother of the twins (Masobesi) was in the new hut with her surviving twin and her husband. All were

---

[1] It was delayed three days to oblige us, as we had another engagement.

[2] *Kajenja* gives a yellow dye used traditionally to decorate bark-cloth, and nowadays also used as a relish like curry, 'but this is a new Swahili custom'.

freshly shaved and anointed; the mother and child were also rouged, and both husband and wife had on new cloths. The women explained: 'The filth is finished now', and, in answer to a question about why they shaved, they replied: 'We throw away the hair in the long grass because it is filthy.' The little girls picked up scraps of hair carefully and disposed of it in the long grass. Mwaiteteja (brother of Mwakobela) said of the shaving:

All the children, Mwakobela's and mine, boys and girls, and our wives, shave. I, Mwaiteteja, do not. Mwakobela shaved last night. At an ordinary birth only the mother shaves. Mwanyilu and other grandsons of Mwaipopo are 'just people' [i.e. not relatives for this purpose] and do not shave, but they are treated with the hot medicines.

MWANYOSO: The anointing is part of the ritual. The shaving and anointing are to show that the ritual is over. Since the birth of the twins neither the women nor the children have shaved or anointed themselves, nor we men either, but we don't anoint ourselves very much anyway. We shall all shave to-day or to-morrow, but I have shaved already because of the funeral ritual of Mwakisisi which took place two days ago.

Husband and wife in the hut spoke in whispers, and not even the doctor entered: 'They fear the legs.'

The doctor ranged everyone in a rough circle and she and her assistant went round smearing the forehead of each with the powder mixed with ointment. The circle soon broke up and people came up to her of their own accord to be smeared. She just dabbed a line on the forehead of each.

Then the banana suckers were cut and frayed at the end. A regular circle was formed. Mwakobela rushed out of the hut (washed, shaved and wearing a new cloth), seized two of the suckers and dipped them in the hot medicine, and splashed it on to the circle. The people yelled and ran away, only to return. He splashed them thus two or three times and then returned to the hut. The doctor continued the splashing.

Then Mwanyoso went up to the hut with a pruning hook and cut it open, crying: 'War has come!' Mwakobela and his wife and the child rushed out 'in the direction of Mwaijonga's place' [Mwakobela's father's home], followed by the whole crowd shouting: 'We are pure (*Tuli belu*).' They ran thirty or forty yards only and came back laughing and talking. Mwakobela said: 'In the old days I'd have taken a spear and shield and danced, alone!'

Two banana leaves were spread on the ground and the doctor

emptied out the two pots which had been cooking, one of meat alone, the other of meat and plantains. She and her assistant divided the meat into smallish portions. Meanwhile all the younger people gathered round and, at a sign from the doctor, fell on the meat, each trying to secure a piece. Some people even took sticks and beat their way into the seething scrimmage.

Then a pot of beer was brought. The doctor added powdered medicine to it and Mwakobela stirred it. All drank in turn, some from the pot directly, some dipping in little pots or cups of leaves. Mwakobela himself did not drink. Mwanyoso, Jane (Kasitile's wife) and others took beer in leaf cups for those at home.

iv. *Showing him the way home*

Mwanyoso was just going off when the doctor called him back: 'You are the *unyago*, you must show him the way home.' Mwanyoso then called to Kasitile's son: 'Come, Kasitile, and we will show him the way home.' The doctor, the two *abanyago*, Mwakobela and four or five others walked about fifty yards in the direction of the sacred grove of the dead chief, Mwaijonga, Mwakobela's father. Then the doctor said to Mwanyoso: 'Tell him where his home is.' So Mwanyoso pointed in that direction and said: 'That is the way to your house, the house of Mwaijonga.' Then Mwakobela took a packet wrapped in banana bark from the doctor, walked a few paces in that direction, turned round and threw the packet over his shoulder towards Mwaijonga's place. It fell in the grass behind him. 'So now we have finished,' said the doctor.

Meanwhile the mother of the twins with her surviving baby, the doctor's assistant, ten other women and twenty-three children set off to her 'father's place' about a quarter of a mile distant in Kibonde, with a calabash of beer. Her father is dead and her brother, Mwaipopo (not the chief), has inherited. The women and children all sat down at the edge of the homestead while the doctor's assistant went ahead. She ranged all the relatives present, twenty in all, in a line with their backs to the oncoming party and smeared their foreheads with powder and ointment. Then Masobesi's party approached, walking backwards, and when they were quite close the doctor's assistant said to the people of the homestead: 'Turn round and say: "We are pure." ' They turned and shouted: 'We are pure!' laughing; and at the same time Masobesi's party turned too.

Then the doctor called for water, added powder to it, and took Mwaipopo, the owner of the homestead, off to the edge of the bananas, some way from the house, to wash. He scratched a hole with his hands under a banana stem, and buried a packet (just like the one thrown over his shoulder by Mwakobela) which the doctor gave him. Then she poured the water for him and he washed his hands and mouth, as the others had done at Mwako-bela's place. The doctor took the mother of twins off to the edge of the swept place, some distance away, and poured water for her to wash her hands and mouth likewise. All this was quietly and seriously done.

A calabash of beer was then brought out of the house, the doctor put powder in, the mother of the twins stirred it, Mwaipopo drank first, and all the others in turn. Likonyela was present and took part in all this. He took off some medicated beer to take to his sister, Kipesile, who lives in Ipande. 'She is sick and I want to go to see her, so I shall take the medicine to her myself.' I asked him why he was not at Mwakobela's (being a classificatory son of Mwakobela). He replied: 'Well, they never sent me a message, to call me, so I came here.' He and Mwaipopo, the head of this homestead, are sons of two sisters. Likonyela's wives were not here—'They are sick'; but one of his children was here carried by a younger sister of one of his wives.

Some medicated beer was also taken by a man, Kikaja, son of Nokile, a cross-cousin (*untani*). 'His father was our mother's brother.'

Then the mother of twins went into the house and took out three baskets of cooked food and one pot of beer prepared for her. Each time she took up a basket the women of the house shouted: 'Ha! The child is snatching food, that is taboo!' She also took out a little pot of ointment and one of rouge. Then she cut at a grow-ing stem of bananas with a spear, while the women of the home-stead shouted: 'The child is cutting a banana stem, it is taboo!' The stem was finally severed by a boy with a hoe—she did not cut it through. Then the women of the homestead rushed at the mother of twins and greeted her and pressed round the infant excitedly. One of them explained to me: 'We, his mothers, are greeting him [the twin], we say to him: "We have never seen you before, how are you standing up to the cold?"' They also tied little pieces of string to the twin's wrists. 'It's to greet him and break the taboo (*ko kumbonola*),' they said.

All the women present, and Mwaipopo himself, had shaved to-day.

We stayed forty minutes there and some of the food was eaten on the spot. The rest of the food, the pot of beer, and the ointment and rouge, we carried back with us to Mwakobela's. The beer was given to Mwakobela who drank it with eleven other men, his kinsmen and neighbours. The food and ointment and rouge went to the women.

26 July 1935

The women had intended to go and visit the maternal relatives (*abipwa*) of the mother of twins yesterday, but her 'father' (Mwaipopo) had sent a message to say: 'Do not come yet, they are all away, some in Mwandosia's country, others planting potatoes.' Mwakobela, asked about his own mother's relatives, replied: 'My own *abipwa* have all died, and even if they had not, it would be too far to go, for they lived in Kukwe country. I did not throw medicine into the grass for them, no, we never do.

'The doctor is coming soon to sprinkle the cattle, all our herd here, my cattle and my neighbours', with medicine.' There are two herd groups in the village.

28 July 1935 (Sunday)

v. *Treating the cattle*

We were called to Mwakobela's place. He told us:

The doctor brought medicine last night, just before dark, and she said to me: 'Sprinkle the cattle yourself.' 'Perhaps it is taboo for me to do so?' I replied: 'No, not at all, you sprinkle them; I am going off to church to-morrow, to the catechumen's class.' Her elder sister is baptized already and she herself intends to be baptized. So I asked her: 'To whom shall we go for medicine then?' She replied: 'I am giving the medicine to my daughter, the wife of Mwakisisile, the son of Mwaihojo.'

When we arrived at about 1.15 p.m. Mwakobela's cattle and some others were standing round a smoky fire, as usual, during the midday hours.[1] The pot of medicine was steaming on another fire at a little distance. 'How do the cattle fall sick, if you do not treat them?' we asked. 'They purge continually. . . .'

Mwakobela's wife said: 'We should send to Mwampona and let his cattle be treated too.' Mwakobela (to us): 'Mwampona herds his cattle with Mwakikato, in a separate herd from ours;[2] she says they should come too; certainly when Mwampona had twins our

[1] cf. Monica Wilson, *Good Company*, p. 34.   [2] op. cit., p. 56.

cattle went up to be treated.' (To his wife): 'All right, they shall come,' and he sent off a boy with a message.

Mwampona came to inquire about the message sent to him and then went back to fetch his and Mwakikato's cattle. Six banana suckers were prepared. The cattle present were splashed by Mwakobela and two of his wives, each holding two banana tails. They were the cattle of Mwakobela himself and those of seven neighbours who herd with him. Then the other herd of the village came in (the cattle of five men) and was splashed. Mwakalobo II and Mwakikato (neighbours) both came up at the end and had their legs splashed with the remains of the medicine. They had both been splashed before—we had seen Mwakikato being splashed —so we asked: 'Why again?'

Mwakalobo II replied: 'We were a great crowd the first time, and I did not get properly splashed.' Mwakikato: 'I feel a pain.'

15 February 1937

Mwakobela and his wife told us that she had been to her mother's people (*abipwa*) after we left Isumba, but that he did not go to his *abipwa* and will not do so.

vi. *The ilibalaga*

We only saw the twin ritual enacted right through once, but the different events mentioned here were repeatedly described to us, and the ritual for Mwakobela's twins may be taken as typical. Two essential actions are, however, omitted from this account, viz. the eating of sausages of porridge from the ground and the ritual intercourse.[1] We describe these in the words of Mwakatage of the plain, a middle-aged Christian, himself the younger brother of twins, who gave a very detailed account of the whole ritual. He said that at the 'bringing out' rite, besides being smeared with medicine and splashed, children are given medicated porridge.

The women cook porridge for the children, medicated porridge, outside on the road. To this cooking and eating of porridge they only take children who are unmarried. The reason that they eat porridge is this: it is a ritual which they do so that when the parents of twins come out of their house, we may not just greet them, but that they may be one with us, we whose bellies are heavy (*tungisakuponanyaga itolo nagwe, fikuti ajege na nuswe tali basito munda*). To eat this porridge they fashion little balls or sausages, one for each child, smear them with ointment

---

[1] This rite was also described by a Kukwe doctor who had just supervised it in a twin ritual.

and stick them in the ground; then each one in turn kneels down and bites his sausage of porridge. . . . The parents of twins are still in the house, with those that accompany them. Then they kill a bull and cook most of the meat outside, because that is for everybody to snatch. But the portion of meat that is for those in the house of twins is put on the fire to cook by the doctor in their hut, for it is the meat of *ilibalaga*, that is of the most important rite. The doctor then approaches the twins' house and tells the man to come out. He obeys . . . and takes the frayed banana sucker heavy with water, and scatters the water in front, and to the sides, and all round, ending up by scattering it behind him, in the direction from which he came, then he runs back into his hut. The doctor goes into the hut too . . . he prepares a bed for the husband and wife and tells them to lie with each other, and they do so. Then he puts powdered medicine into the tiny pot of meat and bananas, which is there in the hut, lets the pot cook, and pours the contents out on to a leaf. He takes a little of this mixture and divides it into four portions, two for the man, two for the woman. Then he brings these to the parents who have had intercourse, before they have washed, while the filth is still on them. He tells the woman to take the food into her hands; she does so and smears filth on to it. Then the doctor makes two[1] little parcels, one for the man, one for the woman, and this it is that is called *ilibalaga* and is the most important element in the ritual.

After this the couple wash their hands and they eat. They eat the food, which the doctor left aside [i.e. which was not touched with soiled hands] and into which he has put a little powdered medicine. The man and his wife eat together. It is to bring them together again and let them eat together after they have been eating separately. The doctor then takes a little beer in a calabash cup and mixes it with water for them and gives it to them in the hut; they drink together there, the man and his wife. At dawn on the morrow the doctor says: 'Put on the fire some bananas and the uncooked meat left over.' He adds powdered medicine to it and it cooks, then he divides it into two portions, one for the man, one for the woman, and each portion is bundled up for the man and woman to take to their respective relatives. The doctor tells them to go each to their grandparents[2] with the filthy *ilibalaga* which he did up into parcels the day before. They take the parcels of meat which he did up this morning—the uncontaminated meat—and

---

[1] Probably four, two for each of them.

[2] According to Mwakatage an *ilibalaga* is taken by the father of twins to his parents and to his mother's people, and by the mother of twins to her parents and her mother's people, and at each meeting the same rite is performed. As we have seen, Mwakobela threw his *ilibalaga* in the direction of his father's grave, but did not visit any of his mother's people, and he denied that it was customary even to throw an *ilibalaga* in their direction.

this is eaten by the relative who receives the *ilibalaga*, after he has
buried it. He who receives the *ilibalaga* buries it, and while he is doing
so he looks up country to the origin of the Nyakyusa, who moved down
to the plain (MuNgonde); the officiant then tells them all to look up
country. . . . The mother of twins meets her family and it means: 'I am
all right now, I am clear, I am your friend, Kyala had bound me. . . .'
On reaching home the woman waits on the path . . . her husband (who
has been with the *ilibalaga* to his people) likewise waits for his wife. . . .
Then they both advance together and meet, and go into their house
[not the temporary hut] and eat and drink together. This eating and
drinking together means that their ritual is finished; they say: 'We
have survived that rubbishy Kyala who had bound us (*tuponile kwa
lyaKyala ili lya tupinile*).'[1] They eat the food which has come from their
two families together, first drinking together the beer. This is the end
of the twin ritual as it has always been performed. People avoid the
parents of twins for they say: 'He brings disease into our family.'

From the time the twins are born until he meets their mother
ritually, intercourse with any woman is taboo to the father of
twins. After the ritual he may live with the mother (though she
should not conceive again until the twins are running about), but
he cannot visit his other wives. Only when she has given birth
again—and had a normal delivery—is he free to live with his
other wives. Should he break this taboo it is believed that the wife
with whom he breaks it will fall grievously ill with swelling of the
legs and belly, and her father is entitled to claim a cow as damages.
Some polygynists are said to circumvent the taboo in this way:

The husband will go to the father of one of his wives and will take a
cow to him and say: 'I have got twins, I petition for your daughter.'
Then he can take her into his house and sleep with her, but with his
other wives he cannot sleep until she has borne a child. When she does
so, then he goes to the fathers of his other wives, taking a bull to each,
and says: 'I have had a twin birth but now it is finished, and I am
taking your daughters.' If the first wife thus taken bears no child, then
he must take a cow to the father of another and try with her.

But several of our informants held that no father in his senses
would permit his daughter to be taken by her husband after he
had fathered twins, until the mother of twins had herself borne a
normal child.

The isolation of the parents of twins from cattle also continues
for some time. The father of twins does does not milk or enter a

---

[1] Mwaikambo, commenting on the text, said: 'It is as if Kyala was *lindu* (rubbish).'
The concord implies *ilindu* not a person, as is usual with the proper name Kyala.

7. *The officiant at a twin ritual anoints a child*

8. *Preparing the meat for the participants to snatch at a twin ritual*

byre or strike a beast with a stick 'until the twins had grown up' (an elastic phrase), 'but if he has no sons to milk a doctor comes and gives him a medicine to drink in the house, then he can milk the cows outside. To enter the byre is altogether taboo.' He and his attendant during his seclusion drink the milk of one cow only, which has been specially treated. All his wives avoid milk until the end of the ritual and the mother of twins herself 'can only begin to clean the byre after she has borne at least one other child'— some say two or three other children. If a cow is given her for milk (after the end of the ritual) it is taboo for others to share that milk. If these taboos are broken it is said that the cattle will purge and die, or their legs will swell.

It is also taboo for a parent of twins to pass behind people—he (or she) must always pass in front. 'They fear that if he passes behind, he (the parent) will always have twins.'

Twins, and their parents who have been through the full ritual, are thereafter immune from the danger of twin birth and may even go in to greet a mother of twins—Mwakobela's sister, who herself had borne twins, entered his wife's seclusion hut. There are, however, two or three taboos which apply to twins in later life. It is taboo for one of a pair of twin girls to get married without the other. Angombwike explained:

If a man comes wooing the first he must do it secretly, and when he speaks to her father he must do it secretly, he may bring cows but no one knows about it; if it becomes known they say the younger might curse herself (*ukwibuna*) and die. Then when another has come wooing the other, secretly, the father tells them both to come wooing openly *on the same day*. They come with cows. Then the father summons all his children, and the twin girls, and tells them: 'These men have come to marry you, do you like them?' And he asks the elder (*mbasa*): 'Which do you like?' She chooses. Even if she chooses the man who came for her sister he must accept, and if he tries to protest people will hush him up at once, for it is the custom for the elder to get married first. Then the younger (*musindeka*) says she likes the other one and their father takes the cattle. If either one is wooed secretly before the other she must stay quietly at home till a wooer comes for her sister. If she did not (whichever way it happened) the other might die. It is common knowledge in the boys' village here that of X's twin daughters a lover has only come for the younger, none for the elder. And so both are still unmarried.

Twins and their parents, the fearful ones (*abipasya*), and other people who have been treated with medicines, eat first-fruits of

M

millet, beans and pumpkin with medicines. 'We fear lest the medicines we have drunk will turn round in the belly';[1] and they must be buried in a hut. 'If they are buried outside there will be drought and famine.'

(b) The overt purpose and symbolism

The overt purpose of the twin ritual is plain to all Nyakyusa. Twin birth is thought to be contagious, causing other twin births, and also to make men and cattle ill. The ritual is to prevent this. Mwambelike, a middle-aged pagan, was explicit on the point:

People are afraid to go to the house of a man with twins. They think that they will have twins themselves if they do, and we do not like twin births; they are taboo in the country. Or perhaps their legs will swell, or their bellies, or faces, if they go to his house. So we go to a doctor and he comes and sprinkles all the people in the village, even tiny children, and all the cattle. He takes a banana stalk to burn the twin birth (*pakokya ipasa*). He burns us because of the twin birth. The water is hot and medicated. He sprinkles us all with it and when we have all been treated we say we have been burnt because of the twin birth.

When a man has begotten twins we are in awe of this Kyala (*tukukeba Kyala uju*). . . . If people drink out of the same vessel as the parents of twins, or if the father of twins sleeps with his other wives, this makes the disease increase, the disease of swelling legs and stomach; men catch it, the wives catch it, the children and fathers of the wives catch it. There is also a twin ceremony for cattle; if a cow drops twin calves we fear the same things. You, your wife and children drink medicines, and the cows are all sprinkled with medicine—but not your other relatives, or neighbours.

Mwakobela himself said:

If I did not wash and went to eat with my relatives, my legs would swell, I should pant and gasp. Swelling of the legs is due to our shades (*imindu gyetu*) or perhaps Kyala beneath is angry (*Kyala pasi akalele*).

References to Kyala as the cause of twins are frequent:

KASITILE: The shades are in twin birth, and Kyala is there—it is he who gives two children. We drive them away. Kyala and the shades are together. When we bury the *ilibalaga* in the banana grove I say: 'Kyala, leave my bellows (which means my wife) for me, you shades leave it for me.' If the shades are angry perhaps my penis is broken in copulation.

MWAIKAMBO: I have not heard people speak of the shades in twin

[1] cf. Monica Wilson, *Good Company*, p. 54.

birth but they commonly say: 'This illness has come from Kyala, in the ritual we drive away Kyala (*tukunkaga Kyala*).'

MWANDISI (asked about the meaning of the phrase 'War has come' in relation to twin birth): It means the war of Kyala, of the twins, the illness. We bring out Kyala. Let him get out of the body, Kyala has caught hold of him, has brooded over him, has given him twins. 'Go out therefore! (*Soka panja lelo*).' At first he was taboo. Kyala was in the house; he could not come out. So then we bring him out, saying: 'We have fought the war there, he has come out.'

NJOBAKOSA (another elderly man—also said that the ritual was to to 'drive off Kyala'): He [the father of twins] comes out, he takes a spear and shield and runs, and we run. One snatches up a shield, and another, and another. Then we give each other beer to drink, and food, and meat, snatching it from one another; we drive off Kyala. When the father of twins comes out of the hut we say: 'You hit us!' He replies: 'I am innocent (*mwelu*, lit. white) because he has been black (*ntitu*) on account of having twins.'

MWANDISI: If the ritual is not completed [i.e. if copulation does not take place], then they go to divine. It is said: 'The shades are angry.' Are the shades not with Kyala?

ANGOMBWIKE: I remember when I was a child, when I had one younger brother who was just beginning to walk, my father had twins. I remember the people sitting round the beer praying that his first ritual copulation should be successful. They began with Mbasi. 'You, Mbasi,[1] support us! (*Gwe Mbasi utwemele*). You, Kyala, support us!' Then they came to the shades. And I have heard that they always said both Mbasi and Kyala but began with Mbasi.

The parents of twins have been singled out by Kyala or Mbasi and therefore remain somewhat fearful all their lives. Angombwike said:

The parent of twins (*umwipasya*) seems like a great person (*alete mundu fijo*), he is not like us, his relatives. See, he has gained two people, he is the child of Mbasi, he is with Kyala, he has seen Kyala. You know that pagans do not eat twin bananas, they fear, saying: 'These are twins (*mapasa*).' They give them to small children. (What I speak of is Nyakyusa custom, not the custom of the baptized.) And the parents of twins (*abipasya*) do not eat the bananas on the sides of the bunch, only those in the middle. When a girl has brought a bunch of bananas to them in the temporary hut . . . they say to her: 'Take away those at the sides,' and she takes away here one, and there one.

[1] There were hints of some special connection between the hero Mbasi and twins (*amapasa*), the elder of whom is *Mbasa*. The younger twin is *Musindeka*, the following child is *Syula*, the next *Kumba*, and the next *Kumbulilu*.

QUESTION: Why?

ANGOMBWIKE: Because they say you are a middle one, Mbasi goes with you. We others are on the sides, you are on the open space between (*mpulo*);[1] he has drawn you apart, you are a man of Mbasi now; no one drives you away; no one makes you move aside to make way for someone who comes later. No one makes Mbasi, the fearful one (*umwipasya*), move aside; he is someone who is not moved aside.

He went on to explain that a father of twins must never move aside for a woman passing on the path; should he do so she would fall ill with swollen legs. 'The man looks at the woman and says: "I am here, I am someone, move aside," then she moves aside, she knows that he is *mwipasya*.'

Kyala creates twins, but they are not part of the natural order which he himself created. 'Kyala made us to have one child, so when we have twins it is like an illness.' Mwaikambo held that twins are both unnatural and animal-like.

The man who has borne twins we liken to an animal, because Kyala has created things so that we human beings bear just one child; it is only animals which have many young at one time. So when our fellow has twins we fear to sleep with him in the house because he is like an animal now, therefore we build for him a little hut at some distance, that his badness (*ububibi bwake*) may not move on to us. We seek a medicine for greeting him with, when he comes into the house. . . . He fears to call out because he is following the customs of animals which do not speak. . . . Snatching food is eating like animals. . . . The parents of twins avoid cattle because they are like animals which bear many cubs in a litter. And the blood in the parent of twins is much and fierce (*ililopa lya gwa ipasa lingi, kangi ikali*); it will make the cattle purge, and their legs swell.

A number of other men assented to this interpretation that twins are like animals, saying: 'Yes, it is so,' but no one else volunteered it. The feeling that twins are unnatural is general.

Part of the fearful quality of twins is their heaviness (*ubusito*), and friends and relatives drink medicines that they may be heavy also, and able to meet them.

When twins are born we drink medicine before we meet the parents, it is as if we were light, our bodies have not strength to escape their illness. So we treat ourselves with medicines that we also may be heavy in the belly, that we may have strength to escape their illness.

[1] *Umpulo*: the open swept place between lines of houses in a village.

The *ilibalaga* is to make the mother's relatives one blood with the daughter's children. 'The food which each of the parents brings to relatives is the blood of the lineage (*lyo ilopa lya kikolo kyabo*) that they may have one body (*ukuti baje mbili gumo*). They do not look at one another when they take the *ilibalaga* because the blood [of the two lineages] has not yet met.'

The statements of two doctors, the one from Selya and the other a Kukwe, throw a little more light on the symbolism of the various actions. Mwakionde (of Selya) replied to a question about why the parents of twins only eat the middle bananas in a bunch:

Those of the sides belong to Kyala, because the twin was with Kyala; Kyala brooded over him, he came to them and gave them two children. After two days they throw away those bananas on the side, they throw them behind the huts, where they throw the rubbish of twins. . . . That means: may Mbasi be driven away when he comes to look at the children, may he be driven away to the rubbish heap behind the huts.

QUESTION: Why are the parents not allowed to call out?

MWAKIONDE: When we give each other medicines to drink? Since you have borne twins we do not meet one another. It's taboo to call out.

QUESTION: Snatching food from one another?

MWAKIONDE: They spread meat and cooked bananas on leaves of plantain and sweet banana. The doctor sprinkles powdered medicine, then we all snatch. Then the doctor gathers up the rubbish (*imindu*), those leaves, and throws them away behind the huts.

QUESTION: But why the snatching?

MWAKIONDE: If we do not snatch from one another our legs swell.

QUESTION: The running to the pasture?

MWAKIONDE: I myself have borne twins, you are my relative. When they have shaved my hair in the house, when you come with a shield to the doorway, 'Come out, Mwakionde,' you cry. 'War has come!' Then I go out. You give me the shield at the doorway. I run off with it. Another comes and snatches it, and another and another. It's to help the legs. Women do it afterwards, and then cry the war-cry. If I just meet a twin then Mbasi is angry and says: 'Why do you kill your fellow by just meeting him?' I am ill, I have diarrhœa, my legs swell, and my face swells, but sometimes the sickness returns to the parent of twins and he himself is ill.

KAKUNE (a Kukwe): In European times we do not fear; we drink medicine, that is all; but of old we feared very much. At the coming out (*ukusoka*) beer is brewed and the people and relatives drink it, and then in the night the man and wife, secluded in the hut, have intercourse, and the doctor stands outside at the door. The doctor asks: 'Is it successful? [i.e. can you have intercourse with her?]' and the man says: 'No, it is not successful.' Then all we *abanyago* (priests, officiants), the fathers of the girl who are there, and the fathers of the man, pray, in words only [i.e. without blowing out water], saying: 'Father, support us, Grandfather, support us, Kyala, support us, let not the ritual go on for ever.' And then the man is able to eject, and he tells the doctor: 'It's all right now.'

The disease comes from the twin birth (*ilipasa*) when a couple have had twins (*bapasile*). If the relatives speak with them or tread in their footsteps when they [the relatives] are empty (*bwasi*), not having drunk medicine, then their legs will swell up and they will have diarrhœa. No, they do not say that the private parts will swell, only the legs. The refusal of the seed to come is due to the shades (*imindu*). If a man has angered his father or mother who are alive, or if they are dead and he gives nothing to his sister, then those below, *balungu*, are angry. *Imindu* catches hold of them and then when he begets twins he will have trouble at the ritual.

The semen refuses to come also if the girl has angered her parents, or if her husband has angered them. It's *imindu*. This copulation is an essential part of the ritual. If the parents of twins do not do this and you meet them afterwards, your legs will swell and dysentery will set in. The fearful ones [the parents of twins] have a fire and create sickness in us. We say: 'Kyala has loved [*sic*] you, he has created you so that you bear twin children. Now we speak with you.'

Yes, the old people said: 'Kyala and those below.' They said those below beg Kyala to give them two children. This was said of old, before the Europeans came. One who has himself had twins will not fear his relative who has twins for he says: 'I also am heavy (*ndi nsito*), I am a fearful one, a parent of twins myself.' No one fears the twins themselves, but their parents are feared.

The child that follows twins (*ndili*), does not anoint himself at any later twin ritual. It is said that he finished before because he followed twins.

When the parents of twins leave the hut they run with a lighted piece of thatch,[1] followed by all the friends and relatives; the friends and relatives call out: 'You hit us with fire [i.e. you give us the disease].' They reply: 'We are pure (*tuli belu*) [i.e. we have no disease, it is finished]. Kyala has prayed for us.'

And at the death of a parent of twins the relatives fear to touch the corpse until the twin doctor comes and puts a medicine in the hand of the corpse and sprinkles hot medicine on the legs of the relatives—then

---

[1] This was not seen or mentioned in the Selya ritual.

they take hold of the corpse. But they wait for the doctor; if they do not do so the same disease will come—a swelling of legs and diarrhœa. An ordinary corpse is not feared in this way.

Yes, a man fears to take his other wives. He says: 'If I just go to them I shall give them the disease of the twins that I begot with this wife.' The wife he takes without precaution will swell in the legs and stomach, and pass blood with her stools. He first tries to have a child with the wife who bore twins, waiting till the twins are walking about. He lies with the mother of the twins but withdraws, and then, when the children are grown, he impregnates her. He does not go to the other wives. And if he asks for another wife before trying to impregnate the mother of the twins her father will refuse. If he takes her without asking, her father will make him pay a cow. He can only ask for another wife if the mother of the twins does not conceive. For one month[1] the husband refrains altogether from intercourse, then after the ritual he goes to his wife (the mother of the twins) but does not impregnate her. . . . A man is supposed to tell the twin doctor before he begets another child with his wife. He must do it openly, and not in secret. It is taboo to do it secretly. Nothing happens, but the doctor is angry, saying: 'Why did you not tell me, the doctor, the owner of the body?'

Themes already familiar from the death and puberty–marriage rituals recur again here. The parents of twins are isolated and cleansed like mourners and nubile girls. Contact with them is held to be dangerous because 'those below'—in this case Kyala and Mbasi rather than the shades—have brooded over them, and must be driven off before normal procreation can be resumed. After their isolation the *ilibalaga*—the symbol of their ritual union—must be offered to the shades of both lineages, that of the man and that of the woman. There is also the eating of balls of porridge, the symbol, in the other rituals, of the actions of a madman, but the fear of madness was not adduced by our informants as the purpose of the twin ritual; rather it is the formidable potency which produces two children instead of one, that is the danger—'the parents of twins have a fire'—and men protect themselves against it by burning themselves with hot medicines. They 'burn the twin birth'.

[1] Presumably longer when the seclusion and ritual lasted longer.

CHAPTER VII

RITUALS OF MISFORTUNE

An abnormal birth is the most dangerous misfortune that can befall a family in Nyakyusa society, and the ritual to ward off its expected results is the most elaborate, but there are lesser misfortunes also, which may be averted by simpler rituals.

(a) Cleansing after spearing

When one man has speared another and killed him, even though the action was legitimate (as slaying an enemy in battle, or a cattle thief or an adulterer caught in flagrante delicto), the slayer and his relatives dare not eat together with the relatives of the slain, or enter their houses, lest they themselves, and the kinsmen of the slain also, fall ill, coughing, spitting blood, and wasting away. This sickness is known as ulukwego, 'the disease of spearing'.[1] Both parties are thought to suffer primarily from contact with each other and both protect themselves by drinking medicines, but they drink separately, each engaging a doctor to treat them. We were told:

If one man kills another it does not finish. He begets children and they die; an autopsy is performed and reveals fighting with spears (isengene)[2] The disease may not injure the slayer or his children, but the relatives with whom he eats and drinks, and so also on the other side; it may not hurt the children of the dead man, but those relatives with whom his children eat and drink.

We all fell ill, especially the brothers of the slain. The murderer always remembered to drink the medicine because he knew that he had killed someone, but when your brother was slain perhaps you forgot to drink the medicine. Then, afterwards, if you drank beer with someone, not knowing that it was he who had killed your brother, you fell ill.

The manner of treatment is as follows:

If I have killed someone they take me to a waterfall and make me

---

[1] Ingwego: a spear.   [2] Ukusegana: to fight together with spears.

vomit by tickling the back of my throat with a hen's feather, while I am standing under the fall with the water coming down on my head. The blood of him you have killed is in the waterfall. May it not come! May it all go out of the body! You vomit because it is there in the body. May it go out! Then a medicine is cooked and the legs of the slayer and his relatives are scalded with it. It is the medicine of twins: the twin medicine and the spearing medicine are one because they are a rejection of the blood. When people's legs have been splashed then we all shave; that is to drive away him whom we have killed.

But even after such treatment the kin of the slayer and the slain fear to eat together. 'We remain enemies. If we eat with them it makes us thin.'

Those who drink protective medicines are the agnatic kin of the slayer and the slain, their mothers' kin (*abipwa*) and their wives, but not their affines. 'Those who must be treated are wives, and blood relatives but not affines. Affines are of different blood, but wives are of your flesh.'

The spearing ritual is not a joint ritual in which a large group of kin participate; married men, even brothers, make their own arrangements for taking protective medicine.

We do not meet together with all our relatives, the descendants of one man, no, it is not like the twin ritual. We drink it each man with his wives and children in his house. If I have a married brother he also goes to a doctor to ask for medicines for himself. He seeks his own doctor, not the one to whom I went. We drink separately, we do not meet together when we drink.

Only if a daughter had been given in compensation for a murder (as sometimes happened) and later he who married her took marriage cattle to her father to establish kinship, then, our informants said, the two parties should drink the 'medicine of spearing' (*unkota gwa lukwego*) together.

(b) Rotting the ropes

A man who has been bound with ropes (*ingoje*), or has committed suicide by hanging,[1] or raided cattle and tethered them, is also

---

[1] What the incidence of suicide is among the Nyakyusa we do not know. The Rev. Merensky, one of the first Europeans to live in the area, speaks of it being 'not uncommon'. We recorded two cases: one of a man whose wife and children had died; the other a woman forced to leave her lover and marry against her will. X, a Christian whom we knew well, swore to his pagan elder brother that he would commit suicide if his brother insisted on the pagan practice of performing an autopsy on the body of their dead sister.

believed to be a danger to his kin and descendants, but in a manner somewhat different from the one who has killed another. The sickness is thought to come from the ropes and is called *ingoje* after them.

Mwaikambo explained:

If one member of a family commits suicide by hanging then his surviving relatives, if they do not drink a medicine, will die of the 'ropes', always. If a man hangs himself all his relatives fear; if a woman only her children.

Kasitile's wife, Kiluleli, had borne ten children, but all save one had died. He said:

It is because of the ropes of her father. They bound him at Tukuyu; he died in gaol; it is those ropes which are killing my children. I said to her father [i.e. the heir]: 'Let us go to divine,' but he has not yet agreed to do so.

The death of Mukwabila, a junior kinsman of the Chief Mwaipopo, whose funeral we attended, was attributed to the ropes used to tether cattle raided by his grandfather. Kasitile, himself a distant agnatic kinsman, explained this case also:

One of the fathers of Mukwabila was killed by the hill people. They seized him on the road. So in revenge Mwamusiku, the father of Mukwabila, took twenty cows belonging to the hill people as they passed north, coming from the salt lick. This was long ago. Then Mukwabila's father omitted to kill a cow for those who had helped him to secure the cows. So they were angry and brought *ingoje*—the disease of ropes—upon him. After seizing the cattle he moved to Mwambebule's country in the hills and he was quite well, but then he came back to live here, first sending two cows to the Chief Mwaipopo, but killing none for the people, who were angry and said: 'Why does he not kill for us? What sort of chief is he?' He got weak and fell ill and died. They did not perform an autopsy, saying it was forbidden to do it on a chief, and his son died also and was not examined, but now when the younger son died, Mwaipopo said: 'Let us examine him so that we may know.' And it is that old *ingoje*. . . .

The sickness of ropes (*ingoje*) is of three sorts coming from: (1) the suicide (by hanging) of a relative long ago; (2) the binding of a man by other people, as distinct from a man binding himself; and (3) the shocked astonishment of men and their breath. In dreams they put the sickness of ropes into his stomach, they say: 'May the sickness of ropes come into his stomach.' The sickness of ropes lies in wait for an heir. A man dies and the sickness comes on his heir, others are all right; so it goes on. Mwamusiku was never bound, but we say it was that sickness of the ropes of the cattle that he seized from the hill people. Perhaps the people of that country were shocked, and the sickness is due to their breath, to witchcraft. Perhaps the owners of the cattle took the ropes they had used for tying up the cattle which were stolen, to a doctor to be cooked with medicine. We have not discovered the details yet, we have not yet been to divine; the divination will tell us, however. But the medicine for rotting the ropes (*imbosyo*) is the same for all these illnesses from ropes, so we cook it immediately, before going to divine. We divine when we clear away the litter. The cooking of medicine at the grave now is to rot him who has died that the sickness of ropes (*ingoje*) may not come on us. Yes, only the heir fears to die, but we others fear lest we fall ill, coughing. The sickness of ropes does not kill us, but makes us ill and thin. Yes, I drank and ate the medicine myself. After the divination we drink another medicine, in beer, not the *itemelo* beer. They brew another lot just for the medicine.

We saw the drinking of medicine 'to rot the ropes' at Mukwabila's funeral. He was buried at Kasitile's homestead and Kasitile was organizing the proceedings. The doctor dug a hole at the foot of the grave and put into it a length of green wood which projected a foot or so above the level of the ground. On this was balanced a pot, and a fire was lighted beneath it. In the pot she boiled certain leaves and roots. She took a large drinking calabash, put in some ash from a fire-brand, added some of the same species of leaves as had gone into the pot, and stirred up the mixture with water. This mixture was drunk by the relatives present and fifteen or twenty leaf cups were made to send to those who had not come. Medicated porridge was also made and some was eaten by the relatives present.

Then the pot was taken off the fire. We were told: 'We are praying (*tulipakwiputa*). We want to take the pot off the fire.' No words were said, but the medicines were taken out of the pot by the deceased's father's sister (the oldest surviving member of the lineage) to prepare more porridge for those relatives who had not attended, and the officiant poured the water into a hole which she made in the middle of the grave. She covered it again with earth.

While the officiant was preparing the medicine at the grave, Kasitile, who was helping her, said to a half-brother of the deceased:

Pray earnestly with this medicine, be on good terms with others.
HALF-BROTHER: Me? What case was there against me?

KASITILE: You sons of Musika had a case against you . . . you fought.
HALF-BROTHER: But that case concerned a woman.

A discussion of the case followed.

KASITILE: Friend, we pray here. Listen carefully.
HALF-BROTHER: I have spoken and not concealed anything.
KASITILE: That's what I say, let us pray well.
HALF-BROTHER: I performed the ritual for him. Let him die with his hair.
SISTER: Let us confess [lit. vomit] we were angry.
HALF-BROTHER: Yes, it is so, we were angry. The cow made us angry.

Mwaisumo described a treatment with *imbosyo* medicines which differed slightly from the one we saw and involved the slaughter of a sheep; according to his account the medicines are coiled in the pot like ropes, and the participants are washed under a waterfall, though they are not made to vomit like the relatives of a murderer. Doubtless the details vary with the officiant, but the principle that medicines are used to rot the ropes remains constant.

(c) *Protection against sorcery or vengeance magic*

Sickness caused by sorcery or vengeance magic is believed to spread among kinsmen in much the same way as sickness due to the shedding of blood or binding with ropes, and the ritual performed as a protection against it is very similar to the ritual for 'rotting the ropes' just described. We saw it performed after the death of E. who died on 23 March 1935. Her elder brother (heir to her father) and her husband, who were pagans, wished to perform an autopsy, but her younger brother, a Christian, prevented their doing so. Soon after her burial her mother and husband fell very ill and three weeks later (April 13) the five-year-old son of her elder brother M. died. An autopsy was performed on the child and the diagnosis was that his mother's father, after quarrelling with M., his son-in-law, had drunk medicines to bring death to M's children. M. explained: 'My wife has already buried two children. This boy is the third. Previously we found evidence of *ilyepa*[1] at the autopsy, and this time it is the same. The disease comes from my wife's father.' However, when M. went to confirm

---

[1] *Ilyepa* is a medicine alleged to be drunk by a senior relative, when he is angry, which, if his anger is justified, will cause his junior relative to suffer in his own person or that of his children.

the cause of both deaths with a famous diviner, Sambo, he was told that the boy's death was due to the anger of neighbours who had not been feasted as they should have been, but E's death was due to the sorcery of her first husband. M's report of the divinations is worth quoting:

I have just been to Sambo in the country of Swebi, he has divined and he tells me that the death of E. was due to the sorcery (*ubutege*) of Mwakyusa, her first husband. He also told me the name of the doctor from whom Mwakyusa got the medicine to kill her, the man is K.; he is both a doctor and a smith in the country of X. He told me that Mwakyusa was angry because, when he tore her mouth, he paid to us a cow in damages; he said: 'I have paid the cow, I should have my wife. But they have taken her back and eaten my cow.' E. had left all her things in his house, her bark-cloths, her cloths, everything. Sambo tells me that Mwakyusa took all these things to K. and spoke four names, saying: 'I wish E. my wife, M., and one of M's wives [mother of the dead child] to die. If these die I shall be happy.' So the doctor prepared a medicine which he put into a calabash. He did this while saying the names, and he addressed the names to the cloths, as if one of them was E., one was me, and so on. If E. had left nothing behind he would have had to send a man up with medicine to our place.

He told me to go to Mwakionde, who is a great doctor. Mwakionde will come to my place and cook medicine, we shall all drink it, not only the three people named but all my distant relatives will collect to drink it, N., E's second husband will come too. About the child, Sambo denies that it is *ilyepa*, he says it is due to the wrong-doing of her father. At first my wife was married when very young, but her husband went away and left her, she never lived with him. So when she grew up she said: 'I am tired of being alone, I am going to get married.' So she came to me. I paid five cows to Mwandosia (the chief) who is the mother's brother of her father. Her own father is dead. She has a father by inheritance, but Mwandosia had looked after her a great deal, so I sent the cattle to him, and he sent them on to the elder brother of her first husband. But her father's heir said: 'That finishes the cows to be paid to her husband, but I want one for myself to make six.' Well, at first I was involved in a lawsuit and did not bring the cow, so her father was angry; he came and took her back home; then after a time I found the cow and took it to him, and he sent her back to me, but he did not, as the custom is, cook food for my friends of the village. He should have cooked some chickens and brewed some beer, so that my friends would be happy and say 'Thank you'. So now my friends are angry, they say: 'Why does he not bring his daughter back properly? Perhaps he is not her father!' The breath comes from my friends, they are angry because of food. If I had not given him the cow it would have been his anger, now it is that of my friends. At the other deaths the doctors diagnosed *ilyepa*, but Sambo denies this. It is just the offence to my neighbours. He says I am to send the woman to him, and he will put her right himself.

A month after E's death (April 25) Mwakionde, the doctor, came to her elder brother's home to perform the ritual of protection. He and her second husband were next-door neighbours. The preparation and drinking of medicines was at her brother's homestead, but they moved to her husband's (where she was buried) to treat the grave. Beer had been prepared and the doctor added medicine to it. The mother of E., and one of her brother's wives, ground millet from their own crop, letting it fall on freshly-cut leaves of the sweet banana. This millet was used for the medicine. Meantime, one of the doctor's assistants opened the grave, digging down until he reached the cave in which the corpse had been placed. Then medicine to cause rotting (*imbosyo*), made with the lees of the beer, was poured in and eight pots of water. Mwakionde explained that 'opening the grave is to rot the poison in the body' and the water is put in that it may reach the corpse—the amount depends on the depth of the grave. Then the grave was filled in again and three small lengths of root, anointed with red pigment, were stuck into the fresh earth. These, Mwakionde said, were 'to close the way so that if the medicine comes again it will be turned back'. 'All three pieces of root are to close the way so that if that man comes again to work sorcery we shall escape, if Kyala keeps us.'

Then the doctor prepared a pot with about twenty roots, two varieties of spiny cactus, one impaled on the other, six packets of medicine, and water, and set it to boil on a fire made near the doorway of her brother's hut. The fire was lighted by friction by the male kinsmen, and the old fire was cleared out of the hut. A small bull was killed and its blood added to the brew. Porridge was made from this and the specially ground millet, and eaten by the participants. Then each of them, beginning with her elder brother, was scarified on the back, arms, legs, and feet and medicine from a horn rubbed in.

All through Mwakionde spoke only of *protection*, but others, speaking of the rite of filling the grave with water, explained it as a means of making the sorcery recoil on the sender, causing his death, and there is little doubt that this was one object of the ritual, though not openly admitted. The younger brother protested at the inclusion of the cactus stems and it is likely that they were an ingredient intended to injure the sender of sorcery.

(d) Prayer to the shades

Misfortune is also believed to come from the anger of senior relatives, living and dead. If a junior has angered his senior kinsman the senior is said to 'mutter over the fire'. 'He is so angry that he cannot speak intelligible words, he murmurs and mumbles to himself. . . .' 'I crouch over the fire in the evening and mutter to myself in a low voice: "I am astonished and hurt at my son. Did I not provide marriage-cattle for him? And he does this to me!"' Then the shades hear him and the wrong-doer falls ill, or is sterile, or his crops or fishing fail. 'No man has the power of making the shades hear like this save Father (*tata*)—he mutters alone and the shades hear him—all of us, pagans and Christians alike, believe in the power of Father to mutter, because whenever a man wrongs his father something always happens to him—he finds blessing nowhere.' The 'father' is a man's own father who begot him, or his heir, or, in a lesser degree, his father's elder full brother, or any kinsman who has given marriage-cattle on his behalf. 'If a man has given me cattle for marriage then he has authority over me (*jo mpala gwangu*)[1] for cattle are important (*imbala*).'

If a senior is at fault (for example, an heir who neglects his wards) the shades may, in theory, punish him also, but more often any misfortune that befalls him is attributed to the just wrath of his neighbours who watch over the interests of the dead man's children. The idea that misfortunes spring from the anger of the living is strong; indeed, one of our best informants, Angombwike, maintained that 'the shades never act alone', and Mwakwelebeja, an old man, said: 'It is really we who get angry, but the shades help a little because they are always with us; we always dream of them.'

The shades are 'the fathers' (*batata*), and prayers are addressed primarily to the men of the lineage, but a father's sister is also classed as a 'father'. Some informants denied that a mother could bring sickness on her children:

Women never murmur against their children, only the father, the

---

[1] Literally, 'he is my great one'.

man. Women murmur but it only makes them sick themselves [laughter]. But my father's sister (*unnasenga*) can murmur, she is a man like my father. . . . If my mother is old and I do not care for her she will murmur and fall sick herself, she will never make me sick. My mother is no relative in my homestead, she is no relative to the shades.

However, Mwakwelebeja (a very old and conservative man) held that 'People sometimes say: "My mother beneath is angry" though it's not common', and Kasitile was quite positive that a mother was also a shade with power to inflict misfortune, as the following conversation shows:

QUESTION: What shades influence a man or woman?

KASITILE AND HIS YOUNGEST WIFE: *Imindu* of father is there, and *imindu* of mother. Yes, indeed, *imindu* of mother exists. Once I had not put beer in the house and I fell ill. The divination said: 'It is *imindu* of your mother. She is angry not to find anything in your house.' Because we chiefs always put beer in a little calabash in the house, it stays there always.

QUESTION: When it goes bad?

KASITILE: We put some more. There is a little millet flour there now. Sometimes we put flour, sometimes beer. And when I come to die they bury beer with me. . . . Once the offering was not there, and my mother who was dead came to look and did not find anything. Then she went to father, who was dead, and said: 'I went to our child. His house was without anything.' Then father said: 'Let us go and look!' They did not find anything, then they shook me up. Then the oracle said: 'It is the *imindu* of your mother.'

QUESTION: And a wife?

KASITILE: Both her father and her mother punish [lit. hit] her at their place, even though she is with me, also they punish her.

QUESTION: But your shades?

KASITILE: How can they punish in-laws? They do not punish her, but the child whom she has borne, their grandchild, him they punish.

Though Kasitile and others denied that the husband's shades could punish a wife, nevertheless she suffers from their anger through the child, through a difficult labour, or through the beer she brews going bad.

PYAGILAMO: It is said that when a woman who has quarrelled with her husband is brewing beer and it goes bad, that means the shades are angry. The shades of the husband have made the beer go bad. The husband has murmured and the shades have heard. When a wife is pregnant it is taboo for her to quarrel with her husband; she will have a difficult labour. The husband murmurs and the shades hear. The difficult labour is from this, not from adultery. And in a case of difficult labour her husband does pray to his shades.

All were agreed that a woman is in the power of the shades of her father's lineage and if her father is angry with her, or with his son-in-law her husband, his shades afflict her, causing her to be barren or to have miscarriages, or ailing children. Hence a woman who is barren or ill, or whose children are sickly, often returns to her father's homestead so that he may pray for her, and she sleeps there on the night of the ritual, for the shades come by night. More rarely, if she has quarrelled with her father, she goes outside her husband's homestead and, facing towards her father's home, she prays herself on the pathway. But in all the cases we traced in which a woman's ancestors were believed to have made her, or her child, ill, there was a dispute between her father (or his heir) and her husband over marriage-cattle or the bull of puberty; and we were told that her father's shades 'are angry only if marriage-cattle have not been paid, and for no other reason', thus it seems that the control of her father's shades over a married woman is in fact somewhat limited.

The characteristic illness sent by the shades is sores round the mouth, and fever—an illness which is not acute and clears up quickly. These symptoms are immediately interpreted as *imindu*, affliction from the shades. Beer going sour before it is mature is also *imindu*, usually thought to be caused by quarrels between husband and wife. But almost any misfortune, mild or serious, is interpreted as *imindu* if members of the lineage are conscious of quarrels between themselves, or with their spouses or fathers-in-law.

The ritual consists in the reconciliation of the living in the presence of the dead and, if the misfortune is serious, a sacrifice of flesh, fish, or fowl. The junior begs pardon of his senior who acknowledges his anger and expresses forgiveness by taking a mouthful of water from his calabash cup (*ulupindi*) and blowing it out (*ukwiputa*) in his sacred banana grove. For the patient to recover, or the blight on crops or fish-traps to be removed, *the senior kinsman must confess his anger*, and spitting, or blowing out water, is a symbol of confession and forgiveness. Mwaisumo was explicit on the matter: 'If a father is angry with his son or daughter he may say, some day: "I forgive you now" and spit on the ground: all the anger that is in him comes out like spit.' *Ukuswa* means both 'to

N

spit' and 'to forgive'. *Ukuputa* means 'to blow out water' and *ukwiputa* (the reflexive form) means 'to pray', with the implication of confessing whatever anger or grudge a man may have in his heart. Full confessions both by the wrongdoer and by seniors who have been angry are held to be essential to the lifting of the misfortune.

The man who prays represents the living members of the lineage and he calls on his immediate seniors, who are dead, for support. 'You, Father, you my elder brother, you so-and-so (his grandfather) stand by me, help me, do not be angry, here I am, your child, your younger brother. I am above here, it was not I who killed you but Kyala alone.'

He may also remonstrate with the shades, asking why they should afflict the living. *Ukwikemesya* (lit. 'to cause oneself to blame', from the root *ukukemela* 'to scold' or 'to blame') is used to mean 'to sacrifice', and the conception of remonstrating with, or scolding, troublesome shades is an element of Nyakyusa sacrifice.

If beer has been prepared, a libation is poured out either on the hearth-bricks or in the banana grove nearest the door of the house, which is used by the owner as his sacred grove (*ikijinja kyake ikikemo*). If an animal is sacrified the blood must soak into the earth for, as already indicated, the 'earth is the shade's'. Furthermore, the rest of the beer or the fish and the *ija mmapa* meat from the foreleg of the beast[1] is left overnight on the ground in the sacred grove, more rarely under the officiant's bed, and eaten or drunk in the morning by young boys of the lineage, grandsons[2] of the last deceased, for they are 'the comrades of the shades'. Other people may finish up the beer or meat, but wives of the lineage may not touch it: they seclude themselves in their huts and remain silent during the ritual, for 'they fear their fathers-in-law (*bikutila abakamwana*)'.

The proper person to approach the shades is (among commoners) the senior member of a lineage of three generations; but if he lives at a considerable distance—perhaps twenty miles or more away—then a junior may pray on his own account, only asking help from his senior in cases of serious illness. 'If father and son, or brothers, live far apart, as here in Selya and at Mwaya

---

[1] The cut is the same as the Xhosa *intsonyama* which is sacred in a Pondo sacrifice. cf. M. Hunter, *Reaction to Conquest*, p. 249. Nyakyusa informants denied that the gall is of importance in their ritual as it is among the Nguni and Nuer.

[2] One case was recorded of a son of the last deceased, still a small child, drinking the sacrificial beer.

(forty miles away), then, if a child is a little ill, you pray yourself, but if it is very ill you send a message to your elder.' The senior knows the shades (*agimenye imindu*) and prays alone.

The wives of a lineage avoid everything connected with offerings to the shades in the same way as they avoid a father-in-law, even though their husband's father is not yet dead and they do not avoid his living grandfather: 'If a cock has grown up at my homestead my wives do not eat it. It is taboo. It is the shades'. But my wives may eat a hen. When the cock crows it rouses the house. If a wife eats it she will die soon and people will say: "She has eaten a cock." ' A wife also avoids bananas from the sacred grove, and sacrificial meat and beer, and milk from a cow that has looked into a grave; she must stay silent and secluded in her hut when prayer is made in the grove, and is forbidden to sleep by the hearth at night.

Mwaisumo's account of 'prayer when a child is ill' and descriptions of four particular rituals will make the procedure clearer.

MWAISUMO: Our regular custom here, when a child is ill with sores on the mouth from *imindu*, is to pray to the shades (*ukwiputa kubasyuka*), especially to my father, or my elder brother if I have inherited from him. Before I pray I go to a diviner. We consult the oracle, and he tells me: 'It is *imindu*, your fathers are angry because you have not performed such and such a ritual, perhaps because you have not killed cattle at the funeral of your brother, or your mother's brother, perhaps you have not performed the later death ritual for them.' So when I come home I tell my relatives and wives all the diviner has told me. Then they complain (*ukwijaja*) saying: 'Why are they angry? Take water and complain in the evening.'

So at dusk, when the cattle come home, I take my calabash cup (*ulupindi*), and water, and a live coal from the fire, and put it in the calabash. I go out to the banana grove of my father where I always pray. I take a mouthful of water, I blow it out and say: 'You, Father, you so-and-so, you so-and-so, why are you angry, Father? Since you left me I have nourished the children. How have I wronged you? Even though I have wronged you, forgive me, Father, may the child recover. Stand by me.' When I have finished I enter the house, and next day I may find the child a little better.

Before I pray, if the diviner has told me that they are angry because I have stinted a certain brother of something, I go to tell him and beg his pardon for neglecting him, my brother. Sometimes, if it is a serious case concerning a cow that I have not given him, I seek for a cow with which to ask his forgiveness.

The diviner does not divine by himself, but he who goes to inquire of him says: 'Perhaps it is so-and-so who is angry, perhaps it is so-and-so because I did not give him such and such a thing, perhaps it is so-and-so, I have heard a rumour that he is angry.' Then if he mentions someone whom the diviner has also heard say that he is angry because his brother has not given him something, the diviner assents, saying: 'Yes, it is that.'

MWAISELAGE (a middle-aged pagan): When I inherited from Mwaki-sisile, my elder brother, I was just about puberty, and my senior brother [i.e. half-brother], Mwakasoule, took me to his place with all the wives, to bring me up. He was there in Mwangomo's country. I went to his home and two years running I hoed millet and it refused to grow. Then my sister said: 'Consult an oracle and see why it is.' So I went to the diviner who said: 'Your elder brother is angry because you left his grave, because you do not sweep his grave.' So I asked what to do and he told me to get millet and brew beer. So I brewed beer and left a little in a calabash overnight in the banana grove, and prayed with water. Also I left a cock. I killed a cock because I had no bull, and I left all the meat there also overnight. Then the next day the children, Angombwike and others [Angombwike was a son of the deceased] drank the beer and ate the cock. They ate all the cock, and took the first drink of the beer, and I finished it off. The diviner had told me to let the children begin first. Then next year the millet was very plentiful. I never did it again because I have never had trouble over food. If the crops had not grown I would have done it again.

AMBILIKILE (a Christian teacher): When I was a boy my mother's brother once went to fish and caught two fish in his trap. He gave them to two of his wives, the third being absent. When she came back she was angry, saying: 'They have stinted me of food'. For a long time after that he found no fish in his traps. At last he consulted an oracle. The oracle attributed it to the third wife, because she had been angry. People said that she had been angry, and that the shades of her husband were angry too, and had stopped the fish entering the trap. So my mother's brother went to the wife and said: 'The oracle attributed it to you, were you angry?' She admitted it, saying: 'I was angry, but now I am satisfied. It's all right.' So then my mother's brother took his calabash cup and went in the evening to the banana grove and prayed with water. Next morning, before noon, when men always go to examine the fish traps, he found his traps full and overflowing with fish: they were leaping about inside. Indeed, it was very remarkable. I was there, for I grew up at my mother's brother's home.

Yes, the shades hear wives, though wives never pray to them; they listen to their anger.

The first catch after such a prayer is offered to the shades.

MWANDISI: The fish, when they have been cooked, remain overnight in the banana grove. No one eats any. Then in the morning the children go there and eat. Are they not the comrades of the shades? But for us grown people it is taboo. We eat later on. That is the old custom. And formerly no one dried the fish which first entered the trap. They cooked and ate them in the house with the children. . . . If they put them to dry in the sun the shades were angry, saying: 'Where are the fish we gave you? We do not see them in the house.'

KASITILE: Sometimes it is her father's anger which prevents a girl from becoming pregnant. Perhaps she runs off with men repeatedly, then her father is angry with her. He says: 'She is squandering my cattle.' He complains (*ikwibunesya*) with his wives at the hearth and calls to mind his fathers, the shades. Then the girl does not conceive.

If later on the father forgives her, he sends a messenger to her husband, saying: 'Send me your wife, let her come and we will pray.' Then, after calling his fellows and killing a bull, he takes meat from the top of the foreleg (*mmapa*) and cuts it into pieces and puts a piece into the mouth of the girl, and she eats. They say that it is to drive the shades from the body of the girl, the shades who have caught hold of her fecundity. Some of the meat from the *mmapa* is thrown down, and the children pick it up and eat it. It is taboo for others to take and eat it.

FIBOMBE (a Christian elder): Perhaps your father has died and people have come to marry your sister; and perhaps the sister of your father (*unyokosenga*) claims one cow, saying: 'I am your father, give me one.' If you grudge it, then there is much murmuring which is heard by the shades, by your brother and your father who died. And so if your sister does not conceive people say: 'They grudged the father's sister, the shades are angry.' Then you seek a fowl and beer, and send them to your father's sister, and she puts the fowl under her bed that the shades may know it. She speaks, saying: 'Indeed I was angry.' The shades hear. That fowl opens the door; she knows that the cow is near, it is coming. She confesses everything (*ikusosya syosa*) on receiving the fowl; this she speaks in her house. You go later with the cow to bring your sister to your father's sister. Then if the girl bears at her husband's everyone says: 'Indeed it was so.'

And if your sister has run off with a man and you are angry, the shades hear. You say: 'I do not know if she will conceive there.' Then she does not bear and people say: 'Let her take her husband to her brother.' If the husband is rich perhaps he seeks two cows and a bull calf, but the cows for bringing back are not sent first, a hen is sent first with a message, saying: 'I come on such and such a day.' The hen is put under the bed. The shades know about it. I, the brother, who was angry, pray, and she bears a child. But this does not happen among Christians; there is nothing of it.

One minor quarrel occurred at a funeral we attended. Kasitile was given only a little meat and he complained, saying: 'Why do you give me a leg, I the owner of the funeral?' He took umbrage and left the funeral with his wives. Then they went to his home to say: 'We are in the wrong, we made a mistake in dividing.' Then Kasitile was satisfied and prayed over a medicine (*nkota*) which they cooked to eat. If he did not pray the medicine would go bad and would not cook. He said in his prayer: 'I have no case against them, let the medicine cook, the young men just played with the meat, it is not a serious case, may the medicine cook at once.'

(e) Reconciliation

A distinction is made by the Nyakyusa between misfortune due to the anger of senior relatives and that due to the anger of neighbours,[1] and the rituals performed are theoretically distinct, though in practice they merge into one another.

A man fears the anger of his fellow villagers who murmur against him when he has offended them, and whose cold breath is believed to fall upon him and chill him with fever or cause a paralysis. Mature men or women fear only the anger of their own neighbours, but a young man and his wife also fear their parents' neighbours. The ritual performed to lift the curse of neighbours consists in acknowledging guilt and making an offering of beer or meat for them to feast upon; then, while they eat or drink, they *admit their anger* and express goodwill.

The doctor comes beforehand and gives the sick man medicine to drink. A cow is killed. People are there and say: 'May this medicine help our child.' To drink without people there is like continuing the quarrel. People are there and they speak (*ukwijaja*), saying: 'Someone was angry, but no one is angry now. May this medicine help you.' They drink beer and eat meat saying: 'We are not angry now.' Those who were angry are present and they are satisfied. *Ukwijaja* is to speak many things, and it is like praying (*ukwiputa*) but without actually taking water and spitting.

Sometimes responsibility is fixed squarely on *either* shades *or* neighbours, but since neighbours are said to 'help a father to murmur' against an erring son, and since they may share in beef or beer offered to the shades, the rituals merge into one another, and some offerings seem to be intended to pacify *both* the shades and the neighbours, though in Nyakyusa theory the sources of

---

[1] Discussed in relation to the age-village in *Good Company*, pp. 96–108.

misfortune and the rituals are distinct. In theory, when the shades are angry the essential offering is that made in the sacred banana grove or on the hearth; it is eaten by the grandsons of the most recently dead, and whether neighbours partake or not depends upon the generosity of the officiant; whereas when neighbours are angry there is no offering in the grove or at the hearth, the neighbours are feasted, admit anger and express forgiveness.

However, neighbours are slow to admit responsibility (for to curse someone comes close to witchcraft) and in some cases there is both a formal feast for the neighbours and a prayer to the shades, and it is left uncertain where final responsibility rests. The following texts illustrate this:

MWAIKAMBO: It is the custom among us Nyakyusa to marry many wives, mature ones and young ones, so if a man has sons at his home it sometimes happens that one of them makes love to one of his father's wives. Perhaps they commit adultery in secret, perhaps he runs off with her to a distant chiefdom. Then the father breaks off relations with him.

The son, wherever he is, learns that he has been cursed by his father and his body becomes like goose flesh. If the son is wise he gathers his property and returns to his father. He takes a friend with him and goes into the house of one of his father's neighbours. His friend and his father's neighbour speak together. 'I have come to return unto my father because I have done wrong.' He tells the neighbour what they have brought to offer the father—usually a cow and a bull. Then that neighbour seeks three comrades or perhaps four or five, and they go to pacify their irate fellow, saying: 'Our child has returned. He knows that he has done wrong towards you, but we have received him because he has confessed humbly and begged forgiveness.' His father refuses furiously and almost spears himself in his passion. His fellows pacify him for the whole day, or perhaps two or three days, then at last he agrees. Then the young man and his fellows bring the cow and the bull. The father also calls together many of his fellows and he seeks beer and cooks food. They gather together at the father's homestead and the father says: 'My son has come and admitted that he has done wrong, asking that I forgive him and saying: 'I did not know what I was doing, these are the cattle which I have brought', and the others agree. Then they kill the bull. They roast some meat. The father catches one side of it, the son the other and the village headman cuts it in the middle, and the father and son each eat their piece. This is the blessing (ulusajo), meaning that there is kinship between them now. They eat together. Then all the people eat. Also with the beer it is like this. The village headman picks a straw and puts it in the beer, hands it to the father who drinks, and then to the son. Then other people drink, and they send the son into his father's house. He walks through the whole house and the mothers acclaim him. This is the sign to show everybody that he has entered his father's house. The women call the *akalulu*. They are rejoicing because he has entered.

There are, however, some who do not return to their fathers. They remain strangers [*abandu* as opposed to *abakamu*] until their death. There is a young man at my home who took his father's wife. Where he fled to no one knows because he is still in hiding. His father separated from him altogether.

A son must always bring something and the father must collect his friends. If they just agree with one another and people do not eat anything, then the son will not be settled in well. He will be ill. They say that the illness comes from the shades. If the father is angry he mutters (*ikwibunesya*) and they hear. At first the people are not angry, but later on, when they have heard from the father about the matter, they also are angry. It is as if they help the father to mutter. Their shades are not there, only those of the father's lineage, but his shades have regard to the people. If the people do not eat anything and are not present, they are not satisfied even though the father is satisfied. The father prays to his shades alone in the evening with water in his mouth, and they pour out beer on the hearth-bricks.

KASITILE: If a rich commoner has died and the heir buries him with only one cow, the shades and people are angry with the heir, breath falls on his body; perhaps he falls ill, or perhaps his child falls ill. But they do not meet; people, the witches, are angry and the shades are angry; the shades because they have buried him with only one cow, people because they have not eaten meat, but the shades and people are independent of each other. The oracle says: 'The shades are angry,' it does not speak of people. It knows that people also are angry, but it speaks only of the shades. And when he makes amends he prays in the evening; the next day he calls people and kills a cow and he throws the *ija mmapa* meat in the banana grove and says: 'Here it is, Father,' and people say: 'Indeed, he did wrong, his father was angry.' But they do not confess, saying: 'We were angry.' No, they say: 'The shades were angry.'

Another type of case is that in which 'the breath of men' is believed to have fallen on an infant because of its mother's disrespectful behaviour towards her husband's parents or husband's father's sister. When a child is thin and ailing with *ingoto*, the cure is for the mother to confess to the doctor who comes to treat the child all the rude things she has said, and provide beer (exceptionally a bull) to offer to her injured parents-in-law. They drink the beer with their neighbours and wish her well. Ambilikile's wife cited a case she had seen in which the doctor smeared the child with medicine and beer, and the mothers-in-law and fathers-in-law of the erring woman drank the beer and said: 'All right.' T. (a Christian woman) quoted another case:

One of my mother's co-wives swore at her mother-in-law. . . . When she bore a child it was very thin and ill, so they sought a doctor, and beat the mother and she confessed all she had said in swearing at my grandmother, her mother-in-law. She and the child were treated by the doctor and when her father saw that the child did not recover quickly he brought a cow in payment . . . it is still at my home. From that time the child recovered. If anyone says there is no such thing as the illness of *ingoto* they lie because I have seen it with my own eyes.[1]

When a junior comes to beg pardon of a senior it is the business of the latter's neighbours to persuade him to receive the prodigal. That was indicated in Mwaikambo's account quoted above and reaffirmed by Mwakwelebeja who cited the case of his wife's father, a youngest brother, who had run off with three of his eldest brother's widows allocated to the middle brother, *after* they had been smeared with ash and the heir had slept with them.

When they had performed the death ritual and finished it and the widows had slept with the heir in the house and had taken the *ilibalaga* to their fathers, . . . then three of the widows ran off with the younger brother. He fled with them to Masoko and to the hills, where he lived a long time and begot children with them. Then later on he brought 'the cow of the ashes (*inombe ja mfwandelo*)' to return to his senior brother. The senior received it and killed it and poured out beer. We ate.

QUESTION: Do people not refuse to receive such a cow, sometimes?

MWAKWELEBEJA: No, they fear to do so, they fear people, because the wrongdoer has come to them and it is they, the neighbours, who tell the senior kinsman: 'He has come, forgive him.' If the senior refuses they will be angry with him. Also we tell him: 'See, that man has strength to beget children with these women, you will eat the cattle.' Then he agrees and says: 'Let us make friends.'

The illness that falls on a widow who rejects the heir after being smeared with the ash is 'like a curse from the ash'. Her lover, 'if he is strong and has medicines he will escape, but if he is not strong he will fall ill . . . because he takes men's lips with him [i.e. suffers from their breath].'

---

[1] A third case, in which the beer was brought to the woman's husband, is quoted in *Good Company*, p. 236.

CHAPTER VIII

THE PARTICIPANTS

(a) Categories of participants

THE people who take part in rituals have been referred to
repeatedly and now it is possible to define who they are. They fall
into four categories: the principals, the minor actors, the congregation, and the officiants or priests. The principals are those who
undergo the full ritual lest they go mad; they are always close kin,
but what category of kin depends on the type of ritual and the
status of the person for whom it is performed. After a death, those
who *must* perform the ritual to drive away the shade are the children and grandchildren of the deceased—all of them, the widows
and the heir, if a man has died, or, if it is a woman and a senior
wife, the widower and her related co-wife if she has one.[1] A man
does not perform the ritual for a junior wife or one he has inherited. Children of a related co-wife are treated, for the purposes
of ritual, as her own children, and all must undergo the ritual, but
only some of the children of other co-wives are selected to perform
it. When a man dies the children of the heir perform it, but only
some of the children of his other brothers and half-brothers. 'We
choose some and leave the others until their own father dies.' The
genealogy given on p. 273 to show who performed the ritual on a
particular occasion illustrates this. A mother (unless she has been
divorced) performs the ritual for all her own children, and the
children of a sister who is a co-wife. A divorced woman may come
to mourn her dead child at her former husband's homestead but
she takes no part in the ritual. 'I, the husband, perform the ritual
alone; the woman comes to weep and returns to her new husband.
I, the husband, say: "The blood is mine; that bag was bought
(*alyokigwa*) with cattle; she was divorced and bought with cattle
again." ' A man performs the ritual for a son and daughter of
each wife, and grandparents perform it for some, but not all,
grandchildren.

[1] Probably also the younger sister or brother's daughter who replaces her as a wife,
but we have no conclusive evidence on this point.

Certain siblings perform the ritual, but not all of them. We have referred already to the heir, who is commonly a dead man's younger brother, and who must perform it whether he is a full brother or half-brother, and to a woman's related co-wife who may be either a younger sister or a brother's daughter. The brother or sister 'who followed at the mother's breast', i.e. the sibling immediately younger, must always perform it. Nyakyusa find it very difficult to formulate the rules—there were lively arguments between well-informed people when the question was posed —but these principles emerge from a study of those who actually participated in eight funeral rituals.

Since the funeral ritual is directed to the shades, men can only perform it in the homesteads of their agnatic kinsmen, or of their maternal grandfather or his heir: they can never perform it at the homestead of affines (*kubuko*) for there they are not kinsmen (*abakamu*) but in-laws (*abako*). Hence a husband performs the ritual for his senior wife at his own homestead and her father (or his heir) at his. 'According to custom "the husbands" (*abalume*) perform the ritual, then, when they have done so, she whom we have put in place of the dead comes to us and says: "Fathers, we have performed the ritual, perform it yourselves." ' We never saw a ritual of farewell to a dead woman at her father's house but believe it to be a modified form of the ritual performed at her husband's.

Because of the rules of avoidance, a father-in-law and daughter-in-law cannot, together, go through a ritual which involves the close proximity of the principals. When, therefore, a man performs the death ritual for a son or son's child, he performs it at his own home, and the daughter-in-law concerned does so at her husband's homestead. The widow or parents must begin, and the father or grandparents follow. Thus when Mwandisi's son's son died, the parents of the child first performed the ritual at their home and Mwandisi and his wife then followed at theirs. But in a twin ritual, where participants can be secluded, father-in-law and daughter-in-law may attend the same performance.

A woman can perform a ritual either at her father's or her husband's (as well as at her mother's father's) and she may even perform it according to two different forms, following that of her father's lineage when she is visiting him, and that of her husband's lineage when she is performing it at his homestead.

It is possible that, on the death of a man, his sisters' children sometimes perform the ritual, but we lack conclusive evidence. One case in which a sister's daughter of the deceased man performed the ritual was recorded, but at other funerals girls in the same relationship did not. Kakune, the doctor, asserted that a boy would perform the ritual for his mother's brother for 'he is mother, the brother of mother (*jo juba ulilumbu gwa juba*)', but in a number of cases we observed women performing the rituals for their brothers though their sons did not. A man's children may possibly perform the ritual for his sister but we traced no case of their doing so.

Those who drink the ritual beer when a widow returns to her father's house after her union with the heir are her father and the men of his lineage—brothers, half-brothers, sons, and some of his brother's sons; the wives and children of these; and daughters of the lineage, her own sisters and half-sisters, and sisters of her father, but *not* the husbands or children of daughters of the lineage. At one *ingotolo* ritual we attended there were present eleven men of the lineage, eighteen daughters, and thirty-two wives, as well as numerous children (cf. genealogy, Table (e)).

When a woman has died those who come to cut the banana grove and give medicated meat to her children are the *abipwa*— her brother (or his heir) and his wives.

The principals at a death ritual, then, are children and grandchildren, parents and grandparents, spouses, and certain siblings of the deceased, together with some of their children. If a woman dies, or a widow is inherited, her agnatic kin and their wives are concerned as well.

The group which takes protective medicine after an abnormal birth is larger. All the wives and children and grandchildren of the father of twins must come, his full siblings with their children and grandchildren, and the wives of his brothers, but not the husbands of his sisters; some of his half-brothers, with wives and children, some of the children of his father's brothers' sons (but not of father's brothers' daughters) and of his father's sisters' sons. On the mother's side her father, or his heirs, must take part with his wives and children, and her sisters. At the ritual for Mwakobela and his wife, previously described, we counted 136 relatives taking part, of which 24 were men, 19 boys, 33 women, 12 girls, and 35 babies (cf. genealogy, Table (a)).

When the mother of twins took the *ilibalaga* back to her 'father', her brother (heir to her father), with his wives and children, her sister immediately older than herself, the sister's daughter, and the sister immediately younger than herself, took part.

At the ritual of spearing, the principals are the children and grandchildren of the slayer and the slain, their brothers, their mother's kin (*abipwa*) and their wives. We were not able to watch any case of treatment against *ulukwego* and are not certain exactly how far the infection is thought to spread. Our informants were agreed that the number of kinsmen concerned is less than in a twin ritual, but we traced one case in which a minor chief, Mwaisumo (B.), forbade the father of a man who had killed S., the great grandson of Mwaisumo's mother's sister, to enter his country lest he spread disease among his relatives.

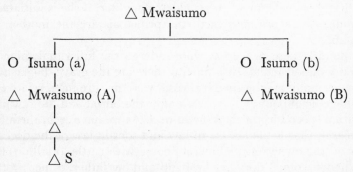

At a ritual to 'rot the ropes' those concerned are the descendants of the one who has been bound and their wives, siblings and siblings' children. At the one ritual we saw there were present 27 members of the dead man's own lineage (3 sons, 2 younger half-brothers, 1 full sister, 4 half-sisters, 3 sons, 5 daughters, 2 grandsons, 7 granddaughters), one wife, the wives of 4 sons, one father's sister's son, one son and 6 daughters of his sisters or half-sisters.

The ritual for protection against sorcery which we attended was performed at the home of the senior brother (heir to his father) of the dead woman. There were present her two brothers, their wives and children; her father's brother's daughter; two wives and one daughter of her sister's sons; her mother, two of her mother's brothers with their wives and children; two of her mother's sisters and the daughters of one of them. Her husband (who lived next door) could not take the medicine at his in-law's house, but some was sent for him to use at his home with his wives and kinsfolk.

In the simple ritual of prayer to the shades the senior kinsman who offers the prayer and blows out water acts alone but, if there has been a quarrel in the family, those members of the lineage who have been at variance must attend and share the meat or beer, and bless one another. Grandchildren, 'comrades of the shades', must eat the offering left overnight in the banana grove.

If a son has quarrelled with his father and comes to beg pardon the father calls his *neighbours* who must be present and partake of a feast and bless the young men. 'If father and son just agree with one another and people do not eat anything, then the son will not be settled in well.'

At a puberty–marriage ritual the principals are the nubile girl and her father or brother, her husband, and sometimes her mother or mother-in-law. A mother goes through the ritual with her eldest son's wife, or with her eldest daughter, if she is initiated at home. At an ordinary birth the principals are the mother and infant.

Besides these principals who undergo the full ritual there are many minor actors. At a funeral there are the grave-diggers who, traditionally among the Nyakyusa, were mature men, relatives or village neighbours.[1] They wash after the burial and are rewarded with a special leg of the funeral beef. As we have seen, the affines (*abako*), that is the fathers-in-law and sons-in-law of the deceased or of 'the owner of the funeral', come with cattle to kill or cloth. When a woman dies, her husband and her father, or her brother, kill cattle, and their affines bring cloths or, occasionally, cattle. Kinsmen—members of the lineage and their wives—and neighbours bring gifts of food to cook for the crowd of mourners, and small gifts of millet which are presented to the shade and used for making the ritual beer. After an abnormal birth, village neighbours have their legs splashed with scalding medicine but do not drink medicines or shave. The cattle of the village are also splashed. At the puberty ritual the bride's maids keep her company during her seclusion. The co-wives and neighbours of her mother and mother-in-law assist in instructing her, and the neighbours of her father join with him first in avoiding her and then in giving her gifts. Her father-in-law is identified with his brothers and his father's brothers' sons, whom she avoids, as well as his sisters, and her mother-in-law's brothers, and sisters' husbands. They, in turn, avoid her sisters, as well as herself.

By the 'congregation' we mean those who attend rituals to express sympathy, and whose presence is felt to be necessary to the

---

[1] In Ngonde they are *abatani*, cross-cousins.

success of the ritual, but who do not play any specially defined part. As we have seen, all who are reckoned kinsmen and all fellow villagers *must* attend a funeral, and a large crowd enhances the status of the kinsmen of the deceased. At a puberty and marriage ritual the 'congregation' is much smaller but is nevertheless important, as is shown by the complaint of the girl marrying a Christian that if she were not initiated she would not be famed. At other rituals all who attend are actors.

The officiants (*abanyago*) for death, puberty and marriage, and birth rituals are almost always elderly women who, by their own choice, have learnt the medicines and observances from some older *unyago* by acting as her assistant. We came across only one man who acted as *unyago* in death and puberty rituals, though at the rituals of spearing, binding with ropes, and protection against sorcery men are more common than women. Often all the elderly women are referred to as '*abanyago*' for 'they help the *unyago*', but the one who has been called upon to provide the medicines and organize the proceedings, and who is paid for her trouble, is clearly recognized. Sometimes she is a kinswoman of the 'owner' of the ritual—if a member of the lineage knows the medicines she will carry out the rituals for all her kin, as did Syungu, wife of Chief Porokoto's half-brother—but she is not necessarily a relative. It is knowledge, not kinship connections, that qualify her. She is the final arbitrator on procedure, and is insistent on exact observance of the details. Because knowledge of medicines is so important Nyakyusa often refer to the officiant at a ritual as *unganga*, a doctor, but *unyago* is the more precise word since *unganga* has other applications.

On the occasion of prayer in sickness, and in the ritual of reconciliation, no specialist *unyago* is necessary. The senior kinsman of a lineage prays to his shades direct, and a father and his neighbours receive and bless an erring son without the mediation of any priest; but the doctor called in to treat a sick man may press the kinsmen to confess their anger and bless one another (as Mwakionde did in the case quoted) and come very close to organizing a ritual of reconciliation.

At a marriage ritual there is a 'go-between' (*umfusya*) representing the bride's father and one representing the groom, and, besides their legal function as witnesses to the passage of cattle, they help the officiant to organize the ritual, and are specifically responsible for conveying invitations to the feasts. The wife of the groom's 'go-between' accompanies 'the mothers-in-law' when they go to induct or instruct the bride, and the wife of her father's 'go-between' is one of the group of mothers which takes the bride to her husband. The duties of a 'go-between' do not end at marriage: the groom's 'go-between' is responsible for taking to the bride's people the hen to announce the birth of the first child, and, among the Lugulu, the 'go-between' of the father is master of ceremonies at the ritual of vituperation.

The ideas that emerge from this analysis are, that in the *protective* rituals—after death, twin birth, spearing, binding with ropes, and death from sorcery—the parents, children, grandchildren, and some siblings, and siblings' children of the person primarily affected undergo the ritual. Links through females as well as males are recognized—daughters' children as well as sons' children attend—but they are not traced so far, and a brother's or half-brother's children attend far more often than a sister's children. Moreover, children of an unrelated co-wife perform the death ritual for a woman rather than her sister's children.

Wives always attend rituals in which their husbands are concerned—indeed, they often come with their children when their husbands stay away—but when the wife is concerned as a sister or daughter, her husband never accompanies her.

The closest relatives, such as own children, children of the heir or of a related co-wife, and proximate full siblings, must *all* participate, but the more distant relatives select representatives.

The range of relations concerned varies with the particular ritual—it is widest in the twin ritual and narrowest for an ordinary birth—and is also modified by proximity, for relatives who live near come when those in the same category living twenty miles away do not.

Affines (*abako*) never perform a ritual together even when they are next-door neighbours and close friends, but *abako* in one generation are *abipwa* (mother's kin) in the next, and a man and his *abipwa* can participate together, as in the protection against sorcery described. More often, however, the members of each lineage act separately.

Our Nyakyusa informants distinguished the officiants—*abanyago* —from those undergoing a ritual but they did not make distinctions of the sort attempted here between principals and kin who do not undergo the ritual. The distinctions they drew were between kinsmen and neighbours and between lineages. At a death ritual they distinguish *abakamu* (kinsmen) from *abandu itolo* (non-relatives) or *abapakipanga* (villagers), and *abakikolo* (those of the lineage of a dead man) from *abako* (affines) and mother's relatives (*abipwa*). These categories have different functions.

(b) Christians

The performance of family rituals is complicated by the fact that 16 per cent of the Nyakyusa are professing Christians, and in almost every lineage there are individuals who withdraw from the full performance of traditional rituals at death, puberty, and marriage, birth, and misfortune. In most cases such a withdrawal is treated tolerantly by the pagan kinsmen: the Christian kinsmen come to mourn, to congratulate the bride, to express sympathy with the parents of twins; and their non-participation in the washing and shaving and avoidance of ritual meat and beer is accepted. At the funeral of Mwamulenga his preceding full brother, who should have been a principal in the death ritual, was a Christian, and he took no part, though his children went through it. At the funeral of Mwampiki (p. 248) one boy was left untreated on the ground that he was a Christian and a Christian 'should not have two gods'. At the puberty ritual of Mwaihojo's daughter (p. 91) the brother called to wash with her was influenced by Christians and was reluctant to take part, though he finally did so.

Only when a son who is heir to family wealth, or to the office of chieftainship or priesthood refuses the inheritance of widows (as a Christian must do) is there very strong pressure on him to conform to traditional custom: the union of the heir with the widows is held essential to their health. Sometimes also there is acute conflict between different members of the family over the performance of an autopsy, the pagans pressing for it and the Christians opposing it. This we saw in the death of E. when her pagan senior brother wished to examine her, and her Christian junior brother opposed him vehemently.

That Christians cannot take part in certain of the rituals[1] and do not suffer if they omit them is generally accepted. The farewell to the dead at the homestead of the deceased, and the treatment of kinsmen of twins, fall into this category. About certain other rituals, such as the ritual of the gasping cough and the protection against sorcery, opinions are divided. Some of our Christian friends insisted that 'the gasping cough is a real illness' and cited

---

[1] There are minor differences in the rules of the different missions.

the case of a Christian who had stayed away from a ritual in his family and 'as soon as he met his relatives he fell sick and coughed like an animal. So they got some of the lees of the beer and gave it to him and he recovered.' A number of Christian kinsmen, leaders in the Church, did not come to the gasping-cough ritual which we attended, but others did come and sipped the beer, or had the lees sent to them at their homes. In the ritual for protection against sorcery which we watched a Christian brother and his wife took part.

And some Christians, though they deny the necessity of many of the pagan rituals for themselves as Christians, still believe them to be necessary to their pagan kinsmen. Hence the anomalous (and to the missionaries the highly unorthodox) position of a woman professing Christianity and acting as officiant in a pagan ritual, as did N. in the death ritual for Kalata's mother (p. 239). N., it will be remembered, came by night. The officiant who performed the ritual for Mwakobela's twins was under instruction as a Christian and was proposing to hand on her medicines to her daughter, a pagan, when she herself was received into the Church. She explained this when Mwakobela (her patient) asked her: 'And what shall we do for twin medicine when you become a Christian?' And we had little doubt that she believed in the efficacy of her medicine for pagans.

Though Christians cannot go through pagan rituals as principals they do not withdraw altogether: they often help their pagan neighbours as grave-diggers at a funeral and in the provision of food for guests at funerals and marriages; and the young men and girls may dance as a separate group, singing their own songs or hymns and ignoring the drums. Sometimes acute rivalry between the two groups of dancers is apparent.

The effect of Christian teaching on pagan ritual is not limited to the partial withdrawal of professing Christians. In those villages most influenced by missions, such as Ilolo, near Rungwe, there is considerable scepticism among pagans, and many of them curtail the rituals in their families, or do not attend them. The Christian view is that 'the pagans see that the Christians disregard the rituals and nothing happens to them, so they begin to ignore them too'. 'Pagans fear much less than they used to do.'

Men who are in European employment either inside or outside the district cannot attend all the rituals. Their case is partially met by keeping the lees of the ritual beer with which to treat them on their return home, but the general effect of modern conditions is that the solidarity of the kinship group expressed in gatherings at rituals is weakened. These changes will be discussed at length in the volume on the communal rituals after the differences between the pagan and Christian conceptions of God have been analysed.

(c) The exchange of gifts

All the family rituals are occasions for the exchange of gifts which pass primarily between lineages linked by marriage. The exchanges at different rituals are connected, and acceptance of a gift at a marriage may necessitate a return gift at a funeral. Thus the groom gives cattle for his bride at the marriage and at a funeral sons-in-law and fathers-in-law must bring cattle to kill so that they may accompany the deceased, and these are counted among the marriage-cattle given or returned. They may be kept and not killed if there are sufficient cattle to kill otherwise, but they must be offered. The obligation of affines to 'bury one another' by providing cattle for each other's funerals is even mentioned in the marriage negotiations. If a bride is not sent to replace a dead woman, marriage-cattle must be returned by her father, or at least one beast representing 'a mother to draw water for you'. So strong is the feeling that acceptance of a gift implies the obligation to make a return, that cattle offered for a marriage or funeral feast may be refused, on the ground that the family concerned do not wish to commit themselves to returning them. Angombwike described how he sweated and could eat little of a very lavish marriage feast, at which he acted as the groom's 'go-between', for he was wondering how he could make adequate return (cf. p. 253).

The greatest gifts are cattle; but fowls, cloth, beer, curds, bananas, pots, mats, firewood, ointment, cooked food and, nowadays, cash play a subsidiary part. At a funeral affines of the dead man who have no cattle, affines of the 'owner of the funeral', and close friends bring cloths. After the consummation of a marriage, or the inheritance of a widow, the new husband must give his wife a fowl, or meat, or cash representing a fowl, to take to her parents, and when she bears a child he sends another fowl. The wife's people, for their part, bring beer, ointment, firewood, mats, pots, and bananas when they take a bride or young mother back to her husband. There are also three or four exchanges of feasts between the groom's lineage and that of the bride during the puberty–marriage ritual.

Within a lineage, also, there is some circulation of property. A young man is provided with marriage-cattle by his father, or father's heir; a father kills a cow at his son's funeral, a son does likewise for his father; and if a son offends his father he begs pardon with a gift. A daughter is given a gift by her father at the close of the puberty ritual, and he or his heir kills a cow at her funeral.

Village neighbours are closely identified with the father, and feast on the bull of puberty and the offering provided by an erring son, and give gifts to a daughter when she reaches maturity.

Kinsmen and neighbours are expected to help provide food, and firewood on which to cook it, for the guests at a funeral or marriage or at a twin-birth ritual. On the first day of a funeral guests are fed on food provided by the bereaved household, on the following day on that provided by their kinsmen, and on the third day on that provided by the village neighbours. Before the marriage-cattle are brought for his daughter, a man asks his kinsmen and immediate neighbours to help him cook for 'the husbands'— not to ask for such help is unfriendly. Kinsmen and neighbours also bring gifts of millet at a funeral and after an abnormal birth, which is used for brewing the ritual beer.

(d) The symbolism of participation and exchange

What is implied by undergoing a ritual or offering gifts? Participation in a ritual implies close kinship. We see, in the rituals performed after death, or spearing, or binding with ropes, the unity of the group composed of parents, children, grandparents, and siblings; the acknowledgement of a closer link between some siblings than between others; a recognition that wives are of 'one blood' with their husbands; and a separation between kinsmen and affines who are of another blood. In the twin ritual the limits of recognized kinship are expressed by participation and in the death ritual they are expressed by attendance. Observance of the taboo of avoidance, like attendance at rituals, is taken as evidence of kinship.

The difference in the status of senior and junior wives, and of eldest and junior daughters and sons, also appears in the rituals at puberty and marriage and at death. The unity between living and dead agnatic kin and, in a lesser degree, mother's kin, is expressed again and again in the pagan rituals. The Christian with-drawal from them implies a partial break with the closed circle of kin, a movement from the nexus of kinship to that of association, from the kinship group to the congregation of believers.

The passage of cattle at marriage implies first the establishment of a bond of kinship with the wife for whom they are given. 'Kinship is cattle' (*ubukamu syo ngombe*) and a woman for whom cattle have not been given is never kin (*unkamu*) to her husband.

The passage of marriage-cattle determines the legal position of the children borne by the woman for whom they have been given. Whoever has given the cattle controls the children; and, if no cattle have passed, the girl's father (or brother) can claim them. If the woman for whom cattle have been given leaves the lineage which gave them, the cattle (traditionally all of them, together with their progeny) must then be returned, even though her original husband is dead; and when she dies she should be re-placed. Kinship between lineages once linked by marriage should ideally be permanent, and the link is reasserted in the ritual in which, when a woman dies, her brother goes to cut down the bananas at her husband's homestead and to seize her children, and has to be persuaded with a gift to desist. The identification made between women and cattle exchanged is suggested in the phrase conventionally used when no girl is available to take the place of a dead wife and a cow is offered in her place 'for drawing water with'.

The killing of cattle at a funeral, and the burial of cloths and other goods, is an expression of the idea that the dead take wealth with them. When a man requires cattle to pay compensation for some wrong committed and has not sufficient stock to do so, he turns for help to his affines, his sons-in-law and fathers-in-law, and so, when he dies, and is in need of cattle, it is felt appropriate that they should help him.

But the gifts offered at rituals have many other implications. Men take cattle and cloths to a funeral '*ukuti ndaga*'—to express sympathy—and gifts are given to a bride also '*ukuti ndaga*', which then implies congratulation rather than condolence. And gifts are used when begging pardon—a son who has sinned against his father first sends a hen and later offers a bull; and a daughter-in-law who has looked at her father-in-law or sworn at her mother-in-law must offer beer or a bull. Lastly, they are used in lifting a ban, putting an end to an avoidance. When a girl's father and his neighbours give her gifts after her initiation it is that she may 'cease to avoid them', and a woman may give a small gift to her husband's father's sister, and thereafter look at her. Nowadays, a father-in-law, in exceptional cases, kills a bull for his daughter-in-law so that she may look at him.[1]

Great prestige attaches to generosity, particularly generosity with food. A chief or village headman is one who *feeds* people, and generosity is displayed both in informal feasts for neighbours and on the formal occasions of ritual. A father who is generous in the feasts provided for his daughter at her initiation and marriage gains prestige; if he is stingy his affines and his neighbours comment on it; he both loses their respect and fears lest he may even fall ill from 'the breath of men'. If the groom's family fail to provide sufficient, the bride's father does not hesitate to scold them for it, and they reply with humility which may be so exaggerated as to verge on boasting. It is conventional for the groom to plead poverty but at the same time he and his kin compete with the bride's family in preparing quantities of fine food. The pride and excitement over feasts is clearly brought out in the comments on funerals, the remarks of a mother on the return of her daughter to her husband after the birth of the first child, and Angombwike's account of marriage negotiations and gifts (pp. 31–4, 148, 253–5). The principals in any ritual are the centre of attention and may gain prestige from its performance, as a bride does, but what concerns the Nyakyusa much more is the reputation of the family serving the feast. Here the emphasis is very different from what it is in the Pondo ritual for the initiation of diviners, or the Lunda rituals of misfortune.

[1] cf. Monica Wilson, *Good Company*, p. 85.

CHAPTER IX

THE NYAKYUSA CONCEPTION OF REALITY

(a) The symbolic pattern

AFTER these lengthy descriptions and interpretations of family rituals, we at last approach our goal, viz. an analysis of the symbolic pattern of the Nyakyusa people. Contrary to the commonly held theory that ritual is always more constant than interpretation, we find variations in the details of ritual related to variation in descent, but the conceptions expressed vary very little. Some symbols (such as the plantain representing a male and the sweet banana representing a female) occur in all the rituals; others are peculiar to one or other of the cultural groups, but recur in all, or several, of the rituals of that group. Our informants constantly made cross-references between different rituals; the more conscious were aware both of a recurrent symbolic pattern in the rituals of their own dialect group and of a common content with the rituals of other groups. It is clearly recognized, for example, that the foods used in ritual vary with the resources of the area; that the Kukwe cast away the shade by allowing pebbles placed between their fingers and toes to wash down-stream and by burning grass necklaces in which they have slept, while the Nyakyusa do it by throwing away a stem of bananas; in short, that differing ritual idioms express common sentiments.

The framework of all the rituals (save those of misfortune) is the *induction* with a formal laying of the litter of banana leaves in a hut into which the participant is brought to live apart from other people; the retreat or *seclusion* during which he lives and eats apart and is regarded as filthy, for he is 'brooded over' by the shades; and the *bringing out* when the shades are driven away and he is purified. During the seclusion not only is the participant filthy, but he *may* not wash or shave or use cosmetics; in the death ritual he embraces the corpse, smears himself with mud and ash, and mimes the actions of a madman, eating filth, casting off his clothes, and, in the Kukwe version, being mocked at as a fool. The madman is filthy like a corpse and mourners accept identi-

fication both with corpse and shade. In other rituals the identification is with the shade alone, but still the participant is felt to
be filthy and close to madness. The symbols of purification are
many: clearing and burning the litter, burning the clothes or
leaves worn during the seclusion, elaborate and repeated washing
and shaving, and anointing the body with rouge and oil. One
aspect of purification is the driving away of the 'filthy' shade
symbolized first by throwing away pebbles or a stem of bananas
into a running stream; and, secondly, by casting seeds into a pot
which is put on the fire, grinding millet in the doorway and letting
it fall on bark-cloth, putting various parts of the body on the fire
symbolically and grinding them symbolically, passing a winnowing basket of millet between the legs, scattering millet, and dancing
the trampling dance. The second group of symbols all represent
sexual intercourse. Seed or grain is identified with semen, fire with
intercourse, bark-cloth and the round winnowing basket—a
woman's basket *par excellence*—represent the woman, and putting
seeds on the fire, grinding, passing the basket of millet between the
legs, and probably also the trampling dance[1] represent the sex
act. The shade is thought to be ejected from the body as semen,
and therefore intercourse is a means of driving the shade from the
body.

An element of the death ritual is the separation of corpse and
spirit, the final disposal of the corpse, and the bringing of the new
shade back 'to warm himself with the other shades' at the family
hearth: he is received as the water which drips from the doorway
of the hut, and welcomed to the hearth with music; but the distinction between the corpse which is got rid of and the shade
which is welcomed is not maintained systematically. Repeatedly
our informants spoke of the shade (*unsyuka*) being driven away
from dreams and waking thought, and from men's bodies, as well
as being separated from the corpse. The aim of Nyakyusa ritual
is not that union with God constantly sought in Christian ritual,
but a separation both from the shades and the heroes; for close
association with the pagan gods spells madness and death, not full-
ness of life. A measure of separation from the shades is a condition
of fertility as well as of sanity. Intercourse cannot be fruitful until
the shades of her father's lineage have 'moved aside a little' from
the nubile girl, the shade of a deceased husband from his widow.

[1] The action of the trampling dance and the contexts in which it occurs at death
and puberty suggest this, but such an interpretation was not explicitly given.

meat is offered in the bride's father's grove; the two symbols of first intercourse—treatment with *undumila* medicine and jumping over fire; the recognition of the end of childhood by calling on the bride's mother to put her down off her back; the insistence that she show modesty before her father and his fellows as before a father-in-law; and the taboo on crossing water lest her menstrual flow become like a river.

The twin ritual is characterized by the fear of infection from too great potency, and the treatment with scalding medicines to 'burn' the twin birth.

Sometimes our informants gave different interpretations of the same symbol and there was no agreement between them, as with the stem of bananas stolen in the Kukwe death ritual, and the bunch of flowers brought back from the stream. Nsyani said stealing the bananas symbolized that 'we may now eat other people's food', and Mwamulenga that it was a symbol of driving away disease. Kakune, the doctor, interpreted the bunch of flowers brought back from the stream as a symbol of the shade which was brought home; Mwamulenga saw picking and carrying flowers as yet another symbol of the actions of a madman. Though there was general agreement over the interpretation of many symbols, it is possible that some have no commonly accepted meaning, but suggest different things to different people. It is clear, however, that with the Nyakyusa, as with ourselves, one symbol has often several associations for the same person, and Kasitile and the more self-conscious of our informants were aware of this. For Kasitile the banana in the death ritual is the corpse and the pumpkin-seeds in it the shade; it is also faeces which madmen eat; it is also, in the puberty ritual, the male organ and the seeds are the semen. Eating a banana is a symbol *both* of copulation and of the actions of a madman. Conversely, the same object or action is symbolized in many different ways—there are nine or ten symbols of sex intercourse, and twenty of driving away the shade, recorded in the texts quoted above.

When an action recurs in different rituals, informants almost always interpreted it in the same way in each context: the exception was the trampling dance (*ukukanya inganya*) interpreted as a way of 'driving away the shade' in the death ritual and a 're-joicing' in the puberty ritual. It was always explained as 'customary'. 'Father and grandfather did it.'

This brings us to the ultimate explanation given for all the rituals: 'they are customary' (*lulwiho*), 'they come to us from long ago', 'our fathers and grandfathers performed them'; and established in the nature of the universe: 'Kyala made us black people like that.'

(b) The nature of the shades

The nature of the shades is revealed in Nyakyusa rituals, and we are now in a position to summarize their attributes.

The shades, 'those who have risen from the dead', are the dead members of a lineage and, unless they were ruling chiefs when alive, they have power only over their own kinsmen, and are concerned only with behaviour between members of the lineage, not with behaviour towards outsiders. As we have seen, the shades of her father's lineage 'move aside a little' from a woman when marriage-cattle and the bull of puberty have been given for her but, if these are still owing, it is thought that her child as well as she herself may be made ill by her father's shades. Membership of a lineage is determined by the passage of marriage-cattle: a child belongs to the group which provided cattle for its mother. Therefore, it is argued, the shades of the lineage which provided the cattle, and they alone, if the payment has been made in full, have power over children. If no cattle have been given the child is in the power of the mother's shades. But there are difficulties over the *ikipiki* medicine, for only that of the genitor's lineage can safely be used, and its use implies membership of the lineage that provides it. There is a further idea that shades only have power over those living in a homestead of their lineage. 'A child is never made ill by the mother's shades when it is in the father's homestead, only when it is with its mother's people.'

The dead dwell beneath (*pasi*), in 'the land of the shades' (*kubusyuka*), which is a shadowy reflection of the land of the living, with homesteads and gardens, wives and cattle, villages and chiefdoms.

MWAIKAMBO: People think that in the land of the shades they build homes like we do, they marry wives, they have children, they plant food and build houses. I heard this always from old men, but they only guess. They say: 'Perhaps it is nice, perhaps horrible.' They do not know very much. They fear to die. I have never met any old pagan man who wanted to die, they always fear. Property is important: People are much taken up with the idea that riches are there in the land of the shades. They say: 'If a man dies his fathers come to receive him, but if they find he has no cows with him they are angry, they do not receive him with rejoicing. If they do not kill some cattle at the burial of a dead man without doubt illness will come to the home. I they consult an oracle then the oracle says: 'Your fathers beneath are angry because you did not kill cattle for the burial of So-and-so.' So then they go and kill a beast. When they kill cattle at a death they do not kill for the mourners to eat, no, but they say it is that the fathers may receive him well, that they may not be angry.

The shades manifest themselves to the living in dreams or as snakes, and they come by night to the homestead to eat food set aside for them in the sacred grove or the senior wife's hut.

Whenever food is cooked a little is left for the shades. It is said that the shades come by night to eat the food. Some people say that they have seen the shades when they come to warm themselves by the fire in the house. If the fire of the shades blazes up, and I look, it is extinguished immediately, and if someone turns round the hut is quite dark. People eat the food which they put for the shades, they do not throw it away. Sometimes, if the food rots, they say it is because the shades have eaten from it. People say that if they do not put aside food the shades will take away the fertility of the fields and we will not have much food.

The hearth is a shrine: the food and beer are left overnight beside the hearth or on the hearth-bricks. Every good housewife has a log of firewood which she keeps by her all her life: she takes it with her when she moves and it is burnt at her funeral. 'It is the shades'. The shades [of her husband] pick bits from it when they want to warm themselves at the fire.' And the wife herself must keep out of the way: 'Some men refuse to let their wives sleep near the fire at night, saying: "You will drive away the shades." '

The association of a small grove of bananas in each homestead with the shades has already been stressed. There meat and beer offered in sacrifice are left. There is also a connection, most obvious among chiefs, but occurring among commoners also, between the shade and a chosen tree. In Ngonde Mwenefumbo said:

The fathers prayed at the grave of their father. If a man moved he took *ilindu*, a branch of the tree at the grave, and carried it to his new home and there put it in a tree he had chosen, saying: 'Now you have arrived, Father.' He poured out beer and flour there and invoked all his fathers and grandfathers and ancestors, saying: 'May I sleep! Gather and eat these things! May the children sleep.' Then he blew out water and finished.

Among the Nyakyusa men spoke often of the obligation of the heir to keep the grave of his father swept and tended. Graves are in the open courtyard of the homestead and the meticulous weeding and sweeping of this space by the owner and his young sons is thus an act of piety, as well as a means of achieving 'dignity' in the homestead.[1]

The shades are also identified with the earth—'the earth *is* the shades (*umfu bo basyuka*)'—and offerings to them are buried, or laid upon, or poured out on it. To say 'the earth is angry' means: 'the shade is angry.' Stories are told of prophets (*abasololi*) who have descended to the land of the shades and returned, and of others who have seen men in the land of the shades while they are yet alive. That is a sure sign of their future death, though it may be delayed. And there are tales of those who have seen the dead with the cattle killed at his funeral. 'We say those are the shadows (*imisyungulu*) which go to the land of the shades.'

A soft, tufty grass, used as bedding for cattle, is called 'blessed' (*ikisajelo*) and is known as 'the doorway of the shades' (*ikifigo kya basyuka*). The tale of three prophets who uprooted a tuft of it and saw the land of the shades beneath has already been related (p. 77).

ANGOMBWIKE: As a child at my grandfather's I heard that the water from the blessed grass reaches the land of the shades, and that if the shades wish to come to our place they stand there in the blessed grass and where they have stood there is no dew. Indeed, there is never dew on the blessed grass.

At this point in the conversation one of us went to examine the blessed grass and called back: 'But there is dew on it.' Another man who was listening broke in indignantly: 'Is there much dew? There is very little!' and, indeed, there was less than on other types of grass.

But though the shades dwell beneath and visit the homesteads of their kinsmen seeking food and warmth, they are also *within* men—*munda* (in the belly)—they create desire, they control conception, and are ejected in intercourse as semen. 'If you have not got a shade you are impotent, sterile, you do not go to women.'

The shades delight in cattle, and though they demand certain sacrifices they are unwilling that cattle of the lineage should die unncessarily. Mwakwelebeja told us:

---

[1] cf. Monica Wilson, *Good Company*, p. 77.

My bull was wounded. When I tried to kill it, it troubled me, it did not die. I took a banana sapling and chewed it and prayed to my fathers, saying: 'This bull has been wounded because it was destroying people's crops. I am killing it because the people are angry with me and they might spear me in the night if I don't kill it.' My son struck it the third time, then it bellowed and I said: 'Yes, they have heard my prayer,' and it fell down and died. The shades were preventing it dying because they liked it to be alive. The whole country liked this bull because of its beautiful bellowing.

The shades are very real to an old man like Mwakwelebeja:

We live with the shades, constantly the fathers come to us, and also a wife who has died. The shades rise and come to us. In the morning I wake up and tell my wife the shades came to me, I slept with them, and with the wife who has died.

QUESTION: Why do they come?

MWAKWELEBEJA: You just dream. Sometimes they speak something, and in the morning I tell my wife they said so-and-so. Sometimes they bring food. If a sick man dreams that he eats their food he will die. If he dreams that he visits them and they drive him away he will recover. Sometimes I dream of my father or of my mother, sometimes of the villagers, So-and-so, and So-and-so. Yes, we fear to dream of the shades, even if we don't eat food. We fear that if they come often we will follow them.

And even to young men like Kititu they seem near:

Yes, the shades come to us in dreams at night. Perhaps I dream of my father who has died, he appears, he gives me a cow, I wonder, it seems that I have gained that cow. I rejoice and am glad. This is all in a dream. Perhaps my mother has died and I dream of her. She gives me food as it were on this table. I eat, I drink beer with her. Our grandfathers used to dream of war. When the Ngoni were in the country they would dream that they and the shades, the fathers who had died, were fighting with the Ngoni; in the dream they would spear them and the blood would appear. All men dream, but those whose dreams come true we call *abasololi*—prophets. These men sometimes dream of public matters, as well as private, they go to Kasitile [the priest] and say: 'Hunger is coming, carry out the ritual in the sacred grove.' Then they take a cow, bananas, and milk to the sacred grove as Kasitile says. Then there are those who fall into a fit and the friends of such a man go to Kasitile and tell what he said.

Perhaps I dream of my father or grandfather, and he comes and gives me food. I know him by his appearance in the dream. Perhaps my grandfather died while I was still a child, but I know him by his dress

P

of which the basic rule is the separation of the reproductive activities of successive generations.

If my wife goes to the inner part of my mother's house, it is a wrong. Perhaps she will bear a thin and sickly child. She has gone to the inner part of her in-law's house and my mother is angry with her for going where my father goes. Perhaps, when she is first pregnant, my wife goes to the back of her own mother's house. That is a wrong, too. Perhaps she will have a difficult labour. The trouble in both cases comes from the anger of the elders, my mother's in the first case, her mother's in the second. It is said that if my wives have seen my father by inheritance, then, when I die, the fathers who are dead will not receive me because I have injured ('kept back') their younger brother. I think, for my part, that the pagans honour this custom [of avoidance] very much because they say that the shades will be angry if it is neglected.

Apart from the neglect of rituals, the types of behaviour commonly believed to be directly punished by the shades are (1) quarrels between father and son or between brothers, turning on the seduction of a senior's wife by his junior, on the sharing of marriage-cattle or, nowadays, on the sharing of the earnings of a young man working for wages, or on his seduction of women which necessitates the payment of fines by his father; (2) quarrels between father and daughter or father-in-law and son-in-law turning on the handing over of marriage-cattle by the son-in-law and the provision of gifts for his daughter by the father; (3) quarrels between husband and wife; (4) quarrels between relatives of all sorts over failure to attend, or to invite to, rituals; and (5) the neglect of his wards by the heir.

Cases of family quarrels over seduction leading to misfortune have already been quoted (pp. 134–5; 187–8). One concerning cattle and earnings was cited by Mwakwelebeja. A young man, X., went out to work and left the cattle he earned with his elder full brother. When he married he took all these cattle and gave them to his father-in-law. His elder brother was very angry. X. said: 'I take all the cattle for you have never given me any of yours.' His brother replied: 'How could I give you cows? I have no children.' Then all the cattle X. had given to his father-in-law died and had to be replaced. 'The shades were angry because when the younger brother took the cows his elder brother complained very much.' And if a young man goes out to work and gives his father no share of his earnings the shades are angry: 'Perhaps I will fall ill; perhaps when I look for work I shall not find it. There are many cases like that. My friends in the age-village will go to a diviner who will declare that the shades are angry because I do not care for my father.' If a daughter makes a runaway marriage her father is angry and it is believed that either she may not conceive or her baby may be ailing until the marriage-cattle and bull of puberty have been given by her husband and accepted by her father.

The respect and obedience due to a father is due to his heir, and in certain circumstances to his sister also; while on his part the heir has the same obligations to his juniors as the deceased had. Fibombe cited the example, already quoted, of a man quarrelling with his dead father's sister over the distribution of the marriage-cattle for his own sister, and the girl failing to conceive because of the anger of her father's sister. If a son, whose parents are dead, neglects to provide his sister with the customary gifts of food when she returns to her husband after a visit to her 'father', he may become impotent: 'Those below are angry and when he has be-gotten twins he will have trouble at the ritual.' Or the girl may fall ill. 'She thinks: "Who is my father? This is my father, but he does not care for me." ' The mystical power of a senior relative is linked directly with his obligation to give gifts:

My father's elder half-brother has power over me only if he has given marriage-cattle for my father or nurtured him. If he has given him cattle to marry a wife then he has power over him. . . . My superior (*mbala gwangu*) is he who gives me everything.

Favouritism in a polygynous family, shown in the unfair division of milk or meat or fish by the husband between his wives, is thought to anger the shades, which cause his cows to bleed from the udder when milked, or prevent fish entering his traps, and so do the bad temper and insulting language of a quarrelsome wife. Mwakwelebeja explained that:

If a woman is bad-tempered when she is making beer the beer goes sour. If my wife and I quarrel my shades are angry and the beer is spoiled. I say to my wife: 'You have spoiled the beer because you do not listen to what I say.'

Neglect of his wards by the heir is a wrong-doing frequently mentioned.

It is said that if I neglect my brother's children he and my father will be very angry, they will not come to meet me when I die, as the

shades usually do, and I shall wander a long time on the way to the
land of the shades because I shall have no relatives to show me the way.
And then when I get there I shall still have trouble. They will drive
me away from them, and I shall live alone, apart from them, quite
separate.

More rarely a shade is said to be angry because his grave has
been left unswept, or he has not been buried where he asked to
be.

The kinds of behaviour believed to be punished by 'the breath
of men' are very similar to those thought to be punished by the
anger of senior kinsmen; and, indeed, as we have seen, kinsmen
and neighbours may murmur together against a son who has
seduced his father's wife, a girl who has behaved insultingly to her
parents-in-law, either verbally or by a breach of avoidance, and
an heir who has neglected his wards or has neglected the customary ritual for his father, more particularly the customary killing of a cow when he enters into his inheritance. It is said that
neglect to provide them with certain customary feasts infuriates
neighbours more than anything else.[1]

The misfortunes that threaten from the neglect of rituals, and
from the anger of kinsmen and neighbours, are loss of sanity, of
life or health or fertility; a difficult labour or a lingering death;
repeated miscarriages; loss of beauty (a wicked woman goes bald
or turns reddish); scanty crops or sick herds, or, nowadays, un-
employment—the man whose father is angry does not find a job.
Only rarely is it suggested that punishment may be postponed
until after death and then what is feared is that the shades of the
lineage will not receive their kinsman.

When Nyakyusa talk about their religion they speak mostly of
external things, of the rituals, of the angry words spoken by kinsmen or neighbours and of the fearful effects upon one against
whom this anger is directed. Misfortune is said to be brought
down on a man by his parents muttering in anger over the fire, by
people murmuring against him (the word used is that for the
humming of a hive of bees). The emphasis is on outspoken complaint or criticism. But it is also thought that 'the shades see what
is within a man': if he stints one wife of fish, then 'even though the
woman herself has not said anything, the shades hear the thought
of the belly'. Sleeplessness and an unquiet mind are taken as
evidence of the anger of the shades or the attacks of witches.

[1] cf. Monica Wilson, *Good Company*, pp. 105–6.

'*Tutigona* (we do not sleep),' is the formal phrase with which the village headman and other responsible people notify the chief that all is not well with the country, or with which a woman or a junior kinsman prefaces the troubles brought to the notice of the head of the homestead, when these troubles have not obviously materialized in sickness. Anger is dangerous first and foremost to the person against whom it is directed, but there is also the suggestion that it may react on the person who is angry. We have already quoted the remark: 'A woman never murmurs against anyone. If she does she falls sick herself.'

How the fear of the shades is inculcated in a child is shown in the following text:

I began by learning the word or name: *unsyuka*, and to know that the shade (*unsyuka*) was someone who had died, and people said that they were like flickering shadows (*imisyungulu*). Also people said a shade is someone very awesome (*nsisya*) if he appears to you. When I began to think of the shades at night I could not sleep because I feared the awfulness (*ubusisya*) of which they spoke. And this was specially told: 'If a person dies to-day, and perhaps you have not heard, then that dead man appears to you with cattle. He is smeared with earth on his face and forearms and knees. Then, because you do not know anything, you say: "Friend," and talk with him, saying: "Where are you going with the cattle?" He says: "I am going to my in-laws." Then if you go home and find they are wailing a death, and you tell your tale, they say: "So-and-so has died, you met him." They say you also will die. But you must be silent, and only speak after they have buried him.' So in my belly, in my thought, the shades appeared very fearful. Many people compare the awfulness of the shades with that of wild animals, and say the awfulness of the shades is greater. If a shade is standing here, and a wild animal there, you will flee towards the animal. So I also thought. But later I changed my mind, and said I would go towards the shade.

Once when there was some sickness at home I heard it said that the shades were angry, perhaps because there had been a quarrel, perhaps because he [*sic*] had not killed a cow for a relative's funeral. Once when I was ill with sores round the mouth, people said: '*Mindu*, the shades have created them'—that was to be 'beaten' by the shades. So, when they had consulted an oracle, they poured a little beer on the fire-bricks and prayed. Then the illness disappeared very quickly. When I asked my mother about it she said: 'The shades were angry, so you were ill. It was because your father was angry, or perhaps on some other account.' Thus I learnt the work of the shades, little by little, from illnesses among my parents and stories of my elders.

There is much more talk among the Nyakyusa of misfortune from the shades or the anger of neighbours, than of blessing, but there is an idea, somewhat vague but real, that generosity and kindliness will bring blessing (*ulusajo*). Ambilikile, a Christian teacher who had grown up in a pagan home, said:

My mother tells me that my father was in the habit of feeding people, those who were not his relatives. People went to a distance and brought medicines for fertility and gave them to him, hence they said: 'He is very kind; food never grows short at his home.' She also told me that my father died very old. He did not die of disease, but of old age, no breath being left in him. This was because men were always saying: 'May they stand by him, may they bless him (*bammwemelege, bansajege*),' not to his face but to others. They said that he lived long because of the blessing of men. Yes, they say that the food of a kindly man never gets finished, that of a stingy man finishes; he himself suffers hunger.

Mwaisumo described a father on his death-bed blessing a favourite son, allocating cattle to him, and telling him:

Care for the children I have left, keep on good terms with them, then you will be rich in everything like your father. I cared for my children, I was not harsh (*nkali*), so complain to me of anything that troubles you. If you are like this the property in your home will be plentiful, people will be astonished and say: 'He is like his father.'

Of a man given a cow by the chief, it was sometimes said: 'The shades have blessed him; he has a righteous (*ngolofu*) shade.'

Although our Nyakyusa informants talked a great deal about the danger of neglecting rituals and angering senior relatives, living and dead, the number of cases of misfortune attributed to their anger is small in comparison with the number attributed to witchcraft or 'the breath of men'. (Ten as compared with sixty-three.) There is no reason to suppose that one type of case was concealed when the others were reported to us, and it is clear that the Nyakyusa prefer to make neighbours in the age-village, rather than kinsmen, the scapegoat for their misfortunes. Even when the wrong done is against a kinsman it is often the neighbours, rather than the shades, who are said to have brought punishment on the wrong-doer.

At the same time, we were assured by one informant after another that people blame the shades or Kyala for misfortune when it is really the neighbours who are responsible! Angombwike argued that men fear to accuse the neighbours, who are slow to admit their anger, and prefer to blame the shades and conciliate the neighbours by feasting. For example:

When someone is ill of a curse the owners of the village do not agree that it is they who have bewitched him. No, that is what others say. . . . When they bless such a person they pray to the shades. As, for example, with M. [informant's father, a wealthy man]. If he falls ill with a disease of the legs, and goes to a diviner, and the diviner says: 'They have bewitched you,' then he goes home and seeks a bull and calls the men of the village, saying: 'Let us enjoy ourselves with this bull.' They say: 'Is it the legs?' He denies it, saying: 'No, I am just giving you something to eat, something with which to enjoy ourselves.' They say: 'Are you a chief to feast us on a bull?' He says: 'I just thought I would like to enjoy myself with you.' He conceals the cause because if he speaks of the illness they will say: 'Ha, he is catching us for witchcraft.' They eat, and at the beer they say: 'You, M., take this stick and stand up. Walk!' And when they go home each prays to his shades, saying: 'Stand by him, may he recover from his sickness!'

In short, the Nyakyusa speak of the danger of angering senior relatives, but they attribute most of their misfortunes to their neighbours, and they say that more misfortunes are due to neighbours and fewer to the shades than is openly admitted!

Perhaps the most striking feature of the family cult among the Nyakyusa is the narrowness of its range. Neighbours are concerned with the fulfilment of family obligations as well as obligations to themselves, but the shades are concerned solely with behaviour between kinsmen. 'If I wrong a kinsman I fear the shades, but not if I wrong another.'

CHAPTER X

THE SOCIOLOGICAL ANALYSIS OF THE
RITUALS OF KINSHIP

(a) The symbolic expression of structural relationships

THE rituals of kinship express, first and foremost, the differentiation and the unity of agnatic lineages. In all the rituals we have discussed members of a lineage act together as a distinct group, bound together by common 'blood' which is symbolized by the *ikipiki* medicine. 'It is our kinship, it is our blood.' A member of the lineage is protected by it, and illegitimate children who are not of the lineage may not share it. The new-born infant drinks it with his mother whose breasts are washed with it; the nubile girl washes with her father or brother, thinking: 'I have fathers, I am no bastard.' Its use is an acknowledgement of agnatic kinship and legitimacy.

A lineage includes the living and dead, who have communion together, sharing *ikipiki* medicine and food and beer, in most of the rituals of the cycle. 'All the food which we have eaten you have eaten.' And the dead receive the dying of their lineage. 'The shade has created us, we come from him, we die, we go there to him; not to others, but to him.' The shades cause menstruation and sexual desire, and men and women cannot produce children without their support. Therefore reproductive power is controlled by the lineage, and virginity is something valuable to it.

A woman is a member of two lineages. At marriage she is partly transferred to her husband's lineage. She washes with *ikipiki* medicine with her husband and 'using it means that the bride is now of his lineage'. When the bull of puberty has been handed over the shades of her father must 'move aside a little' that she may conceive by her husband, but still the bond with her father's lineage is not severed. 'The blood' of a married woman is created by her shades and those of her husband together. Both sets control procreation, though the inference is that her father's shades cease to have control when *all* the marriage-cattle have been handed over.

Yet still she remains a daughter of her father's lineage and shares in its rituals as well as in those of her husband's.

Lineages are linked by marriage and kinship between them is established by the passage of cattle. The son-in-law becomes 'one blood' with his parents-in-law when they drink the beer brewed or eat the chicken killed at the consummation of the marriage; some of his semen is buried in his father-in-law's grove, and his spear is placed in his father-in-law's hut. The significance of the link is magnified by the thicket of taboos which surrounds 'mixing bloods', and once forged the link should be, and commonly is, retained long after the deaths of the individuals by whom it was created, for each is replaced, the husband by a brother or son, the wife by a sister or brother's daughter. For each heir the ritual of 'mixing bloods' is performed afresh reminding them of their separation and union.

Cattle are closely identified with men and therefore with lineages. The shades watch over them. Like men, they are in danger from women who are ritually impure; at the death of their owner they, too, mourn; and kinship relationships are established and expressed by their transfer from one lineage to another. 'Kinship is cattle.'

The distinction and opposition of lineages is apparent in the ritual of puberty and marriage which expresses both hostility and conciliation. The two lineages dance in rivalry, haggle over cattle, and exchange feasts. Among the Nyakyusa, the opposition is not between men and women, as suggested by some recent writers on rituals elsewhere,[1] but between lineages; though the men and the women, both of the groom's party and the bride's, act separately. The hostility and conciliation reach their culmination in the ritual of vituperation among the Lugulu, when groom's group and bride's insult each other by word and in action and then, at the instance of the master of ceremonies, praise each other and feast together.

Among the Nyakyusa there is no clan organization and no common name for a lineage of many generations like the Pondo *isiduko*, which identifies agnatic kinship within a large group. A common name is used by members of a lineage of three or four generations at the most, and among commoners there is no invocation of a distant ancestor as among the Pondo. The hero

[1] E. Fromm, *The Forgotten Language*; M. Gluckman, 'The Role of the Sexes in Wiko Circumcision Ceremonies', in *Social Structure*, edited by M. Fortes (1949).

referred to is not necessarily an ancestor of those who speak of him. In the rituals the participants look towards the direction from which their ancestors came, and the details vary both with the cultural area and with the particular lineage, but similarity in ritual observance is no ground for claiming kinship. The one recognized bond is common participation—attending one another's funerals and observing the rules of avoidance.

The segmentation of lineages is by houses. Ties between full siblings are closer than those between half-siblings and this is immediately apparent in the attendance at, and participation in rituals, as the genealogy of Mwakobela (Table (a)) shows. Full siblings, particularly successive and linked siblings, are closely identified. The most important link between men or women is inheritance. The heir takes the name and social position of the deceased, succeeding to his or her rights and obligations, and observing the same avoidances. 'A shade is resurrected in the body of his child.' The heir is a junior[1] man or woman of the lineage, preferably a full brother or sister, but possibly a half-brother or sister, or parallel cousin, or a son, or brother's son, or brother's daughter.

When the heir is a son, or brother's son or daughter, the separation so strictly maintained between generations is bridged for that individual only; he or she changes generation and a man is treated by his former comrades as a 'father' and referred to by his wives as 'father-in-law', even though they are still his wives and live with him.

The identification of alternate generations is expressed in calling grandchildren ('the comrades of the shades') to eat the sacrificial meat or fish, or take the first sip of beer, as well as in the absence of taboos between affines of such alternate generations. A woman does *not* avoid her husband's grandfather. Thus, though the lineage is treated in some respects as a unit, one man (or woman) of it being able to replace another and override the distinction between successive generations, the unity is not pushed as far as among many other peoples, such as the Pondo, where the form of behaviour appropriate to a father-in-law applies to *all* senior members of his lineage irrespective of generation.

Differences in status within the lineage are clearly shown in the rituals. In their observance seniors precede juniors, men precede

---

[1] If there is no junior full brother, a senior full brother may inherit provided that he has not previously inherited from his father and so become 'father'.

women, daughters of the lineage precede wives. Seniority, of course, does not depend solely on age, and we once saw a little boy precede his father in the performance of a ritual for his grandmother, with whose generation he was identified. The relative status of husband and wife is expressed in the taboo on a woman 'overstepping' her husband physically or metaphorically, and 'overstepping' is symbolized (oddly to a Christian) by the sign of a cross. The precedence of the chief wife is very marked. In commoner families she alone washes with her husband using the *ikipiki* medicine, and he performs the death ritual for her only. A chief may do this for two wives. In Selya a father washes in the puberty ritual with his senior daughter, and among the Kukwe a woman washes with her daughter or eldest son's first wife. 'To wash is to admit that I have lived, and borne a child, and grown up.'

All the rituals celebrate a change in status, and danger lies in not recognizing or admitting the change, in clinging to the past. This is most obvious in the death ritual, which is directed to the separation of the living and the dead. The mourners have the corpse 'on their bodies', they may not separate themselves from him by washing till the appropriate moment, and they share their food and *ikipiki* medicine with the shade, thereby recognizing him as a kinsman; but in due course they drive him off: 'You were our kinsman before but now it is finished, you are a stranger.' 'You are no relative of ours.' 'We are not corpses.' And at the same time they bring him back transformed, as a beneficent spirit in the home. The pattern is a common one in Bantu Africa: the Nyakyusa peculiarity is (1) the speed with which the transformation is achieved (commonly the 'bringing back' of the spirit is delayed a year, whereas the Nyakyusa may delay only a month); and (2) the close correspondence between the change in status of the dead and the change in status of the older generation, who 'move aside' at the 'coming out'. Each generation has its day and must give place to the next.

All through the rituals the dominance of the agnatic lineage is evident, but it does not exclude the recognition of kinship in the female line. Daughters' children *must* perform the ritual at death, twin birth, spearing, and binding with ropes, for their grandparents, while some sisters' children, and father's sisters' sons, may do so also. What is clear from the genealogies is that kinship links in the female line are not traced as far as in the male line and, though wives are assimilated to their husbands' lineages for ritual purposes, men play no part in the rituals of their wives' lineages.

The second fundamental principle expressed in the rituals of kinship is that a moral law holds within the lineage. Senior kinsmen, living and dead, have a mystical power over their juniors, but their anger is dangerous only if it is just. They cannot mutter irresponsibly. Kinsmen are 'members of one another' in the sense that the life and death of one affect the others. The sins of a father are visited on his children, his juniors in the lineage (though a woman's sins affect only her own husband and children), and the very fact of kinship makes a mystical bond between agnatic kin, descendants of a common great-grandfather, and a man and his daughters or sister's children. The moral law is thought to operate also within the age-village, where the just are protected and the evil punished by 'the breath of men'; but within both lineage and village irresponsible and malicious injury by witches or sorcerers is possible.

When misfortune occurs the sufferer, and his kinsmen and neighbours, seek an explanation in conflicts and ritual omissions, and interpret the misfortune in terms of these, putting the possible alternatives before the oracle. Thus the danger of conflict with kinsmen and neighbours, and of neglect of ritual, is constantly before men's minds. In practice, there is a strong tendency to push the blame for misfortune outside the lineage of living and dead on to the neighbours.

(b) *The celebration of rituals and maintenance of the structure*

In any society the practical, intellectual, and emotional aspects are mutually dependent; the practical organization is dependent upon, and at the same time supports, an intellectual system— certain cosmological ideas—and attitudes. It has been argued very cogently that these ideas and attitudes are maintained by their expression in myth and rite[1] but little evidence for this has been published. Can objective evidence be collected? The anthropologist cannot look into men's minds; he is not concerned with personal religion—with the varieties of religious experience. Can he observe any effect of participation in ritual upon the behaviour of groups and categories of people? It must be admitted that our evidence here is thin.

[1] A. R. Radcliffe-Brown, *The Andaman Islanders* (1922), pp. 236 ff.; *Structure and Function in Primitive Society* (1952), pp. 157 ff.

It has been shown that participation in rituals compels the gathering together and co-operation of kinsmen and of affines, most of whom live dispersed in different villages; it compels the provision of lavish feasts; it compels respectful behaviour to senior kinsmen and, more particularly, affines; it compels an erring son to beg forgiveness of his father, and the father to receive him; it compels confession of anger and formal forgiveness between kinsmen. In short, the rituals compel outward conformity to an approved system of co-operation and respect; the expression of certain sentiments is compulsory whatever the individual may feel. It is clearly understood that not all feel the sentiments they express: Nyakyusa women commented on the fact that certain widows were not really grieved at their husbands' deaths, though they wailed and smeared themselves with mud: but the corporate expression *tends* to induce the appropriate feelings. Even to an outsider the pressure of the ritual is strong; the sense of terror and grief in a throng of women, close packed, and weeping and wailing, is intense. Moreover, though the emphasis is on outward conformity, there is constantly the suggestion that inward attitudes are significant: anger 'in the heart' is dangerous; the medicine will injure any who do not indeed forgive their kinsmen (p. 182, 266 ff.). It is because they think inward attitudes matter that the Nyakyusa lay so much stress on confession (*ukusosya*), admission of a grudge or anger, as the essential preliminary to reconcilation.

This brings us to the next point: the rituals provide for the public expression of anti-social attitudes or tendencies, and their public rejection. The Nyakyusa hold that merely to suppress grief or hatred is useless, and likely to increase it, and they constantly press on one another the need to *ukusosya*, to 'bring out', to confess, that which is within.[1] The admission of anger against kinsmen and affines is the prelude to reconcilation; the open expression of antagonism between two lineages, which are then reconciled by the exchange of gifts and feasts in the Lugulu ritual of vituperation, is but the most dramatic instance of a common theme. The violent expression of grief and anger in the death ritual precedes an assertion of life, and joy in living. The miming of the actions of a madman, and identification with the shades, in the rituals at death, puberty, and twin birth, may be interpreted as an expression of the desire to wallow in filth and the desire for death, preceding purification and rebirth. In short, the rituals are both

[1] Monica Wilson, *Good Company*, pp. 99–100.

degree. Sir Charles Darwin has suggested that those societies which put a premium on fertility will ultimately be dominant, by the weight of numbers,[1] but the evidence from Africa suggests that those societies which have in fact survived have regulated reproduction. Of the concern of the Nyakyusa with fertility there can be no doubt. The gods *are* the reproductive principle expressed in the idiom of a patrilineal society—'the shade and the semen are brothers'. One of the express purposes of the rituals of kinship, as well as of the communal rituals, is to secure fertility; one of the major sanctions of religion is the fear of the loss of it. And further than this, all their major activities are expressed in terms of the reproductive cycle and thought to be linked to it. The association of crops, and cattle, and hunting, and war with pregnancy and menstruation in women has already been indicated, and a more general connection between fertility in crops, and cattle, and men will be shown in the account of communal rituals. The two principal crafts, iron smelting and bark-cloth making, are associated with the act of coition. So also are fire-making, grinding, cooking, and eating; and the hearth and hut are identified with the union of husband and wife, and with childbirth. Whether such a preoccupation with fecundity, and the tendency to express all activities in terms of the reproductive cycle, are stronger among the Nyakyusa than among most other peoples we do not yet know, but at least they do not minimize its importance. It is the more significant therefore that, though maximum fertility of soil and stock was sought, there was a limitation of the human reproductive rate by deliberate spacing, and by limiting a woman's period of child-bearing to the years before her son's marriage. The Nyakyusa appear to have been an expanding people in relatively empty country, and the six or seven births per woman which this system allowed, combined with an infant mortality of perhaps 50 per cent, did not cause undue pressure upon their resources.

The particular form of limitation was linked to the structure of age-villages. The very wide spacing, with four to five years between pregnancies, and the taboo on a woman bearing after the marriage of her eldest son, ensured that, as a general rule, full brothers built in different villages. Thus the most closely-knit kinship group, that of full brothers and their sons, did not coincide with the local group, and the fissiparous tendency of lineages was checked by village loyalties. A group of full brothers and their

---

[1] Charles Darwin, *The Next Million Years*, p. 171 *et passim*.

sons, between whom economic and religious bonds were strong, might be liable to isolate themselves, but could not do so when each brother and son lived in a different village. As among the northern Nguni and Tswana, who were organized in age regiments,[1] the principle of generation balanced the lineage principle, each holding the other in check.

Every society values co-operation: 'mutual aid' of one sort or another is a condition of social survival. The Nyakyusa rituals of kinship constantly reaffirm the mutual dependence of members of a lineage. They are 'members of one another' by virtue of their common blood, and what injures one may injure all. This is very clearly expressed in the rituals of death, twin birth, spearing, rotting the ropes, and protection against sorcery. The desire for health and plenty is the lever used to compel co-operation.

The elementary family of parents and children exists in every society of which we have evidence and may be taken as an institution necessary to survival, biological and social, though its form varies. In the death, and puberty, and birth rituals the close character of the bonds between parents and children, between siblings, and between spouses, is expressed; and the polygynous form of the Nyakyusa family, the closer bonds between a man and his first wife and those of the same 'house', and the identification of alternate generations, are also manifested. Thus the importance of the primary ties of parents and children, and of the 'house' within the polygynous family, is enhanced.

Differences in status exist in every society and must do so since leadership is necessary. Individuals move from one position to another during the course of their lives, and all societies celebrate such changes, thereby compelling public acceptance of them, and impressing on the individuals concerned their new duties and responsibilities. These are expressed very pointedly in the Nyakyusa admonition to a bride, or widow, or the mother of twins; in the greeting accorded to the heir to the father of a family; and in the oration to the shade. The rituals are a symbolic weaning from childhood, from the bride's father's lineage, from a former marriage, or from deceased parents, and compel acceptance of a new position; clinging to the old spells madness and death. The conception of being 'born again' and making a new start, is directly

---

[1] Among the Pedi it was taboo for full brothers to be initiated into the same regiment. G. M. Pitje, 'Traditional systems of male education among the Pedi', *African Studies*, 9 (1950), p. 109.

linked to the physiological cycle of individuals and their close kin, and cannot be detached from it as in Christianity.

Law is a condition of social survival; no society can exist without it; and in so far as religion helps to maintain law and order it fulfills a necessary social function. Among the Nyakyusa (and perhaps in all societies) order is maintained partly by fear of supernatural sanctions. The rituals we have described both enhance fear and relieve it. They harness fear to social ends.

The preceding chapters are full of the pagan fear of death, menstruation, childbirth, and shedding blood. The rituals express the fear and teach men what they must do to be saved. They teach them to co-operate with their kinsmen and to follow traditional custom, for in that alone does salvation lie. The fear of madness or sterility compels each generation to follow traditional custom as ordained for them by the heroes: thus is the dependence of man upon his society instilled. The death ritual illustrates this most dramatically. In every society men must overcome death emotionally, they must turn to life. In the death ritual the mourners are distraught, terrified; they express their grief and put it behind them; their relatives and neighbours gather round them, share their sorrow, and help them to overcome it. The dead is replaced. Death is associated with fecundity and so made tolerable. It is no accident that the Nyakyusa interpret all the rituals, and especially the death ritual, as a protection against going mad, against the disintegration of the personality. And safety is assured to the living by following minutely the traditions of their lineage.

That the nature of men's fears is culturally determined is clear from the Nyakyusa evidence, for Christians and pagans alike are agreed that 'the Christians fear much less' than do pagans, and the Christians do in fact ignore taboos which the pagans feel to be binding. But the rituals do not create fear out of nothing. All the situations in which they are performed—birth and death, marriage, and misfortune—are situations of emotional tension in all societies. The rituals heighten the emotions and canalize them. They both teach men to feel, and teach them what it is proper to feel.

Many writers have shown us that the conception of sacred includes both the idea of holiness and of pollution;[1] that the awful, the fearful, may be conceived both as pure and as filthy. In

---

[1] See particularly W. Robertson Smith, *Lectures on the Religion of the Semites* (1889), pp. 153, 446–54 (1914 ed.); R. Otto, *The Idea of the Holy* (1923).

Nyakyusa thought the emphasis is almost exclusively on the filthy. Awe is expressed in terms of pollution. As we have seen, there is a clear conception of resurrection, of separation between rotting corpse and shade, but still the shades are 'filthy', and the mourner, or the bride, or the mother and newborn child, who is identified with them, is filthy too. There is a conception of purity, innocence, whiteness (*mwelu*), which is applied to those free from witchcraft or other crime, and to virgins, but it is not cited as an attribute of the shades or of the heroes; indeed, it is those who have been *separated* from the shades or Kyala who are pure.

Nyakyusa religion is characterized by two things: the general linking of misfortune with sin—the conception that if someone falls ill physically or mentally it is usually because he or his kinsman has done wrong—and the preoccupation with pollution. These are connected. The chief sins are neglect of ritual and quarrelling between kinsmen. Now neglect of ritual is, in essence, failure to purify oneself—failure to separate from the filthy shade —therefore sin and pollution are linked, though not identified. The connection between pollution and quarrelling between kinsmen is less direct but it exists, for rituals, the means of purification, are also the occasion for composing quarrels, and cleansing oneself of anger by confession—spitting it out—is a condition of their efficacy.

That the Nyakyusa are dogged by the sense of guilt is clear, but whether it is more overwhelming in their society than in others, or merely more openly expressed, is arguable. Why some people look down to earth, to the rotting corpse and bodily excretions which are buried in the earth, and express their awe in terms of pollution, corruption, and others look to the sky and express it in terms of light and purity; why some people seek union with God and others separation from Him, we do not know. The answer to these, as to many questions regarding Nyakyusa religion, lies beyond the field of this investigation.

SELECT RECORDS

I. REPORTS OF PARTICULAR FUNERALS

(a) Farewell to Mwamulenga III,[1] son of Mwegama (Selya)

Record of G. W. 10/3/37

Mwamulenga III hanged himself seventeen days ago, after the death of one of his wives and his only child. This ritual was held at his own house in Katumba but he was buried at the place where his father, Mwegama, had lived, and the mourning was carried out in the hills by Mwakapesa, the head of the family, who has moved there. The litter was at Mwakapesa's and was taken out about a week ago.

Mwaikambo and I arrived about 10 a.m. with Sikatula (wife of Gwamungonde), who is a cross-cousin (*untani*) of the family. The women were gathered inside the house wailing dirges—words were clearly audible but not, to me, distinguishable: one woman was the leader. There was more wailing than singing. The dirge was punctuated by slow handclaps. Mpogo, the eldest full brother of the dead man, and the heir, told me: 'It is the custom to wail just before the ritual, like this.'

Food was brought out about 11 a.m. The women had come close to talk to me; when food came out the men told them to go away. I asked why. 'We wash constantly, but women only wash a little, also they look after children and their bark-cloth belts are dirty. When they cook they wash, but for eating they wash little.'

I asked who would perform the ritual.

Mpogo: 'Kalukwa (the widow) will perform the ritual, also each of his brothers and half-brothers will select one or two children to do it too. The rest of our children just look on, for we ourselves are not yet dead.'

Kana Nsambe: 'It is our custom to leave some people over, not to perform it on all.'

Later I asked why Bapala (Kana Lwesi) did the ritual and not Kana Ipalu whose relationship to the dead man was exactly the same. 'We leave some out, they will do it at some other later death.' Actually thirteen people performed it. 'Mwamaloba (son of Mwegama II) will not do the ritual when he returns—it does not matter; but if he'd been a son of the dead man then he would do so. The wives of the dead man's brothers never do the ritual. The ritual for Lukosa (dead wife of

[1] cf. Genealogy on p. 273.

234

the dead man) has been done already; that of to-day is for the dead man
and his child together.'

c. 11.30 a.m. The women left the house empty; suddenly the men fell
on Mpogo and dragged him struggling into the empty house; the
women likewise dragged in Kalukwa—still smeared in ashes. The pair
were left alone there with the officiant but, as I heard afterwards, they
made no attempt to mate now, it is taboo until the beer. After three or
four minutes Kana Nsambe called Mwaipalu (see genealogy) to summon them (*ukubasosya*). He went with a stick to the door and pushed it
open. Each then came out with a string of green creeper (*nkolonowa*)
over the right shoulder. 'This is the sign that we have given him the
inheritance.' 'They do not have intercourse, however, until the beer.'
Each went to bathe, separately, escorted by friends of the same sex—
'to keep them company'.

The two chief officiants were non-relatives, Sikabile, wife of Mwen-
nganga, and her assistant Mwanyengenye; but the older female relatives assisted them too, and were referred to as *abanyago*.

Sikabile brought a plantain flower, carefully wrapped in a plantain
leaf, into the swept place near the door. She dug a little grave and
buried it. There was a discussion about the right direction, and it was
decided that the point represented the legs of the corpse and must be
set to face BuKinga. The leaf was not buried. 'They take a plantain
flower because the deceased was a man. If it had been a woman, they
would have taken a sweet banana.' Then, one by one, the principals
came and rubbed forehead, right elbow, right hand, and right toe in
the pile of earth there—once facing BuKinga and then, all over again,
facing the other way. Then they went to bathe. One infant was touched
with earth in the correct places by the officiant. Boys and their father
bathed separately—'it is always taboo for them to bathe together'.

Mpogo told me that he lives in the hills at Mwakilema's, but all the
ritual, including the drinking of beer, will be done here. 'If there was
millet available,' he said, 'we would start the brewing now; as it is, we
must wait for the new millet. We have sown all our millet.'

After all had bathed, the officiant poured water for them with powdered medicine in it, at the doorway. One by one they stood in the
doorway and she outside, and they washed hands, and mouth, and both
knees; then her assistant handed her for each a banana, roasted and
unscraped, with the end broken off and with a pumpkin-seed and a
lentil, stuck in it, and some powder on it. The officiant held it near the
ground and each stooped to bite it, then took hold of it and ate it—
some bit first without touching with the hand, some caught hold of it.
To each she gave more roast bananas and seeds separately too. In all
the ritual Kalukwa (the widow) came last and Mpogo usually last but
one. Now he was last but one.

The women then all gathered inside the house and the sisters of

Mpogo began to admonish the wives. This went on for two hours or more. I heard one of the sisters remark: 'The wives tremble now, their husband has died, their Kyala has died.' There was a great noise. Mpogo said to me: 'Our sisters are men, those our wives have married. It is the custom to admonish the wives because our sisters have been angry.' 'And at a twin ritual?' 'Yes, then also.'

I was told later: 'Mpogo's sisters punished all their sisters-in-law because when they had gone to their brothers the sisters-in-law did not receive them well, they were stingy to them with food. One said: "I went to my brother's home. When I was approaching I passed through a sweet potato garden; I took a potato without fearing because I said to myself: 'It's the garden of my mother.' When I arrived with the one sweet potato I had dug up she said: 'Who are you with a sweet potato?' And she began to shout, saying: 'Whose is it? You do not listen.' My body began to shrink and I said to myself: 'Ha! Why does she not come to look closely? She says a thief comes by day.' And I sat down." And so they went on.'

While this continued the principals were all given ointment (*inyemba*) by the officiant and smeared themselves. 'This is the first time they've done so since the death.' Then at the other door of the hut all the principals were collected 'to see the litter (*ukuketa ulufumbo*)'. They watched while the officiant sat inside the door, took some dry banana leaves handed to her, and sprinkled powder on them in the form of a cross. Then she went out of the door holding the leaves and rubbed them lightly on the ground in the form of a cross, and put them outside to be thrown away.

At last the admonitions of the brothers' wives stopped.

Then came the putting of food into the pot. The officiant held an old pot in her hand and circled round the hearth-bricks with it while her assistant dropped in food and all the women sang '*Ilinwanwa*'. The food was transferred to another pot and put on the fire. The officiant then touched the hearth-bricks with different parts of her body, or made gestures as if to do so, while she and they said: 'The foot is also put on the fire,' and so on. For all the parts the prefix *un* was used, implying 'his'. The officiant also said, stamping: 'You pass by me, I your wife, your friend.'

Then came a symbolic pouring out of millet into a basket. The gifts of millet were not available, so a little, provided by the family, was used symbolically. Two small winnowing baskets were emptied into a large grain basket by the officiant, while another woman said names— of relatives for the first basket and of neighbours for a second: 'So-and-so and So-and-so has brought millet'—ending up with 'all' in each case. 'This,' they said, 'is a symbol (*ikimanyilo*), we shall each bring our gift of millet later.'

Four stems of bananas had been brought and were now divided up—

one by the wife of Mwabufugo (she had returned home the day before yesterday), one by the wife of Mwamgobole, one by Sikatula, one by Kana Ipalu (cf. genealogy).

A fresh bark-cloth was taken from the tree and hammered a little: 'Until this moment it was taboo to hammer bark-cloth, the hammer belonged to the dead man.' The bark-cloth was placed on a fresh banana leaf beneath a grindstone and a little millet ground into it. Then leaf and bark-cloth were taken away. This flour was used for the shaving. Another leaf was put under and more flour ground for porridge.

Roast plantains were handed round for eating. There was a discussion about shaving the 'hair of the corpse'. As it was late, Mpogo wanted to leave it until the gifts of millet were brought, but the others overruled him: 'It must be done now.' They decided to smear their heads with millet paste in preparation for shaving now, and to shave to-morrow.

Kalukwa has to avoid Kana Nsambe (her husband's father's sister) as an in-law. Once, when she came close for eating of mash, Kana Nsambe put a cloth over her head. But when Kalukwa was in the hut at a distance (e.g. standing in a line) no precaution was taken. Kana Nsambe said: 'It is I who buried Mwegama, she avoids me.' Mpogo explained that 'She avoids, but only a little, if she gives a gift to Kana Nsambe she can look at her'.

Then all the principals stood in a line, the assistant officiant crawled round them sweeping the dust on to their legs, while they, and the other women, began to wail a dirge: 'Farewell, Mwaikono!' The women, cheerful a moment before, were weeping at once. This continued for five minutes or so. The principals stood with legs apart while the officiant pushed a flat basket of millet, pumpkin-seeds, and lentils, between the legs of each in the row—she crawled along doing so and then dragged the basket back to the right side. Then she put it on the head of each in turn, and she put a pinch of millet flour on the left shoulder of each.

A stem of bananas and a bunch of feathers (representing a hen) were brought out, and each of the principals in turn sat on the feathers. Kalukwa who, as always, was last, picked it up and put it over her shoulder on a string. The officiant took a leaf for each principal, touched her own body in various places with it, and then put it round the wrist of the principal—to each in turn she did this. As they came out of the hut she held a banana sapling across the doorway so that as each stooped coming out his head collided with it.

Another line was formed outside, facing BuKinga (as in the hut), and again the basket was put by the officiant on the head of each, but this time she threw a few seeds out over their left shoulders and the basket rested for a moment on their heads. They then went to bathe, and Kalukwa threw away the bananas and feathers in the stream.

A mash made of beans, lentils and pumpkin-seeds was salted, to be eaten with millet porridge; one unsalted was prepared to be eaten with bananas. Each principal then washed again with water and powdered medicine at the doorway. The unsalted mash and bananas were handed to each of the principals to eat. The salted mash and porridge (in one ball) was placed on one of the hearth-bricks and each one came and stooped and bit (as with the bananas before outside), then took away the mouthful to eat. 'We used to put it up on the wall, we have abandoned the custom nowadays.' Mpogo begged for 'only a little'. Finally, each principal sat in the doorway and the officiant smeared a cross on his head with a paste of millet flour (previously ground on the bark-cloth) and water.

It was 6 p.m., the sun sinking, as I left.

The kinsmen present are marked on the genealogy on p. 273. There were also three neighbours one of whom was a younger full brother of the village headman, Mwambuputa. The headman was not there himself.

(b) Farewell to Kalata's mother (Kukwe)

Record of G. W. 6/11/36

Kalata's mother died on Monday evening, November 2, and was buried the next day.

KALATA: They will perform the ritual on me and my younger brother and on my son; if we had a sister alive they would do it for her too, but we have none. . . . The officiant is Sijele, wife of Mwainombola. He is a relative of ours, our mothers avoided him. He was their 'father-in-law'. . . . My father is already dead.

A young man present had gone for the *ikipiki* medicine to wash with and brought back a plant, *nyasati*, but the officiant (Sijele) had seen it and gone for another, saying 'that is the *ikipiki* of the Sangu'. However, two older men and the dead woman's younger sister disagreed with her and said *nyasati* was right.

There were present one classificatory father of Kalata with a small son, Kalata's own small son, Kalata's younger brother, Kalata himself, a young man *untani* to Kalata (son of the dead woman's brother) and a small son; the wife and the sister of the *untani*, a younger sister of the dead woman, and another young woman, all with mourning belts tied round them. A fifth young woman had no belt.

The sister's daughter began to grind millet. A young woman went off to look for medicines for sweeping out the rubbish (*imindu*). Everyone gave her advice as to where to find them. Sijele came in with a bunch of twigs for sweeping, and a separate one for washing. There was more discussion of *nyasati*. Sijele said that *nyasati* was for bathing with after the burial, not for washing with now.

A young woman began to clear the rubbish (*ukusosya imindu*) with the bunch of twigs and to carry them into the bananas. Sijele took over the grinding of the millet.

K's younger brother went off to fetch the wife of M. (who himself died the day before yesterday). As soon as she arrived she insisted on the grinding stone being moved opposite the door (it had been to one side of the door). 'That's the ritual,' she said. She changed two other things: first she said that *nyasati* was the correct plant to wash with, and they accepted her judgement; then she was furious that they'd begun to sweep out the hut: 'You must not do that, to-night you have to dance to the harp on the litter. Actually, you should have started yesterday washing and eating porridge, and swept to-day, now you must sweep to-morrow.' After much discussion it was decided to eat the porridge now, dance to-night, and sweep to-morrow. Some of the litter was still left inside unswept.

M's wife, N., went away again. Kalata told me: 'She is a Christian, she is our officiant, she also is related to us, she and Sijele are those we get to perform the ritual for us.' He also said: 'The rubbish (*imindu*) or litter (*ulufumbo*) is sickness.' The three young men—K., his brother, and *untani*—all took the women's argument over the ritual as a great joke.

The millet porridge had now been cooked. Kalata's son (aged about 4 years) was stood by the door and a little piece of twig, *nyasati*, put between his hands. Three times the officiant poured water on his hands; and twice she made him hold it in his hand, suck it into his mouth and spit. Then K. and his younger brother in turn each did likewise, washing hands three times and mouth once and spitting. Two leaves were put on the ground, one of sweet banana, one of plantain, on top of each other, in front of the door. Sijele put porridge on them and then, taking a leaf-rib of *isege* she gave a little to each twice in turn, in the same order. To each she gave once when he stood to the west, once when he stood to the east, of the door. She shoved the porridge in great lumps into their mouths amid laughter. The porridge has no medicine in it. The rest of the porridge was finished by 'the officiants'—i.e. Sijele and the dead woman's elderly sister.

I asked the reasons for all this.

'Our ritual is of great importance. When anyone dies they treat us, the children, ritually; they make us lick porridge, they make us wash— for if they don't treat me thus then, if I go to eat other men's ritual food, the disease falls upon me. There are many kinds of ritual; in our Kukwe ritual we eat mash (*ikufuge*). If I come across other people eating maize with beans, as the Ngumba and the Penja do, or anything else but mash, then I don't eat that food, I avoid it and don't go near, I say this is a different ritual. But if I find people eating mash then I eat too. Even then, however, if I haven't had all the ritual performed for me, both of father and of mother, the disease will fall upon me.

'We perform the ritual upon the immediately-following younger brother of a man, on his wife, children, and grandchildren. On the husband, the immediately-following younger sister of a woman, children, and grandchildren. My mother's sister here did not immediately follow her, therefore she does not have the ritual done for her.'

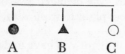

A   B   C

B. died first. A. performed the ritual for him. A. has now died and C. does not perform the ritual.

K. has no wife with him, she's left him.

I returned the same evening just before sunset, as they told me to. We waited a long time. K's classificatory mother asked him: 'What about the stem of bananas?' And he went off to arrange with a neighbour that he should cut and 'steal' a particular stem. As the light faded from the sky, Sijele, the officiant, arrived, walking as she always does with the help of a stick. Still we waited for N., and by the time she came it was full night.

From the moment of Sijele's arrival there was a prolonged discussion as to whether or not we should include maize in this evening's ritual food, or whether beans alone were correct. Precedents were quoted from previous rituals, including that of the dead woman's husband and those of the local chief's family. Sijele left declaring that to include maize was a Sangu custom. After N. arrived, the argument continued and it was finally decided that beans alone were correct. For about half an hour after we were all gathered ready in the hut, round the fire, the talk continued. N. and S. described, with immense enjoyment, the rest of the ritual, particularly the bathing with stones. Although, as we shall see later, the stones symbolize death and the corpse, there was no atmosphere of awe about the description—it was vigorous and expressive and punctuated by the laughter of the listeners. There was no solemnity; no evident sense of awe; the two officiants, the principals, and the rest of us laughed and talked all the time. It was clearly thought most important to perform the ritual correctly, but not, apparently, the least important to spread a 'religious atmosphere' over it.

'Who shall begin? Let the young gentleman (ulifumu) begin!' The child was made to begin, K. followed and K's younger brother came last. Kalata held his son's hands open to receive the beans and powdered medicine, in front of the fire. A pot was put on the fire and beans brought in calabash spoons. Sijele began by opening her little packet of powdered medicine and putting a pinch into the pot with a few beans, then she poured in some water from a drinking calabash. As she did each of these activities she said: 'This is the ritual of my wife.' (N.B. she was speaking for the child, grandsons call their grandmothers 'my wife'.) Then the child was helped to do the same thing. Sijele put medicine and beans into his two hands and K. helped him to throw them into the pot. As he did so K. and N. both said for him: 'This is the ritual of my grandmother.' Then Sijele gave him the water calabash and K. helped him to pour, while the same words were said for him again. Sijele did the same for K. and his brother in turn. She began each time by putting powder and beans and pouring water into the pot, and then K. followed suit, and his brother after him. For K. she said: 'This is the ritual of my mother,' and he repeated: 'This is the ritual of my mother, Sandumi'; for the brother she said: 'This is the death of my mother,' and he repeated the same words.

The ritual was interrupted once or twice by discussion. The child's hands got burnt in throwing the beans into the pot and there was a pause for comment and comfort. When Sijele said for the child: 'This is the ritual of my wife,' N. said: 'Let him say "of my grandmother". ' Neither of the young men was very serious, and each laughed as he finished his words.

We went quietly (by pre-arrangement) to a neighbour's homestead, stumbling in the darkness, and cut a stem of banana. We made a noise doing so but the householder stayed quiet. K's younger brother picked up the stem from the ground and ran off home with it, while the rest of us set up a hue and cry, following him at a run and calling: 'Thief, thief, he's stolen a banana stem!' Still the householder stayed quiet. This is the custom, the owners say nothing, it is the party of the 'thief' that pursue him. This stem, they told me, would be kept and used later.

So we entered the house again. Kalata had previously borrowed a harp (*ilipango*) of four strings and asked a neighbour to come and play it. The three principals, Sijele, and the player, stood up and began to circle round the fire slowly, stepping rhythmically and saying: 'Good-bye, go to father! Good-bye, go to mother!' Sijele and N. had previously told them the words and the tune. The fire burned up brightly and flickered on the circling figures, the leader crouching to his harp, while the beans steamed in the pot. Sijele held a winnowing basket full of dry pods of oil-seeds (*inyemba*) in her hands. The three principals reached into the basket as they circled and crushed them in their fingers till the seeds fell out. Then N. called out: 'Now then, stamp the stamping dance (*ukukanya inganya*)!' The harp-player stopped playing while the three principals stamped and stamped near the fire calling the war-cry as they did so. No words were spoken.

Two leaves were then placed on the ground, one sweet banana, one plantain, on top of each other. Sijele and the three principals knelt round them, and N. told them the words and the tune. Then these four beat the leaves as if they were hand drums, singing: 'The ritual of my father (*syeku, syeku*), the ritual of my mother: the ritual of Mwaijagila, Mwalibuti, Malambaiaga, Kisinile, Lambwe (these are the praise-names of their father); Sananbi, Mwilwa, Maluhajegila (these are the praise-names of their mother). The next day they explained their song: 'It is to perform the ritual (*ukusyekula*). They call it *isyekula* (i.e. the ritual) and they say that if they don't perform it the child will be like an idiot, he will run about naked and mad.' In all the songs Sijele acted as leader and the principals as chorus.

Then, finally, a grain basket was brought and turned upside down. Sijele and the principals beat on it with a new rhythm, but still syncopated, singing: 'The two ways of the parent! The two ways of the parent!' And so it finished.

I was told that the next morning early the three principals would eat the beans which had now been cooked, but that they must stay for a night first in the hut.

Kalata commenting later said: 'We Kukwe circle and dance the stamping dance, but we beat neither the ground nor the basket. Beating the basket is a Sangu custom.' Kalata is a Kukwe but his mother was a Sangu.[1] 'We Kukwe sing farewell and "*Syeku, syeku*", and we dance round to the harp; but we don't sing "the two ways of the parent" at all!'

November 7

I arrived at 8 a.m. to find that the beans had been eaten. 'We came out in the morning cold very early, we washed our hands and ate the beans. Then Sijele, who had slept the night with us, swept out the rubbish (*imindu*) with the bunch of medicine twigs.' When I arrived Kalata was finishing the sweeping outside with an ordinary broom.

November 16   Record of Mwaikambo

They began by building a little hut on the pathway that goes through the bananas to the stream, near the house. The path went right through the hut, which was built only by the officiants, not by the others. After they had finished building they planted hearth-bricks inside and lit a fire; then, taking some dry oil-seeds and powdered medicine, they called out to summon those for whom the ritual was being performed. When they came into the hut the officiants gave powdered medicine and oil-seeds to the child who received them in both hands and poured them into a potsherd on the fire, saying as he did so: 'This is the death of my grandmother.' They gave them to the two young men likewise, who said: 'This is the death of my mother' (that is to say: 'This is the ritual of my mother'). And then the officiant took all the rest of the oil-seeds and put them in the potsherd to roast.

When the seeds were roasted the officiant ground them up and began to prepare ointment. Meanwhile the principals poured water into a

[1] Strictly the ritual should have been Kukwe since a wife follows the ritual of her husband.

small pot for cooking the beans; each poured a little in turn, as they had done with the oil-seeds, and said the same words as before. The officiants then picked the flowering head of a banana and selected a petal or two to use as a basin to prepare the ointment in. The beans, however, they did not throw into the pot, because they had done this before, they just put some in to cook. When the beans were all ready for making the mash, but before they took them off the fire, the officiants shaved the principals' hair. The officiants made them sit down on a bark-cloth spread on the ground and drew lines where they were going to shave with a bunch of grass called '*ifisajelo*', which had been dipped in some lees of beer. They began by shaving along the lines marked with the lees, one from forehead to neck, one from ear to ear over the crown. Then, as they shaved each in turn, they mocked him, saying: 'Poor fool, it found its mother (grandmother) was dead. Went stealing and they've speared it on the head!' After the officiant had shaved the lines and mocked them they helped each other to finish shaving their heads.

The mash was made by mixing the beans with the plantain that they had stolen previously, and with a sweet banana which they cut for the occasion. The plantain they say is the man, the sweet banana the woman. While mixing the mash together they took out of it a bean, a plantain and a sweet banana for each of the principals. And to some of the mash they added salt, to some not.

Then they went to bathe. They cut leaves of plantain and of sweet banana. First they tied the plantain leaves round the principals' loins and then the sweet banana leaves on top, and round their necks they tied one plantain leaf also. Then they stuck one plantain in front, and a sweet banana behind, and went to bathe. The principals wore cloths under the leaves because of the women present.

When we reached the stream the principals sat down in the water looking downstream. The doctor twisted grass into pads and put a pad on each one's head with a pebble on the pad. Then she put pebbles in the forks of all their fingers and toes, and in their mouths and ears, and made them hold a flower in each hand. They lay down in the water looking first upstream, for that is the direction of BuKukwe, and then finally downstream again. Stones, leaves and bananas fell into the water and then they bathed themselves in the ordinary way, each still wearing a cloth.

On the way back the doctor picked a kind of water grass (*ulukeke*) and a certain flower called *utungengelenge* and made each of the principals hold some grass in one hand and a flower in the other. When we reached the little hut (in the path between house and river) the principals threw the grass and the flower on to its thatch. Also they had brought water in a calabash from the stream, and this they poured on the thatch where they had thrown the flower. As the water dripped down from the thatch to the ground, a principal ran through the door-way so that the water trickled on to his body, then they poured more and he ran out again. Each of the three principals did this twice.

One officiant had been left behind to roast a chicken and some plan-tains, and when they had run through the drips they ate the food. They began with the roasted plantains in which they had stuck cooked len-tils, then the boiled plantains and the beans which they had left separate from the mash, then the unsalted mash and finally the salted mash. When they had finished the officiants smeared patches of oint-ment on themselves and on all the principals—on the little toe, the navel, the forehead and the elbow—and then each anointed his whole body. Then the officiant took some banana bark, twisted it up and smeared it all over with powdered medicine. This she first made as if to tie round her own neck but did not, and then she tied it round the neck of the first principal. She put similar necklaces on the other two and they slept with these necklaces on.

November 17

Early in the morning when they first woke up the officiant brought some medicated millet porridge which they moulded into little sausages, then they went to the path some way off from the village, and there, on the path, they dug little holes into which they inserted the sausages. Then they bent down and put their lips to them, biting a piece off and leaving a piece in the ground, and this they buried. Returning to the little hut, they took off the necklaces and threw them inside, and they pulled down the hut and destroyed it. Then they went to bathe and washed off the ointment they had put on the day before. When they got home the officiant stroked each on the forehead with a razor but made no cut. So it was over.

They said that if any detail was omitted or done wrong the principals would go mad.

II. LOCAL VARIATIONS IN THE DEATH RITUAL

(a) *The funeral of Mwampiki and his wife* (see Table (c) p. 272.)

This document illustrates the differences between lineages in the details of ritual, and the adjustments made for the children of married daughters. Mwampiki, whose funeral is described, was of a Sangu family, doctors of the chiefdom for the 'coming out', who had lived for two generations in Selya.

Record of G. W. 16/3/37

Kakuju, the village headman, called me to the funeral of 'the wife of Mwampiki' in Ijesi village. Mwampiki (Mwamwenembanga) himself is dead but his homestead and several wives have been inherited by a younger half-brother, Mwaisalwa. The dead woman is a wife of Mwal-emba (Kanjesi) another half-brother. Kanjesi was an old inhabitant of this village but he moved to Masebe. His wife was on a visit to her 'fathers' at Mwakalobo's place in the hills. She went to a funeral there and fell sick and died there yesterday. The corpse was brought here this morning. It is now 10 a.m. and the grave is half-dug. The owner of the homestead, Mwampiki II (Mwaisalwa), is not here, he is sick at Masoko where he had gone for a case. The husband is not yet here either; they have sent for him to Masebe. The dead woman's elder sister and co-wife is here, and their mother.

They went to fetch a doctor to perform an autopsy, offering him 20 cents, but came back without him. 'He refused,' they said. 'Well then,' said Kakuju, 'take him a cloth, doctors do not agree to come for just a little.' So they took him a cloth.

Kakuju told the women to come out of the house as it was too small to hold them all. The corpse was carried out into the shade of an *unsyunguti* tree. All the women gathered round wailing, about seventy of them, and about twenty men.

No cows have been killed yet as neither the husband nor Mwampiki II are here. No drums are here yet either. The grave was finished about 11 a.m. I asked Kakuju about dancing at death. He agreed that in the old days they had only danced the war-dance. 'That was our old cus-tom. Formerly we fought and killed people—the men of Mwangomo (another chief) who came to the funeral!' Mwambuga (the husband of the dead woman's husband's sister), who had been quite cheerful heretofore, suddenly began weeping and crying. He walked over to the women and joined in the wailing. Some small and naked children started climbing joyfully on the piled-up earth from the grave.

Now it is noon and there are thirty-five to forty men present and ninety to one hundred women. A doctor has agreed to come (to perform the autopsy) but has not yet arrived. Although the corpse was outside male mourners went into the house on their arrival to weep. An older woman got up and led a dirge. I heard her say a number of names, among which 'Mwampiki' was distinguishable. Clapping followed her words. Often she just called the war-cry (*akalulu*). The others wailed and joined in the war-cry. She accompanied her wailing with rhythmic movements of the body and arms. After a time she sat down but con-tinued to lead the wailing.

Mwakalabela (Mbalakatela) arrived with a cow. His daughter is married to young Mwaijumba, the son of Mwampiki. The autopsy followed (for description see *Good Company*, pp. 247–9).

17/3/37

Angombwike told me at breakfast that now Mwampiki himself was dead. He died yesterday at Masoko and was carried here last night.

R

They arrived with him in the middle of the night. The message reached
Kakuju at cock-crow. I arrived at 9 a.m. to find the grave finished and
one cow (a young one) killed. 'It was his own, and slept with the
children'—i.e. it was stabled in his long house in the compartment in
which the herdboys, his sons, sleep at night. The drums were being
beaten—I heard them begin as I approached—but there was no
dancing as yet. The corpse was being held upright (wrapped and hidden in cloths) by the women chief mourners, under the *unsyunguti* tree,
in the middle of about 150 women. Wailing was in full progress. Two
women were standing up to lead the dirges; one was the one who led
yesterday. She called out: 'Mwampiki, Mbembela . . .' and other
words. She stretched her hands towards the circle of women, towards
the men and called out: 'You men, you young men . . .' and she called
the villages by name: '. . . Lupondo, Njesi, Bujege, Bujenga'. I asked
about this because Angombwike had told me that the Mwampiki family
were Sangu and did not wail at a funeral. 'Yes, indeed,' I was told,
'they have changed now, but at the beginning [of the funeral] they did
not wail, they were silent, they dug the grave and finished it, they
killed a cow, and have only begun to wail now.' Two men stood by the
corpse (among the women) wailing, his own eldest son and his brother-
in-law. About seventy men were present. Dancing was begun by
Mwaisyelage of Ibale who seized a spear and shouted the war-cry and
danced. Half a dozen men followed him and several bananas were cut.
Kakuju began to shout out words as he sat and then leapt up and
joined in the dance. After five minutes the dancing died down and the
drums stopped.

The grave, like that of yesterday, is an unusual shape. The hole is
small and square and the cave is much bigger than usual. The corpse
is laid down with the forehead pointing to Sangu country. 'Yes, the
woman was buried just like this,' I was told in reply to my question.
'For though she is a Nyakyusa by birth, since she married a Sangu she
looks towards Sangu country.'

A cow was brought by Mwakibilingwa whose daughter is the wife of
one of Mwampiki's sons. 'Have you accepted the cow?' I asked. 'No
one can yet,' said Mwaiʻumba, 'the real owner of the cattle is her child,
the "owner" of the woman. Mwampiki's younger brother should not
receive the cattle. No! But her child, the owner of the woman. If
he wishes he will receive it and tell us. If he does not wish he will
drive it away and tell us: "I am killing my own cow." We do not
know yet.'

The corpse was carried with shouts and the war-cry and wailing
about 100 yards, and the dead man's cattle were driven by the side
(six full-grown beasts and two calves). 'It is to do honour to him here
where he walked about, now that he has died. We do it for all senior
people like him, not for juniors. Yes, and for women too, and even

though there are no cattle they carry him thus.' The corpse was then taken to be washed. 'We do not examine him; yesterday's corpse we did indeed examine but not this one. He was a senior, a chief,' said his son, and Kakuju confirmed it. 'We do not examine him. We refuse because he was a senior person.' More cattle appeared—'those of his son at Masoko'. 'It is the custom,' I was told. 'All the cattle come to mourn. These are the cattle of Mwansasu, the first lot were Mbembela's own. Most (or all of them) were kept by Mwaipungu, the eldest son.'

The drums began again and dancing recommenced. The drums had been warmed up by a fire. About 200 women and 100 men were present.

Mbasuke, father-in-law of Mwansasu, brought a heifer calf. Three cows were killed, two after the burial, all belonging to Mbembela and his sons. The heads of the cows killed point towards Sangu country. There was a dispute about one of these cows. They had killed one already which had come for the marriage of a daughter of the family, and they had taken another from the same son-in-law. There was objection, some saying: 'No, we should take one which came from another son-in-law.' All the cattle of Mwansasu and of the deceased were driven through the homestead together, a herd of twenty or so. Then they were gathered at the side, facing the grave. The corpse was carried out to the side of the grave. The chief mourners stood holding the corpse and all the men and women stood up to watch. The noise of wailing was terrific. A son seemed entirely to have lost control. 'Alas Father! Alas Father!' he cried, his body trembling and sweating, the tears running down his face, his hand pointing, shaking, towards the corpse and the grave. A friend was wailing, holding his head with his hands: 'My friend, my friend!' The corpse was laid down by the women and wrapped in more cloths. This took about half an hour. Still we stood and watched while the women began to sit down. Two men (Mwaisalwa III and a half-brother) and one woman (his widow) got into the grave—a tight fit. The corpse was buried with a new pot (a small one, used for serving food), several calabashes including a calabash cup, and a calabash of beer. Some of the beer was taken out just beforehand and left above ground. 'That means he should not go with all our fertility.' A huge calabash had been smashed before this by a son, in an ecstasy of grief. Now another was brought but it was decided not to bury it.

Kititu explained about the beer: 'Always, when a person has drunk beer during his illness before his death, the remains are buried with him. If he has not drunk beer during his illness none is sought.'

No door was available so a cloth was fixed across the opening of the cave. The women got out of the grave while the men remained in to stamp down the earth. Many people threw handfuls of earth.

Farewell to Mwampiki   2/4/37

Women began to wail about 9 a.m. I saw some arrive with bananas. They stopped wailing after ten minutes or so. Imilanwa (Mwaisalwa) was present. Mwaijumba had not yet come. I met Kakuju on the way. He had not yet been told of the ritual. Mbapa and Maleja (widows of Mwalingo) did most of the work, with Ijumba, widow of Mwampiki. Isalwa sat near and watched while Maleja ground up the ointment. Seeds for making ointment were put on the fire. This was the ointment for anointing oneself in the ritual. Beans were brought in a flat basket. 'We mourn', they said, 'with bean mash and the meat of a cow.'

There was some discussion about killing the cow and a dispute between Imilanwa and Simeni. Just as the cow was about to be killed a woman came and made them bring it to the side of the swept court away from the graves. 'If you kill it near the father-in-law's grave the wives will fear to eat the meat.' The cow was killed by Imilanwa. He then called the men of the family to discuss whether or not they should kill a bull also. One had been sent by the Chief Mwaipopo who is 'our son-in-law. He married a daughter of Maleja'. Imilanwa said: 'Let us kill it,' and they agreed. Only thirteen men were present so far.

The meat from the fork of the right foreleg (*ija mmapa*) was taken to eat with the mash. This is a Sangu not a Nyakyusa custom. The men of the family follow the Sangu custom. The women, daughters of Sangu, do likewise, and the women who are wives of Sangu, but the children of daughters who are married to Nyakyusa men from Selya do the Selya custom. If the daughter of a Sangu marries a Selya man then, if her father dies, she does the Sangu ritual at his place, but if her husband dies she does the Selya ritual at his place even if she has borne him no children, and even if she is herself a child or an infant who has not yet been to him. But her children always do the Selya ritual both at their father's home and at their mother's.

The burying of the banana flower and rubbing in earth is a Selya custom and is only done by the children of Selya men. I saw five or six children do it. Then more children came to rub in earth. One was under instruction at the mission. The women told him to rub himself but Mwaijumba broke in: 'If he is a Christian he ought not to perform the ritual.' 'He's under instruction.' 'Very well, he does not perform the ritual, for a Christian should not have two gods (*ba Kyala babili*).' The bull was killed a little way off among the bananas. Mwaijumba explained: 'It is just for meat, it's not for the ritual, the further off one. Christians will eat it.'

Shaving of the sprouting hair   *Record of Mwaikambo*, 22/4/37

First the men and women began drinking beer separately. Then they began the ritual. They went to the grave with beer in a small calabash.

The officiant prepared some beer mixing it with powdered medicine, and they came one by one to drink. The other officiant made as if to shave them, taking a little hair from the forehead and the neck. When she had done this she put her hands between her legs. Thus the people of Selya perform the ritual. In another calabash they put the lees of the beer that had been drunk, with two pots of water. These lees are poured on to their heads and the water runs over their bodies. When the officiant has done this she puts her hands and the calabash between her legs. They look towards Sangu country. Then they shave their hair. When they have finished they throw away the cloths and bark-cloth which they wear when they wash. Then they anoint themselves with oil, and sleep with it on them, and wash in the morning. The people of Selya shave in the morning; at this time they do not really shave, they only cut the sprouting hair.

In the evening there is the ceremony of handing over the inheritance. The heir sits on a banana stump in the doorway and the chief wife hands him a billhook. Then they say: 'Care for these children whom your elder brother left as if you had begotten them yourself, do not be hard, be kindly as he was.'

And at night he will sleep with the widows. In the morning the chief wife goes to her father without washing off the filth and gives her fathers beer, then they greet one another. Ndingania also goes to his mother's people. They said one woman did not go because her fathers did not know the custom, they are Lugulu. There were only these two women, one grown up and one a girl, to be inherited.

Mwaijumba told me that for Kanyosa their affines will not cut the banana grove for they have no girl to give in her place. 'They will give us cattle, we divide (the marriage-cattle) with them.'

(b) Ndali funeral rites   Record of Mwaikambo

When someone has died the Ndali mourn for five days, and the sixth day they sweep and shave the hair. When they are shaving it they take a potsherd and put in it all the hair that is shaved off. When they have finished they choose one senior woman, the chief wife, and they hand her this hair and they go to throw it away at the cross-roads. Giving the woman the hair means that the shade should be at his place and leave others. Shaving is to get rid of the shade which was on their bodies (*ukunwa ko kunsosya unsyuka uju bali nagwe mu mbili*). And the people who held the corpse in their arms and dug the grave step over a trench of fire when they have come from the bathing. The doctor gives them medicines to bathe with. They say that if they do not step over fire it is as if they had the dead on their bodies (*balinagwe mumbili umfwe*), and he will always come in dreams, so they drive him away.

When some considerable time has passed—a whole year—they do the *ilyengulo*. This word comes from straining beer. To strain the *ilyengulo* they seek two or three officiants, and they build a temporary hut behind the living huts where they strain three pots of beer, which they call 'the beer of the shades'. These officiants do not bathe their bodies because they say: 'Let us be with the shade when we make the beer (*tujege nagwe unsyuka bo tukubomba ubwalwa*).' The rest of the beer is strained in the house.

When they have brewed it they take one potful from the temporary hut and pour the contents on top of the grave; then they dig a hole on the grave and place in it a little pot of beer. What is left in these two pots they drink, together with the rest of the beer, and there is much drumming.

After a long time has passed, perhaps two years, if there has been sickness in the home, they think that the deceased is making them giddy, is causing them to be ill. So they dig up the corpse and take all the bones and finger and toe nails. If one is left the sickness is not cured. When Mulape, the grandchild of Mwakafunga, was ill they dug up the corpse and the illness ceased very quickly. They pile up the bones which have been dug up.

III. MARRIAGE NEGOTIATIONS AND GIFTS

Angombwike: One of our comrades in Kabembe heard that there was an unmarried girl at the Chief Mwasumbwe's, so one Monday he said to three of us: 'Don't go away, friends, we are going to woo the chief's daughter at Mwasumbwe's.' So we put on our best clothes, those we wear to church, and we went to the home of the father of the girl. He was the younger brother of the Chief Mwasumbwe by the same mother, and he told us: 'I am not the father (*ugwise*). She is my own child, but the father is the chief. Go to him' [i.e. authority over his daughter rested with his elder brother]. The girl had reached puberty. Someone else had married her, but her father had received only one cow, so the elder brother, the chief, was angry and took away the girl from her husband. My friend had never met her, never. He had just heard that there was an unmarried girl at that place, because the custom of making love to girls in the long grass is not a traditional one: a girl used to stay at her father's house. A young man went to the father before he spoke with the girl; he never spoke to her in secret. Then the father would send the girl to speak with the young man. She came and sat down and the young man looked at her closely and his friends who accompanied him helped him. Formerly a young man did not wear many clothes, he only wore one cloth in front, and a brass body-ring, so that his whole belly might be seen, and she might look closely. Also he sits high on a stool, while his fellows sit on the ground, that he may be seen by the girl. Then the girl asks his fellows: 'What is he like, friends?' And they reply: 'He's a real man.' Then she agrees to the 'go-between', saying: 'Indeed, I love them [sic].' But if she does not like them she refuses, and the young men go away. Yes, indeed, the girl always had power to refuse; no one ever compelled her to agree, even though the man had many cattle. The fathers always agreed for their part, saying: 'My daughter is good, she refuses at my house, and tells me (i.e. she does not accept and then run away, which is bad).' And if the girl has refused the young men go away, but others laugh and jeer at them, saying: 'So-and-so's daughter refused.'

'Oh?'

'Yes. Indeed, they are horrible young men, their bodies are very ugly.'

And the young men also look closely at the girl, they look very closely, and if they see that her breasts are thin, and her face is ugly, then they go and tell her father's friend, saying: 'We are leaving her, tell her father that we will not marry his daughter. Then he tells her father, who just says: 'All right, let them leave her.' But the custom of wooing in secret first, before a man has been to the father, began among Christians. The Christians say: 'It is good to woo in secret first,' but pagan fathers still object, saying: 'We will not eat the cattle properly.'

So when the father of the girl had told us thus, we went to the chief's place, and sat down under a tree. The chief's wives sat down at a distance. Then we trembled and sweat came on our bodies. I said to my fellows: 'Do we just sit? Let us ask.' And I got up and asked the chief's wives: 'Is the chief at home?'

'Oh! Do you wish the chief?'

'Yes, we wish to see him.'

'But he is at another's wife's place. Shall we call him?'

'Please.'

'Where have you come from?'

'We come from Kabembe.'

Then I returned to my friends and the chief's wives called him, saying: 'Four young men from Kabembe have come and want to see you about something.'

Then the chief came with three of his men, and they greeted us. . . . Then the chief called to his wives: 'Bring some food for them to eat,' and he got up himself to cut a stem of bananas.

Then I said to my fellows: 'Friends, do we just chat to the chief without asking him? One should get up and tell the councillor that we had come to ask for a girl.'

Then they all said: 'You are brave, Angombwike, you get up.'

'No, I am ashamed to get up twice, let So-and-so get up.' He got up and told one of the chief's men: 'We have something to discuss; we have heard that there is a girl who is unmarried here, it is about this we wished to see the chief, there is nothing else. But we are poor, we know that we have not got cattle.'

'Oh! But here there is no girl. There is a nubile girl at the home of the younger brother of the chief, across the stream.'

'It is she we want, indeed.'

Then they told the chief this, and he came and sat among his men, and I went with my fellow who had told the councillor, and we sat down with them.

Then the chief said: 'You have come to seek a girl?'

We: 'Yes, indeed, Chief, it is for this that we wished to see you. There is not anything else. But we beg you, we know that we are very poor. We have not got cattle. That we know. But we will make ourselves your servants, and hoe for you.'

Then he said: 'Who are you?'

'Do you ask our names before we have agreed? I am a son of Syelage.'

'That Mwaisyelage who has built in Bulindanajo in the country of Mwaipopo?'

'Yes.'

'Indeed, you are like your father, and Linolemu[1] himself, you are like him, we were friends, they were always clever fellows. But who wants the girl?'

He asked all our names, then I pointed out the suitor and told him his name.

Then he said to his councillor: 'Tell them that M. (his younger brother) has many funerals in his family, his children die frequently. Perhaps it will create quarrels later on if the girl dies. We have lazy people in our lineage.' So he told us. Then I replied and said: 'We are all like that. . . . We have come to create kinship, we want funerals, to bury one another. If one has died, let his fellow come to mourn at his place.'

'Yes, but some of us exceed in dying.'

'That is what we want, funerals, and burying one another.'

'All right, I agree.' (To the councillor): 'Call the girl and let them speak with her.'

And he went to call her.

Then we put our fellow, the suitor, on a stool, and I and my friend and the councillor, the go-between of the father, went closer to the girl than the others to hear what she said. Then I spoke to the girl, saying: 'We sought you, we want something else of you, we love you. It is L. M. there who wishes to marry.' . . . We spoke with her. . . . Then she agreed and said: 'Indeed, I love them, he is my husband, I love him. I am startled looking at him, I am startled indeed.' Then the coun-

---

[1] Angombwike's grandfather who was dead.

cillor said: 'Give the girl a betrothal gift.' The groom gave her 3s., and I gave the councillor 1s. Then the councillor told the chief, saying: 'The girl has agreed.' 'Thank you, tell them that they must bring four cows.'

Then they called us to eat. They put us in a house which they had prepared with many fine mats, and we sat down. They gave us four calabashes of curds, and a wooden spoon, and we were four. Then we trembled and sweat came on our bodies, especially I, because I knew that they would come to me, the go-between, and I thought 'cleverness is bad!' [i.e. his ready tongue had put him in the most prominent position]. I trembled, thinking: 'When they come to my place what shall I give them?' But the others ate joyfully. I only ate a little and with fear. Then we saw much food. Indeed, very much. What should we do? We called our wife [sic] and gave her one big calabash. Then we gathered together and looked at the food. What should we do? Then we called the councillor with whom we had spoken and said: 'Help us, we are defeated.'

'No. The chief will be angry, saying: "Why are you depriving them of their food?"'

Then I went to the chief and said: 'We beg people to help us, the food is so much we are overcome.' He laughed, all of them laughed. 'Are you overcome, Mwaisyelage?'

'Yes.'

Then he gave us four of his people, and they entered the house, and we gave them the curds and went off quickly because we feared lest they compel us to eat more and we should be ill. I put 50 cents in the basket which the chief's wives had brought us with calabashes. It was my 50 cents because the groom had finished what he had; he had only brought 4s. But it was not really mine, it belonged to my mother who had given it to me to buy groundnuts but I asked all of them, saying: 'Friends, who has fifty cents?' None of them had it, so I thought: 'How about this? Will my mother beat me? Is she not my mother? According to custom I will give it.' And the chief's wives accompanied us on the road and praised us, saying we were men of wisdom, because we had put 50 cents in their basket.

So on Thursday we went with four very good cows, some of them in milk. Because it is the work of the go-between to give the owner of the woman wise advice, saying: 'Choose good cattle to begin with, the weaker ones will follow.' And I told them: 'Let us be many friends; the first time he defeated us with his food; let us be many.' So ten of us went, and when they arrived they gave us six calabashes of curds with the whey drained off. They praised us because the cows were very good, but I told them: 'There is another which is sick at home, it will come when you have called your people to hoe, you will kill it to rejoice them.' All laughed and said: 'Let him bring it, it is Linolemu indeed, as Linolemu always was with his cunning. And they are alike in their shortness.' [Angombwike was short of stature.]

Then they told us: 'Bring five marriage-cattle (*ukukwa*), then we shall agree to hand over the girl. We will send a messenger to call you.' And we went off.

Then the husband sought four cows, because we always took less than they asked, even though there was another available, we did not take it because they would say: 'They are rich, they boast of their property,' and ask for further cattle, more than they would otherwise have done.

One day we were surprised by a messenger, saying: 'Come to-morrow for the *ukukwa*.' Many of us went, people from Mwangomo's country and from Mwaipopo's, many Christians and many pagans. The pagans danced and the Christians sang songs. The groom had relatives in both countries. Before his conversion he had lived in Mwaipopo's country, but after it he moved to Kabembe, to Mwangomo's country, so he brought his fellows, the sons of Mwaipopo, and those of Mwangomo. And I, the go-between, brought my fellows from Mwaipopo's country, for it is always customary for the go-between to have a following.

When we arrived the older ones among us told me, saying: 'Cut the banana grove!' I said: 'How can I cut the banana grove?' 'Cut.' Then I cut. That is to show 'We have come, we sons-in-law of the chief (*balenga*), we marry the daughter of a chief (*undenga*).' Then my fellows said: 'We will marry another, we will come to marry a sister, a daughter of the chief again.' And I cut another.[1] Then the chief's wives sang: 'Is there only one? Is there only one?' (meaning: 'Have we borne only once? Are there not other little daughters?'). For our part, the pagans danced and danced the war-dance, and thrust their spears in the ground, and sang: 'We shall marry her little sister, she has a little sister.'

And the Christians sang hymns.

Then the go-between of the chief called me, and I went to the chief. There they told me: 'See, we are shouting you have brought few cattle, bring what we mentioned.' And the chief's wives also sang: 'We are shouting, Mwambandele, we are shouting!'

Then I crouched down and said: 'Indeed, I told you, I am a poor man; indeed, you did mention the number of cattle, and I have not brought them, and about those which I brought at first I do not boast at all, they were as good as none.'

'But you know that I have many sons who are crying out, who wish to marry wives.'

'Indeed, but I told you that we are poor, if one cries out I will hoe

---

[1] In other contexts cutting bananas is a symbol of death. It is possible that here the symbol is of a girl dying to her father's lineage, at marriage, but this is only a guess.

for him, let him cut a garden and call me to hoe, I will come, I will make myself his servant.'

'But to hoe for a man and to bring him cattle are different things; you hoe for a man when he has married a wife. Who hoes for a bachelor?'

All the time the young men who came with us danced and sang: 'We have brought many cattle, all together they are eight, we have given marriage-cattle indeed.' . . . That is Nyakyusa custom.

And I replied: 'Yes, indeed, I am a child. You correct my childishness. I have no wisdom at all, you told me to bring cattle and I did not bring them. Also my comrade, the bridegroom, you correct his youth, I am like a fly which is killed by your milk, it dies because of it!'

Then he was satisfied and gave us a spear. We grasped the spear and danced with it: 'We are sons-in-law of the chief, we have married the daughter of a chief.' And we brought 2s. to beg for the girl (*ukwasima*) but they refused, saying: 'We chiefs eat a bull.'

Then they brought us food: great quantities of food; and we were many. No one counted us. They brought twelve grain baskets of meat and bananas, sixteen calabashes of milk, and eight grain baskets or basins of banana and chicken, and much food which I have not mentioned; I have only told of the fine food. There was porridge and relish and milk, much of it. And I, the go-between, was like a chief, I divided it to my fellows, all was brought to me and I told my fellow Enoch (he who went with me to speak to the girl when we wooed her), saying: 'Take this to the So-and-so's and the So-and-so's.' Because it is not proper that I should carry the food, but another. We called our wife [*sic*] to receive the choicest food, which she ate with her sisters-in-law— the sisters of the groom had also come with us. And I chose the choicest food for the groom too. We three who had gone with him the first time to woo the girl ate with him, and we each called a friend to join us.

During the feast they showed us a cow, saying: 'Eat it.' But we refused, saying: 'We are poor men.' Then they showed us a bull which we also refused: 'We are poor men, we have plenty with what you have cooked.' Because we feared that if we ate it they would ask for another cow later on. Then we left, but there followed us fifteen grain baskets of food which they had not brought out at first.

On a later day I went with one friend, just the two of us (the groom did not come) to give 6s. to take (*ukwasima*) the girl. They received it. There was much food, but we ate only a little because we were only two. Before they came to bring the girl to her husband I began working for you, so I told my friend Enoch to see to everything, and I told them to go to his house.

MISFORTUNES ATTRIBUTED TO SHADES

Ref.	Category of sufferer	Misfortune	Category of shade	Alleged sin	Investigation	Ritual performed
1.	Man. Katasya	(a) Crops did not grow (b) Katasya died	'Abapasi'	Quarrelling with kinsmen	Autopsy disproved this. Found to be sorcery	Killed a bull for family
2.	Children of village headman	Death of several children	Father of village headman	Village headman moved to father's homestead though told by father's neighbours he should remain in young man's village where he was headman	Autopsy	Prayer
3.	Cattle	Cattle died at father-in-law's (and would have to be replaced)	Shades were angry. His brother complained very much when he took all the cattle	Younger brother took all cattle he had from elder full brother to whom they had been handed on his return from work, and gave them for his marriage	—	—
4.	Two girls	Girls died	—	A wrong (inongwa) not specified	Autopsy Divination	—
5.	Younger brother	Died	Elder brother	Elder brother not buried where he asked to be	Divination	Buried where elder brother had asked

Ref.	Category of sufferer	Misfortune	Category of shade	Alleged sin	Investigation	Ritual performed
6.	Son	Millet crop cultivated by son failed	Father	Had moved from father's homestead. Left grave unswept	Divination	Prayer
7.	Husband	No fish in traps	—	Stinted one wife of fish	Divination	Prayed in banana grove. Wife confessed her anger
8.	Kasitile	Kasitile fell ill	Mother	Neglected to leave flour or beer in his hut for shades	Divination	—
9.	Married woman (wife of Mwakobela)	Woman delirious		Her newly-married daughter returned from husband without bringing a hen or anything, and drank from mother's calabash cup	Divination	—
10.	Child	Death of child	Father's sister?	Father neglected death ritual of his sister	Autopsy. 'The ritual entered the stomach of the child'	Neglected death ritual performed

V. CAUSES OF MISFORTUNE

(a) The death of Katasya

The following account of the death of Katasya is quoted in full because it illustrates how several possible causes of misfortune were considered. Possible causes mentioned were:

(a) The anger of his junior kinsmen

(b) The witchcraft of his wives

(c) The anger of his shades

(d) The anger of his neighbours because he had given them too small a cut of a bull killed as a sacrifice to his shades

(e) The adultery of his son with three of his wives

(f) The sorcery of his half-brother's son, Mwamukinga, with whom there was a long-standing quarrel over inheritance and whom he had accused of killing his (Mwamukinga's) full brother

(g) The sorcery of the Chief Mwaihojo, for Katasya, a man of the neighbouring Chief Mwaipopo, had built and cultivated on land claimed by both Mwaihojo and Mwaipopo

Record of G. W., 4/1/38

Angombwike told me at midday that Katasya had died. He was a village headman of Mwaipopo, the fellow of Mwainyopolela. His case (*inongwa*) was thus:

The millet did not grow in his field, so he called all his children to his homestead and killed a big bull for them, saying: 'Perhaps my children are angry at home. Perhaps my wives have worked witchcraft.' But to the neighbours he gave one leg and the children at home ate the rest. He did not, however, live long. He died immediately. It is said that the meat is still there. They have not eaten it. Such is the case of his death.

Kasitile, when I called on him yesterday, was out and his wife said he had gone to see Katasya who was ill.

Later in the day—4.1.38. Likusyila came in and I asked about Katasya's death.

But he has not died, he is still just alive. We heard that the millet failed in his field and the maize and beans in all his gardens. They all failed. One of his wives went into a trance repeatedly. She said: 'Those beneath are angry. Seek a bull and kill it.' Then he sought one, but now they have killed him. Perhaps he stinted his fellows in the village of meat, because if a man kills his animal alone and his fellows hear that he has killed, they are astonished and say: 'He should have called us. Does he perform ritual alone?'

QUESTION: But why were those beneath angry in the first place? They are not angry without cause.

LUKUSYILA: Indeed, they are never angry without cause. There is always some wrong. But we do not know what it is in this case. If you do not kill cattle for your father's burial they are always angry. But we do not know what wrong Katasya committed to make them angry.

Later Mwanifu came in. He told me that Katasya is still alive, but perhaps he will die this evening. We do not speak with him. He is just breathing. We only ask his wives: 'Does he sleep?' The case is thus: the millet failed in his field and he said: 'I shall pray to my shades and it will grow again.' Then he went to a certain man to get his big bull and gave him a cow in calf, saying: 'Take this and give me your bull,' and later they will give him a little calf worth 30s. The bull was very big. He killed it. Before he did so he was already slightly ill, but when he had killed it the illness became very much worse. We say they have bewitched him because he stinted his fellows in the village. But they themselves deny it, saying: 'But we always kill and eat ourselves alone. I, Mwainyopolela, killed my animal and ate it alone. Have I died therefore? According to the custom, if I have killed my beast as a sacrifice (*jakwiputela*) then I give my fellows one leg.'

QUESTION: Did Katasya not do so?

MWANIFU: No, Katasya did not give them any. He ate alone. Some wise men give the chief the breast because the chief is the owner of the country. Katasya did not give him that. Yes, if someone dies then the chief is usually given the breast. But when a beast is killed for sacrifice, no one having died, then many eat by themselves. The mourner gives to the chief.

QUESTION: Did he inquire of a diviner or not?

MWANIFU: We do not know. Some inquire of a diviner. Some think for themselves that the fathers are shaking them. Concerning his death, we are only speculating, saying: 'Perhaps they have bewitched him. They were angry on account of the meat.' But perhaps it is sorcery. See, he was sweating very much on his face. Let him die. We will look in his belly. Perhaps he has been speared. They have bewitched him. Perhaps it is sorcery. We only speculate.

In the morning Mwaipopo (the chief) was very, very angry. He said: 'Why have you gathered together, you people? Go off home. Do you want to finish off a dying man? It is taboo to gather together. First let a man die, then come to lament the death.'

QUESTION: Is it a Nyakyusa custom to be angry if people gather together at a sick man's house? Is it as if they bewitch him?

MWANIFU: Yes.

QUESTION: Why the gathering?

MWANIFU: We were startled to hear that he had died. They raised the lament of death in the morning and his cattle went home when Kasitile and I were on the pasture land. We were startled to see Katasya's cattle going home and said: 'He has died.' But his relatives saw that he had not died. They said it is taboo to lament when someone is still alive.

QUESTION: Why do cows come home when a man dies?

MWANIFU: It is a form of mourning. They should also weep and say farewell. He had property. For if I, Mwanifu, die, though I do not have cattle myself, yet because I am the son of Mwaipopo cattle are killed at the funeral. It is impressive. But if I were a commoner and had no cattle, then the funeral would be a flop. There would be no meat and people would say: 'He has not yet died, he has left one head.' They count the cattle to kill. If an important commoner dies, one who has cattle, then his funeral is impressive. People dance at his homestead and say: 'Our fellow, who has died, was a strong man who danced the war-dance in the homesteads.' And if he was tough in disputes, if he always got the better of them and no one ever got his cow, then they say: 'A tough fellow has died. May he leave a son as tough as himself. He died with his toughness.' They praise him.

QUESTION: Tell me about the killing of Katasya's bull.

MWANIFU: He killed the bull without telling his neighbours, but when he poured out the beer he called Mwainyopolela and Kapuguso and two others. There were four. He had built in Busikali village in which there are ten homesteads, but, customarily, we do not call all the neighbours, only those who are nearest. Only if I have killed a full-grown beast do I call them all and give them a leg. Yes, it was a big bull and perhaps it is on account of that that they are angry. When they came they were startled, saying: 'They are drinking beer! And there is meat lying outside!' They entered and drank a little. Then Katasya divided the meat for his relatives and took his own. He gave to Mwainyopolela and his fellows three ribs. Then M. said to his three fellows: 'Let us go home. I will not take this little piece of meat.' So they all went away. The other three ate the meat, only M. did not.

QUESTION: So they were angry?

MWANIFU: Perhaps! We say sometimes: 'They were angry and ate him.' But perhaps it was sorcery, because just now three snakes entered the house of his chief wife—the *inelesi* snakes. One entered and they killed it. Another entered and they killed it. Then they caught the third to take to a doctor, the son of Mwakanyamale. The doctor said: 'This snake is sorcery,' and he will find a medicine to give them to drink that the illness may be slight. But he has not yet done so.

QUESTION: When he says it is sorcery, does he mean that the snakes have been sent by someone?

MWANIFU: Yes, Mwaipaja (G. W.), you understand.

5/1/38

Katasya died during the night. I came to the burial with the doctor, Mwakanamale, meeting Mwamalunda on the road. They told me that the son, Mwakanjwike, had fled from the funeral. 'It is said that he had made love to three of his father's wives. They all fled, the three women and the young man. Yes, they will take them to a waterfall to cleanse them.'

I sat by Mwaipopo, the chief. There was a dispute about the autopsy. Kasitile came to the chief to say: 'They are refusing to examine him.' 'Why are they refusing? There is much illness about. Let us examine him and *know*.' Mwaipopo spoke with heat. Then a relative came and told him: 'Katasya said: "Do not examine me when I die."' Mwaipopo: 'Why? There is that case of the son (incestuous adultery) or perhaps it is sorcery, or perhaps, if the neighbours refuse to examine him, it is a confession that they have bewitched him. Let us examine him. It will trouble us later on. Also, he was praying to the shades, saying: "The millet failed." Then he died! Let us examine him and know.'

Five cows and a bull were killed. About twenty cattle were standing in the herd. The corpse was carried around with wailing and drumming and the cattle were driven round also. Then followed the autopsy. I went with Mwanyoso, with Kasitile's relative, Mwakasenga, and with the brother of the dead man. A woman doctor performed it with a bamboo knife. Another woman kept a hand on the head of the dead man meanwhile. 'You brave ones!' was the comment of the other women, two or three of whom stood watching. The doctor hesitated, as if in fear, before the first cut. Mwanyoso encouraged her: 'Go ahead!' As she pulled out the bowels we all crowded round to look. Mwanyoso said: 'Ropes,' but no one else took this up, and he did not mention it again. They looked into the chest and found something wrong. 'He is burned within! It is sorcery!'

MWANYOSO: We chiefs do not fear the commoners, we look for wounds and speak if they are there. But there are none. Look well! If he had been speared there would be much blood, and wounds. But he is burned within. They have worked sorcery against him with Mwangwala. That is the name of the medicine which some Nyakyusa plant. It's sorcery! Then is that of the country (i.e. witchcraft) not there?

It is not there.

How about the son?

That we do not find. He just has diarrhœa.

Mwanyoso then told Mwaipopo (the chief): 'We have examined him, it is sorcery.'

S

As we came away various people stopped us and asked: 'Have you examined him?' 'Yes, it is sorcery.' Great interest was shown by all in the cause of death.

When we first arrived, we found the son a little distance from the funeral and he did not, so far as I know, come near at all. He did not go near the grave when the corpse was buried. I asked Kasitile about bathing at the waterfall. 'They will wash him to-night. Katasya died in the afternoon. At night the son and three women fled. They will wash them at night.'

6/1/38

Kasitile came in to see us at breakfast time. I asked why the son of Katasya had not come near the burial though they had bathed him at the waterfall.

KASITILE: It is forbidden, but they have made a mistake. They have washed him irregularly. According to custom they should first have buried the dead, then, on the evening after the burial, they take them to the waterfall to wash them. When they come from washing, then the son takes a torch of burning grass, he throws it down on the grave, and jumps over the grave. Then they say: 'Let him strike the cattle.' He kills one of his own because he does not eat of those which they have killed previously. This is what they did yesterday afternoon, so it is finished now.

QUESTION: What does it symbolize?

KASITILE: It means it is I who overstepped you.

QUESTION: And when he steps over the grave and the fire?

KASITILE: It is the fire which the women kindled for him who has died.

QUESTION: Do they know who worked sorcery against him?

KASITILE: Yes, it is the son of Mwaikilaja whose name is Mwamu-kinga, because when their father, Mwakyandwike, died, the elder brother, Katasya, was a child, and the son of the second wife, Mwaiki-laja, inherited. But when Katasya grew up they refused to be on good terms with him and quarrelled with him. But they never worked sorcery against each other. So then when Mwaikilaja died, his sons in-herited. Katasya lost the inheritance because they said: 'You are not on good terms with your kinsmen. Let the sons inherit.' So he said: 'I, Katasya, agree.' But later on he was on good terms with those sons of his brother. There were three of them. But the eldest and the youngest quarrelled. The youngest, Mwamukinga, worked sorcery against the eldest, so Katasya told them: 'Do not be friendly with Mwamukinga who is working sorcery against you. Let him be at a distance.' Then Mwamukinga was angry and said: 'Is that wretched elder (*ikulu eli*) never going to die?' and he worked sorcery against him. This is the case.

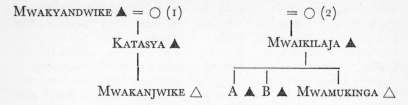

Mwaikilaja, the son of the junior wife, inherited, because when their father, Mwakyandwike, died, Katasya, the son of the senior wife, was a child. Mwamukinga is accused of killing Katasya by sorcery.

Mwakwelebeja came in to take me to the funeral of Katasya. 'It is not the day of burial to-day, but the day of war. On the day of burial they weep very much and it does not go well (*jikanoga*) but to-day it will be well performed.' He was eager and excited at the prospect of good dancing. 'The chief Mwabuga from Masoko, his son-in-law, is coming. He is coming with his drums. The people of Masoko dance well.' At first I refused to go, but he would take no refusal. 'You must come,' he insisted, so finally I went.

On the way we discussed the cause of death. Some say the witches have eaten him. They say that Mwainyopolela is angry on account of the meat. Some say it is the sorcery of Mwaihojo (the chief) because Katasya (a man of Chief Mwaipopo) hoed a big area in the disputed ground. He built a temporary hut and lived there. But we say no. If they had roused up a war between the witches, would they not have gone to Mwakagile (Chief Mwaipopo) and his fellows? But we have not done that. We argue and say: 'Why are you taking our country?' but we are only fighting with words.

QUESTION: The war of the witches?

MWAKWELEBEJA: Yes, the war when they call the witches of a chiefdom by night to fight against those of another chiefdom. But Katasya was indeed wrong to stint his neighbours in Busikali of meat. If he had been wise he would have given them a leg. Mwainyopolela is very generous. Always when he kills a beast he shares the meat with his fellows.

We arrived at the funeral. The women were packed together under a tree to the left, where they had sat with the corpse yesterday. The girls and young women stood watching the dance and occasionally strolling rhythmically out into the midst of it. The errant son was with the other men to-day. The son-in-law from Masoko came with all his cattle (seven cows, one bull and five calves) of which one will be killed and the others returned. The bull was unusually large with an enormous hump and it caused comment. It was well known. They told each other how, when his father, Mwakabulwa, died, this bull was quiescent. It did not move about at all, and it was a very small calf. It was quiescent

s*

and sniffed at the grave. When this son-in-law arrived, the chief women mourners got up from under the tree and went with him into the hut to wail. They came out all wailing. The women under the tree were wailing all the time with a leader standing up in the middle. But the wailing was drowned by the drums of which there were three sets.

Three young men were got up with white clay spots and some had bells on their ankles and loin-cloths. They held spears, and danced and leapt wildly. 'What', I asked Kasitile, 'is the meaning of the white clay?'

KASITILE: It is war paint. During war we painted ourselves with white clay formerly. Then if I saw one with white clay I did not spear him. It was my comrade. But he whom I saw without it was an enemy and I speared him. It was the sign.

QUESTION: But did the other side not use it?

KASITILE: We took them by surprise.

Mwanyoso came to visit me in the evening.

QUESTION: And what steps are they taking about Katsaya's death from sorcery?

MWANYOSO: They sought the doctor, Mwangolombe, for the burial yesterday. He pounded a medicine and burnt it on the grave. Then they buried the dead man and danced on the grave. That means they destroyed the sorcery. The dead man should take it away with him.

QUESTION: And has the doctor given them medicines to drink?

MWANYOSO: He has not yet done so. They will fetch him again to cook the medicine at the home.

QUESTION: What about the payment?

MWANYOSO: For yesterday they did not pay anything, now, but when they have fetched him to their home, then they will pay some shillings. But if many people have died, then they fetch a famous doctor such as Mwakionde. Then he comes with all the protective medicines (*amapingo*) and treats them. Then such a doctor gets a cow. The famous doctors in this country are Mwakionde and Kapuguso and Mwakanyamale.

QUESTION: Will they consult an oracle?

MWANYOSO: Why should they consult an oracle? They know what it is. It is the sorcery of their brothers!

QUESTION: But it might be the sorcery of another. Some say of Mwaihojo (the chief).

MWANYOSO: They are liars. See, Katasya had just come from his brothers. He got the illness at their place. It is they. If it was from Mwaihojo and his people, they would have speared him by night. We would have found wounds and much blood, but we did not find them.

QUESTION: He came from his brothers?

MWANYOSO: Yes, there was a ritual because their father, Mwaikilaja, had died. Their senior brother inherited and he also died. Katasya went to catch the junior brother who was there, but from that time he has been ill.

QUESTION: Did Mwamukinga (the sorcerer) come to the funeral and did they give him meat?

MWANYOSO: Yes, he came.

QUESTION: Is he not ashamed? Do people agree that they have worked sorcery against someone?

MWANYOSO: They deny it.

QUESTION: Did they give him meat?

MWANYOSO: Yes, they gave it to him.

(b) Sickness in the lineage of Mwakyona

The following case also illustrates how several possible causes of misfortune were considered—sorcery between kinsmen who were quarrelling over inheritance, the anger of the shades, and the jealousy of neighbours were mentioned. It shows, further, how expression of goodwill by those thought to be injuring a man is necessary for his recovery. The doctor treating the patient made the kinsmen confess their anger and gave them a medicine guaranteed to kill anyone working sorcery.

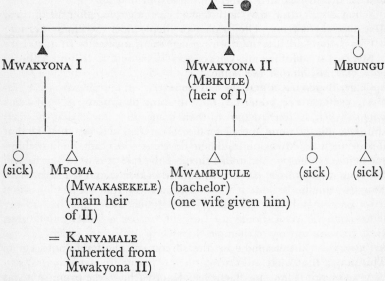

MWAIKAMBO: When Mwakyona died, his younger brother, Mwakyona the younger, whom they call Mbikule, inherited. But Mbikule also died, so they sought Mwakionde (the doctor and brother of the chief) and they asked him: 'To whom shall we give the inheritance?' The village elders, their fathers—those of the house—and their father's sisters, were those who saw to the matter of the inheritance. Then

Mwakionde let Mpoma (Mwakasekele) take the inheritance because he is the eldest. Mwakionde said: 'Let him be their father.' But when they gave the inheritance to Mpoma, they talked to one another and said that Mwambujule should take one wife because he did not have any wife. He was a bachelor. So they gave him one wife, but four wives of the father were inherited by Mpoma. After a little time Mwambujule said: 'My fellow has made a mistake with the property and he has not given me anything.' So he strove to attract the mothers. He said: 'Come to me and let me inherit you myself.' The mothers agreed, they ran away and came to his place. Mpoma was angry and went to Mwakionde to tell him that Mwambujule had attracted the mothers and taken them to his house. Mwakionde said: 'Do not make a case.' The village headman went to Mwambujule to admonish him together with the mothers. Then he returned them to Mpoma.

Later on, illness appeared. The sister of Mpoma fell ill. They gave her medicines to drink and she recovered. Then the brother of Mwambujule fell ill and the doctors said it was sorcery (*ubutege*), that is, Mwakionde thinks it is sorcery. This is also a common rumour. But, as will be seen later, the diviners, when appealed to, said: '*Mindu*,' that is, the shades.

When Mwakionde saw the sick man, he called together all of them that they might grumble (*bijumane*) and drive away the illness, because it is said that when people pray (*ukwiputa*) the sickness from sorcery gets less. It is said if one has worked sorcery against his fellow he always hides himself, he does not appear at his friend's home, because, if he appears, if he comes and says: 'I am sorry for the illness (*ndaga ububine*),' even without praying at all, the illness disappears. Also, if a sick man has died, he does not go or he will die soon. It is said that the dead rise. Yes, it is the same in the case of witchcraft. Then also they say that if someone has 'eaten' his fellow he does not go to him, he hides himself at his own home, and if his fellow has died he does not go or he will die very quickly. The dead rise. In the prayer they especially drive away the shades, because it is said that sickness from the shades comes from us living. If, for example, I have done something bad to my fellow, and the shades are angry, but if he forgives me, they also forgive. He must express forgiveness openly in words of prayer (*amasyu gamo ga lwiputo*). If he forgives me only in his heart, the shades do not forgive. This prayer that we heard during the day had power both against sorcery and against the shades, they spoke of both. In the evening it was completed.

Mwakionde called them all together and said: 'Friends, I am astonished that the illness has come again.' The people: 'Hu; this illness puzzles us very much.'

MWAKIONDE: 'For what reason does this man fall ill in the summer, and that man fall ill in the summer, and the other fall ill?'

MPOMA: 'I am ashamed, and also I am very angry, because people say it is I who am working sorcery against them, although when they were ill I carried them to my house.'[1]

Mpoma turned back on the road when they sent medicine for the sick man (i.e. he did not go to the sick man).

A WOMAN: 'Why do they work sorcery against one another when they are both left?'

ANOTHER WOMAN: 'The wives of Mbikule say Mpoma says: "Let me be alone, let me kill all of them and get everything for myself by cunning." '

MWAMBUJULE: 'Since I carried him to my place I said the illness would not be serious. He also sent a message to *your* place, Mpoma, saying that he was ill, and asking for some milk, but you did not send any.'

MPOMA: 'No one told me.'

THE WOMAN: 'The widows fight with Mpoma. They say: "You have eaten a medicine to work sorcery against your fellows." '

KANYAMALE: 'Also they speak of his wrongdoing, in not approaching the sick man.'

ANOTHER WOMAN: 'Yes, and also you are angry.'

MPOMA: 'See, when they said the present patient was still ill, I prayed, I said aloud: "What am I doing? Get away, what am I doing?" and I sent a medicine and he recovered.'

A WOMAN: 'We consulted an oracle, it said: "It is Mwakyona who is angry," but I said: "What is he angry about?" The oracle said: "He is angry on account of cattle." He says: "Why does he fear me when he has taken cattle?" So we said: "Mwakyona is angry because he has taken cattle." '

THE MBUNGUS (Mwakyona's sisters): 'We like him (the shade), let him come.'

WOMAN: 'They are jealous of the sick man [i.e. a third cause suggested. The unreasonable jealousy of his neighbours]. He dies like his father. People say: "He eats meat in our houses, he borrows our cloths," and he dies of their unreasonable jealousy (*akabini*)!'

The women and the men said: 'Thank you, Mwakionde, because you have made us think of these things [he had taken the initiative in prayer]. You make us make friends, and make us love one another, and bless one another.'

Mwakionde spoke, saying: 'There are many, many roads on which people travel and there is one road through which illness enters.' They say that if many people are with a sick man then the illness spreads.

They also prayed, confessing their anger in the case of Kanyamale,

[1] 'It is the custom to carry people to the "father", the head of the family, when very sick. This is not supposed to cure them, but it is customary (*lolwiho*). That is where we all are ill, at their father's place.'

the wife of Mpoma, but about this I do not know much. When they stopped speaking Kanyamale was ill. Then her husband charged her with witchcraft and she said: 'What is the case about? I have been ill since we came from confessing anger.' Then Kanyamale grew sulky and gathered up her mats and went with them to her child's place. Mpoma said: 'I must follow her,' but his fellows soothed him and he turned back. Then he borrowed a spear from his fellows and went to drive off the game which were eating his crops. When he found no animals he went home. On his return, when he was still outside, he heard the wives whispering about some case. He asked them to open the door for him, but they were silent and did not open the door of the hut. Then he pushed it open. When he entered the hut he closed it and he cross-examined the wives, asking what they were talking about. One said: 'I was just asleep.' He said: 'With whom were you speaking? You are hiding a man in this house.' One woman got up immediately and opened the door. Mpoma cross-examined them hotly. He said: 'Why did you open the door if indeed there is no man in the hut?' Mpoma got in a passion and went elsewhere. He returned again and said: 'Marry the child. I will not destroy him,' and he went away alone. He took the case to Mwakisisya, the village headman, and lost it. Then the court said: 'You get the children. Let them come here, though their mother is not here.'

Later on it was like this: Mwakionde went to attend to the medicines to give to the sick man to drink; they began by putting powdered medicines in a pot, then they put in some water, then they put in three sorts of powdered medicine, one black and two red. Mwakionde, because he was the doctor, began; he put in the water first. Mpoma, the senior, followed him, then all the others. When the water boiled, they stirred up porridge with a spoon, then they gave the sick man some to drink, and the relatives drank. If there were one who was working sorcery against his fellows, he would die when he drank that medicine. But the sick man, before he drank this medicine, drank something else. When the water boiled, they mixed a medicine and scarified themselves all over their bodies.

VI. PARTICIPANTS IN RITUALS ILLUSTRATED BY GENEALOGIES

MASOBESI (10)

2 sons and 2 daughters

8 children

TABLE (c) *See pp.* 244–250.

TRUNCATED GENEALOGY OF MWAMPIKI TO SHOW
RELATIONSHIP OF PERSONS MENTIONED IN TEXT

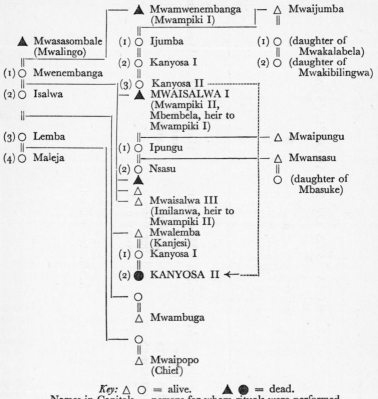

Key: △ ○ = alive.   ▲ ● = dead.
Names in Capitals = persons for whom rituals were performed.

GENEALOGY OF MWAMULENGA III, SON OF MWEGAMA (DEATH RITUAL)

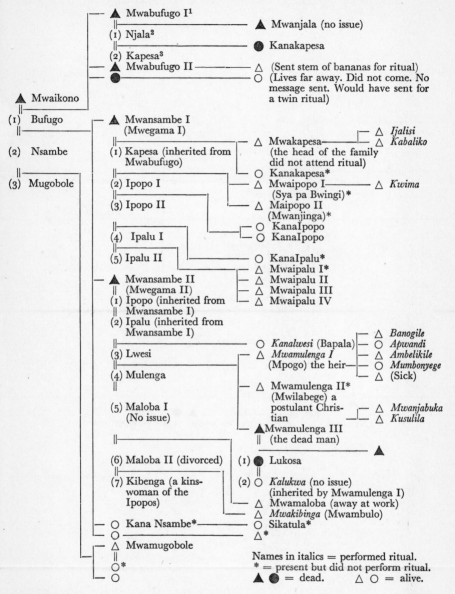

¹ Mwabufugo I was a village headman. The people refused Mwabufugo II (his rightful heir) as headman and the office fell to Mwansambe.

² Njala was divorced. Her cattle went to Mwabufugo II.

³ Kapesa refused Mwabufugo II and went to Mwansambe.

Note. Inheritance by an elder brother was possible in this case because he had not inherited from his father.

(1) ○ *Nyambele* children

Children

own full brothers, 3 wives of half-brothers, 1 widow of grandfather, 4 wives of father's half-brother's sons.

of brothers, of father's brothers, and half-brothers.

N.B. Sons-in-law do not participate.